TRUTH IN PUBLISHING

TRUTH IN PUBLISHING

*Federal Regulation
of the Press's Business Practices,
1880–1920*

Linda Lawson

Southern Illinois University Press Carbondale and Edwardsville

Library of Congress Cataloging-in-Publication Data

Lawson, Linda
    Truth in publishing : federal regulation of the press's
business practices, 1880–1920 / Linda Lawson.
        p.   cm.
    Includes bibliographical references and index.
    1. Government and the press—United States. 2. Press and
politics—United States. 3. United States—Politics and
government. I. Title.
    PN4738.L36   1993
    071'.3—dc20   92-34828
    ISBN 0-8093-1829-6   CIP

Contents

Acknowledgments

Many people helped me in the research and writing of this book. I received much assistance from librarians, including the interlibrary loan and government document staffs at the University of Washington and Indiana University; Aloha South, assistant chief of the Civil Records Branch, National Archives; Hilary Cummings, curator of manuscripts at the University of Oregon; Pamela A. Wasmer, manuscript librarian at the Indiana State Library in Indianapolis; and Sarah Paulson, executive director of the American Advertising Museum in Portland, Oregon. Thank you.

I also want to thank my colleagues in the School of Journalism at Indiana University for their encouragement and support. Special thanks go to my family and to the late Bill Ames, Gerald J. Baldasty, Robert E. Burke, Pat Dinning, Anthony Giffard, Richard B. Kielbowicz, Don Pember, and Lewis O. Saum.

TRUTH IN PUBLISHING

CHAPTER ONE

Introduction

For the Progressive-era press, publicity—that "great purifier" of societal ills—was a paradoxical weapon.[1] Publishers used it to expose wrongdoing in other institutions but resisted public exposure of their own business dealings. Many had good reason to squirm under publicity's disinfecting light, for the press was guilty of many of the wrongdoings that reformers ascribed to businesses generally. Publishers commonly lied about their circulation figures, adapted their editorial policies to favor advertisers, and printed advertisements disguised to resemble news stories and editorials. Others concealed the identity of their publications' owners and stockholders to hide conflicts of interest. And still others were not "publishers" at all, but actually manufacturers who created advertising sheets to look like news publications in order to qualify for the highly subsidized second-class mail privilege.

Until the waning years of the Progressive period, many reformers looked upon the press as an ally in their quest to expose corporate corruption and to educate the public to make moral, pragmatic decisions. Indeed, various periodicals published about two thousand exposés on virtually every aspect of American society in the early years of the twentieth century. Some journalists, particularly those writing for reform magazines, publicized so many social and economic abuses that President Theodore Roosevelt, a masterful publicist himself, criticized them for "look[ing] no way but downward with the muck-rake," like the man in Bunyan's *Pilgrim's Progress*.[2] Historian Richard Hofstadter credits this segment of the press with helping to bring about many of the Progressive-era reforms.[3]

1

It was inevitable, however, that the press would be called upon to reveal some of its own seamy business operations. As early as the 1880s, the Populist party had accused the press of being in league with Wall Street interests. While no federal legislation was forthcoming at that time, critics continued to worry about the seemingly unhealthy alliance between the press and corporate America. By 1912, with the Democrats in power in the House of Representatives and influential progressive Republicans in the Senate, Congress was ready to act to curb some of the press abuses. Oswald Garrison Villard, publisher of the *New York Evening Post*, recognized the irony: "[W]e of the press are to be muckraked and uplifted as some of us have been muckraking and uplifting others."[4]

Like other business leaders targeted by reformers, some publishers and advertisers welcomed the scrutiny and encouraged lawmakers to enact strong legislation to purify the profession. They reasoned that government regulation would add legitimacy to the industry and would help keep their competitors in line. This attitude of seeing government as a friendly ally was common during the Progressive era. Several historians have aptly demonstrated that businesses often formed alliances with policymakers during these years to regulate their respective industries.[5] Studies of the banking, railroad, and steel industries, for example, reveal that "legitimate" elements within each industry worked with lawmakers to clean up corporate excesses and to preserve the economic status quo. Businesses were also instrumental in persuading Congress to create the Federal Trade Commission in 1914 to protect honest firms from unfair competition.[6]

To Progressive reformers, publicity was the preferred antidote for corruption. Public disclosure would alert people to problems and motivate them to work for reform, these idealistic activists believed. It also would provide the public with necessary information to make informed consumer decisions. And it made good business sense, University of Michigan political economist Henry Adams noted. He reasoned that disclosure of ownership data, financial reports, and other business details would build consumer confidence and would help industry avoid more stringent government controls.[7] Many of the Progressive reforms relied on publicity to curb business excesses, including the Pure Food and Drug Act of 1906 and the Publicity Act of 1910, which required representatives to disclose their campaign contributions.

It was natural, then, that reformers considered publicity as the preferred remedy for abuses in the press. Congressman Henry Barnhart, sponsor of the regulations and publisher of an Indiana newspaper, confidently predicted that "every honest editor and every deserving periodical reader . . . will approve this method of compelling all editors and publishers to stand out in the broad sunlight of day."[8] Many publishers agreed with Barnhart's approach. "We Have Certified Milk And Certified Checks, The Day Of The Certified Ad Is At Hand," *Editor and Publisher*, a leading trade journal, enthusiastically announced in July 1912.[9] But other publishers shielded themselves with the First Amendment and resisted any attempt at government regulation of their business practices. While eager to accept the government's substantial postal subsidy, they did not want government officials—or the public—privy to ownership, advertising, or circulation records. After all, they asked, did not the First Amendment protect the press from any type of government interference? Their constitutional defense was not persuasive, however. For one reason, First Amendment law was nonexistent in the early twentieth century. The U.S. Supreme Court would not begin considering First Amendment protections until 1919 and even then it would take several decades before the Court developed a strong First Amendment precedent. More germanely, Congress was able to bypass the constitutional question in 1912 by attaching the regulations to the press's highly regarded mail privilege as eligibility conditions, believing that the courts would uphold lawmakers' authority to establish standards for the subsidy as they had in years past.

Thus, the press was brought under the "purifying light of publicity" when lawmakers approved the Newspaper Publicity Act, the only federal regulations placed on the press during the Progressive years. This consumer-protection law, still in effect, requires most newspapers and magazines using the preferential mail subsidy to identify their owners and investors and to label advertisements that resemble news stories or editorials. Daily newspapers are also forced to disclose circulation data along with their ownership statements.[10] These truth-in-publishing regulations predated by three decades the public debate on the social responsibility of the media expressed in the findings of the Hutchins Commission on Freedom of the Press in 1947.[11] When irate publishers challenged the law's constitutionality, the U.S. Supreme Court resoundingly ruled that government did indeed have the authority to regulate the press's business operations, particularly when the regulations involved a congressionally established press privilege—the subsidized second-class mail rate. The press, in these circumstances, was like any other business subject to government purview, the First Amendment notwithstanding. This obscure 1913 decision actually foreshadowed the Court's reasoning decades later in three well-known cases, upholding the constitutionality of applying labor, tax, and antitrust laws to the press.[12]

Most media histories paint the early twentieth-century press in the role of a crusader, working closely with reformers to weed out abuses in society.[13] This book examines the flip side of that textbook image—the press as a business susceptible to corporate abuses and government regulation as much as any other enterprise. Specifically, the study addresses two sets of issues: the first deals with the internal dynamics of the press, particularly its business practices, in turn-of-the-century America. The second examines press relations with government—state legislatures, the federal bureaucracy, and, ultimately, Congress and the U.S. Supreme Court. Both areas involve matters of press regulation, economics, management, and ethics.

Part 1 looks at the press's inner workings as it evolved from a collection of small businesses in the mid-1800s into an established commercial institution by the twentieth century. With commercialism came business excesses. Chapters 2, 3, and 4 examine three of the industry's most common abuses as seen by reformers: hidden ownership, advertisements masquerading as news, and wildly exaggerated circulation claims. Why did so many Americans believe that the press was secretly owned by financiers intent on manipulating public opinion? How much had news stories and editorials in the Progressive-era press become mere adjuncts to advertising? And how did doubts about the veracity of publishers' circulation statements affect relations with advertisers? Such questions came to public attention partly because of the intra-industry battles among publishers and advertisers that erupted in the late 1800s. Large, urban newspapers challenged small, rural ones at the same time burgeoning popular magazines and trade journals competed fiercely with all types of publications for advertisers and readers.[14]

These divisions within the industry propelled some of the regulatory action discussed in the second half of the book. Chapter 5 discusses the policy making that gave birth to the Newspaper Publicity Act and describes how Congress, the Post Office Department, and the courts reacted to the precedent-setting regulations. Chapters 6, 7, and 8 take each of the troublesome business practices explained in part 1 and examine how various levels of government responded to the problems. Why was the Post Office Department so concerned with verifying publications' ownership, advertising policies, and circulation statements? What prompted Congress finally to become involved in scrutinizing the press's internal business operations and in enacting legislation to curb the abuses? Why did the Supreme Court affirm the law's constitutionality despite the First Amendment? And, finally, what does this episode in policy making reveal about the Progressive ideology and its reliance on publicity and regulation to solve social and economic problems? In the process of answering these questions, chapter 9 attempts to integrate many of the paradoxical strands of scholarship on the Progressive period.

PART ONE

Business Excesses
in the Press

The press had solidified its position in corporate America by the twentieth century. Newspapers and magazines were "great 'business proposition[s],' holding infinite possibilities of profit," journalist Will Irwin wrote in 1911.[1] Publication data confirm Irwin's inference that entrepreneurs considered publishing a lucrative enterprise. In the twenty years before 1912, the number of American newspapers increased by more than three thousand. Likewise, magazines almost doubled in quantity from thirty-three hundred in 1885 to about six thousand in 1905.[2] And they were making money. The *New York World*, for example, was worth $10 million by the mid-1890s and netted an annual $1 million profit. Arthur Brisbane, managing editor of Hearst's *New York Evening Journal*, captured the capitalistic flavor of twentieth-century journalism when he remarked, "Journalistic success brings money. The editor has become a money man."[3]

As profits soared, so did corporate ownership. In 1899 corporations owned 17 percent of the nation's publications;

by 1914, they controlled 71 percent of newspapers' revenues.[4] Millionaires routinely bought publications, often secretly, and ran them like any other business. Inevitably, the press assumed corporate characteristics. No longer was a newspaper or magazine devoted to personal journalism, run by an editor-publisher who was readily identified with the publication. In the days of the political press, readers knew who controlled the papers they read. By the twentieth century, editors of large papers seldom held controlling interest in their publications, and management was anonymous—and unaccountable.[5] Stories and editorials usually appeared unsigned, written by faceless individuals with unknown motives. This anonymity fueled critics' claims that "[m]odern American journalism is menaced by the absolute dominance of the counting-house. . . . The Almighty Dollar rules the day."[6]

Profit was an overriding concern for many publishers, because publishing a newspaper or magazine took much more capital in the early twentieth century than seventy years earlier, when most publications were cottage industries and often subsidized by political parties. More important, however, was a change in focus. Where before editor-publishers saw their publications as a means of reaching voters, corporate publishers viewed them as revenue-producing businesses. The key to financial success rested in providing the link between consumers and producers in the newly industrialized American marketplace. Advertising became that link.[7]

Manufacturers and retailers alike needed the press to publicize their merchandise to a mass audience of potential buyers since profits, particularly in department stores and mail-order houses, were made on volume, not markup.[8] By the 1890s, more than four thousand businesses were advertising outside their immediate localities, often using advertising agencies to place their advertisements in newspapers and magazines. Some manufacturers, such as the Royal Baking Powder Company, were spending at least $500,000 each year for advertisements in more than fourteen thousand newspapers nationwide. Census data show the growth of this symbiotic relationship between publishers and advertisers. In 1879, publications' revenues amounted to approximately $89 million; of that, 56 percent came from sales and subscriptions and 44 percent from advertising. By 1914, revenues had climbed to almost $419 million with advertising contributing 61 percent, and sales and subscriptions dropping to 39 percent.[9] Will Irwin reported, however, that one New York newspaper confessed its revenue ratio in 1911 was nine to one—nine dollars from advertising to each dollar from subscriptions and sales. Similarly, Joseph Blethen of the *Seattle Times* admitted that advertising financed his paper; in 1910, circulation revenues did not even cover newsprint costs.[10]

The growing importance of advertisers could be easily seen in many publications as display ads crowded out news columns. One New York newspaper, in fact, apologized to its readers "for cutting down its reading matter to make room for advertisements."[11] Furthermore, many stories and editorials were actually disguised advertisements, known as reading notices, which added to the widespread public perception that advertisers and corporate America were unduly influencing the press. Publishers' cavalier attitudes toward news and information fueled the suspicions. Treating their news and editorial columns as commodities, some publishers tried to produce omnibus publications—all things to all people. To attract advertisers and readers, editors were forced to "discuss only those things about which everyone agrees or nobody cares," a critic complained.[12] Sometimes the censorship was subtle, as in the case of patent medicine firms whose advertising contracts stipulated that the agreement would be void if the government placed regulations on the industry. Other times it was blatant, as when advertisers opposed to the free-silver movement in the 1896 presidential campaign warned publishers that they would pull their ads if free-silver supporters were elected to office. "In making the choice of which cause to espouse in the present campaign," publishers were told, "it behooves every newspaper in the country to consider the question of its own individual commercial interest."[13] The largest national advertiser in the 1890s, the Royal Baking Powder Company, also flexed its power by refusing to advertise in any publication that carried competitors' advertisements.[14]

Not surprisingly, fierce competition for advertisers and readers sprang up among the various types of publishers—magazine, newspaper, weekly, daily, urban, rural, popular, trade. Publishers developed elaborate schemes to boost circulation, including offers of insurance policies, death benefits, premiums, and contests. Lying about circulation also became commonplace. "Legitimate" publishers found it difficult to compete against "illegitimate" ones—labeled thus by the Post Office Department—who garnered enormous circulations by giving away their publications. Sometimes they even paid people to get their circulars in order to convince postal officials that their publications were regular newspapers or magazines, deserving of the highly subsidized second-class mail privilege. In reality, the publications were advertising sheets or catalogs, often secretly owned by manufacturers or retailers intent on advertising their merchandise. Not only did these publishers cause immense problems for the Post Office Department, they also were scorned as unfair competitors by members of the "legitimate" press.

In one sense, these advertising circulars, making up the majority of second-class mail by post office estimates, stood as exaggerated manifestations of the press's big-business ties. At the other extreme was the muckraking press, although by 1912 its influence was fading. After exposing political and economic corruption at all levels of society, the muckrakers, often former newspaper reporters now working for reform magazines, took on the press, primarily the dailies, which they condemned because of their unhealthy alliance with advertisers.[15] Samuel Hopkins Adams, Mark Sullivan, George Seldes, Will Irwin, Hamilton Holt, and Upton Sinclair were among the journalists who exposed publishers' questionable business practices, including the prevalence of secret ownership, disguised advertisements, and fraudulent circulation figures—all abuses addressed by Congress in the 1912 Newspaper Publicity Act. Joining in the criticism were Socialist papers—*Appeal to Reason*, *Chicago*

Socialist, Milwaukee Social-Democratic Herald, and the *New York Call.*[16]

The muckrakers and Socialist editors, however, were not alone among journalists in calling for business reforms. Professional press and advertising associations, organized in the late nineteenth century, spent much of their time discussing how responsible members of the industry could protect themselves and the public from the irresponsible segments.[17] Three common abuses—hidden ownership, disguised advertisements, and lying about circulation—came up regularly in their discussions. Chapters 2, 3, and 4 explore these problems and explain how the industry tried to handle the abuses before Congress intervened in 1912.

CHAPTER TWO

Hidden Ownership

Who owned the American press? This question troubled reformers and policymakers in the early twentieth century. They had already begun to expose the pernicious influences behind other industries, but the press remained shrouded in veils of corporate secrecy. Suspicions abounded. Many Americans suspected that financiers such as Jay Gould, J. P. Morgan, and John D. Rockefeller secretly owned or controlled newspapers and magazines that they used to influence public opinion. In 1911 muckraking journalist Will Irwin reinforced this distrust with his twelve-part *Collier's* series exposing press corruption. When several popular reform-oriented magazines seemed to soften their stance on corporate America, rumors quickly spread that monied interests were surreptitiously buying up liberal publications, leading Walter Lippmann to write that "not once but twenty times have I been told confidentially of a nation-wide scheme by financiers to suppress every radical and progressive periodical."[1] This Populist belief of a corporate conspiracy to control the press and then the country has made the Progressive era, in the words of historian Richard Hofstadter, the "high point of anti-big-business sentiment in our history."[2]

Publishers squirmed under the attack. Some came out for ownership disclosure, reasoning that the publicity would make their publications more credible to advertisers and readers. Most, however, steadfastly maintained that they were different from other businesses and should not be held accountable to the same standards. The First Amendment, these publishers said, shielded them from government or public scrutiny of their

12

business dealings, and they would be foolish to give up their constitutional rights to quiet criticism.

This chapter discusses two types of hidden ownership in the press around the turn of the century. The first type—corporate magnates and politicians secretly owning newspapers and magazines to influence public opinion—captured the public's attention and sparked much political debate. Government officials, publishers, and advertisers, however, worried much more about the second category—merchants camouflaging advertising sheets to resemble legitimate publications in order to qualify for the highly favorable second-class mail subsidy.

Financiers and Politicians Infiltrate the Press

Many Americans believed powerful interests had "purchased the press," according to reform journalist Hamilton Holt.[3] "[T]he plain people think the newspapers—not all, but many of them—are controlled too much by their business ends and their class prejudice," a political science professor at Hamilton College told New York publishers in 1906. "They say: 'There is so-and-so, but it represents the [August] Belmont interests; and there is so-and-so, but it represents the [J. P.] Morgan interests.' "[4] Oswald Garrison Villard, publisher of the *New York Evening Post*, acknowledged that the public even suspected him of selling out to corporate interests.

I have so often heard this rumor that I have mortgaged myself to Wall Street, with the name and address of the banker, that I am surprised at nothing. Not if he should throw his private books open to a [Senator] Bristow or a [Senator] La Follette, could a New York editor hope to down this entertaining fiction. He would only hear that his books were doctored, or that he was hiding behind somebody else's skirts, or that it was the point of view of the men he associated with that really did the mischief—so discredited are newspaper managers with certain sections of the people and certain cross—very cross-sections of the politicians.[5]

Populist Democrat William Jennings Bryan perhaps articulated the popular sentiment best when he said in 1911, "The greatest menace in this country today is the pollution of the editorial pages and news columns by the interests that are committing grand larceny."[6]

While corporate pressures on editorial content often came in the form of advertising coercion or bribes, the most effective method of controlling press coverage was generally thought to be the secret purchase of a publication or at least a majority of its stock. By the late 1800s, many people—within and outside the industry—saw the press as a chief molder of public opinion. Financiers and politicians undoubtedly recognized the press's powerful ability of "guiding the minds of the multitude," reformer Henry George, Jr., wrote in 1906. With this recognition, "[p]rivilege at once stealthily moves to get control of that mouthpiece."[7] The power to mold public opinion made newspapers "one of the greatest clubs in the hands of the masters," Socialist writer Herr Creel contended.[8] Almost all of the richest families in America, according to another critic, either owned or secretly controlled one or more publications.[9] After all, "it is cheaper to buy newspapers and through them control legislation, than to buy legislators direct. Besides, newspapers when once bought stayed bought," a cynical writer asserted in 1909.[10] These acquisitions often were not verified until years later. As Will Irwin explained in his "American Press" series in 1911:

> [T]he process comes now and then to the surface—sometimes years after the fact. We know now, as we suspected then, that Senator [William A.] Clark secretly owned a string of newspapers, and that Marcus Daly [owner of Amalgamated and Anaconda Copper] subsidized another string, during the copper feud in Montana. The world has long believed that [railroad baron] James J. Hill exerted an undue influence over certain newspapers of the Northwest. We know now that the Great Northern Railroad owns $170,000 worth of bonds in that excellent newspaper, the Seattle "Post Intelligencer."[11]

Press ownership was—and still is—an elusive subject to document, requiring a disturbing reliance on muckrakers' impressionistic accounts of the abuses. It was, however, a common perception in the early twentieth century that many corporate interests did indeed secretly own or hold majority interest in many national and regional publications. In the words of William Jennings Bryan, "So many newspapers are owned by, or mortgaged to, speculators, capitalists and monopolists, and are used for advocating or excusing legislation, having for its object the conferring of special privileges upon a few of the people at the expense of the rest of the people, that the press has been robbed of much of its legitimate influence."[12] Reformer Henry George, Jr., described the special interests that sought press control. "There are steam railroad, pipe line, street railroad, telegraph, telephone and gas privileges; there are electric lighting, heating and power privileges; there are mineral, oil, timber, agricultural, grazing, urban and suburban land privileges; there are incorporating patent and tariff privileges, and a brood of less[er] privileges"—all looking to acquire a secret mouthpiece, George wrote in 1906.[13] Press critic William Kittle divided the interests into three categories: the railroads; the industrial firms such as Standard Oil, United States Steel, banks, and the sugar and beef trusts; and the public utilities, including transportation, gas, electric, and telephone companies.[14] These were the same monied interests that Populists and Progressives feared were taking over the country and robbing the press of its legitimacy.

Railroad magnate Jay Gould was one of the first industrialists to recognize the power and influence of daily newspapers. In 1872 rumors circulated that Gould had acquired stock in the *New York Tribune*, after loaning money to publisher Whitelaw Reid. New York newspapers relentlessly harassed Reid for being "Jay Gould's stool pigeon" and "hireling" when knowledge of the relationship leaked out and criticism of Gould's activities disappeared from the *Tribune*.[15] In 1879 Gould bought the *New York World*, and although Joseph Pulitzer purchased the paper from him in 1883, critics speculated that

Gould still held controlling interest a year later when the *World* printed a vicious article about rival industrialist Cornelius Vanderbilt. Denying that Gould still controlled the paper, one of Pulitzer's assistants nevertheless admitted that the railroad magnate continued to have a financial interest in the *World*.[16] Gould used these newspapers and others he secretly purchased to publicize his various business endeavors just as he had acquired Western Union, the nation's largest telegraph company, to expand his communications regime and to exert influence over the Associated Press.[17]

Gould was not the only railroad czar who quietly owned publications. Henry Villard, promoter for the Northern Pacific Railroad, bought the *New York Evening Post* in 1881 and secretly subsidized *The Northwest*, a publication designed to encourage immigration to the region.[18] Railroad baron James J. Hill owned the *St. Paul* (Minn.) *Daily Globe* as well as other publications. "The fact that Mr. Hill owned at the time all the stock of this newspaper is a guarantee that the statement appeared exactly as he wrote it," the *Globe*'s editor noted, while at the same time maintaining that Hill did not use the newspaper to promote his business interests.[19] In California, the Southern Pacific Railroad owned the relatively obscure *San Francisco Evening Post* "under cover of an ostensible ownership of Hugh Hume," Fremont Older, editor of the *San Francisco Call*, recalled.[20] Railroad interests also reportedly owned the Republican morning newspaper in Kansas City and invested in publications in North Dakota, Minnesota, and Florida, while United Railways, a streetcar company, bought several San Francisco weeklies as well as *Sunset Magazine*, the *Sacramento Union*, and the *Fresno Herald*. It also started the *San Francisco Globe*.[21]

In keeping with the public's suspicion of big business, reformers accused industrial barons such as John D. Rockefeller and J. P. Morgan of systematically buying the press. Rockefeller and his Standard Oil enterprises began to invest in newspapers in 1879, when Ohio Standard unobtrusively bought $10,000 worth of stock in the *Cleveland Herald*. Six years later, Patrick Boyle, one of Rockefeller's associates, purchased the hostile *Oil*

City (Penn.) *Derrick* and immediately turned the paper into a Rockefeller apologist. Boyle bought the *Toledo* (Ohio) *Commercial Gazette* in 1889, and Charles Mathews, another Standard Oil employee, purchased the *Buffalo* (New York) *People's Journal* that same year. Although Boyle repeatedly denied that Standard Oil owned any part of the publications, the rumors persisted and Rockefeller continued his quest to gain control of numerous newspapers across the country.[22] According to Upton Sinclair, he or his associates acquired publications in Colorado, Ohio, and Florida, and purchased almost every newspaper in Oklahoma. In Colorado, Rockefeller's interests owned the *Trinidad Chronicle-News and Advertiser* and the *Pueblo Chieftain*, but they were unable to buy the *Rocky Mountain News* in Denver.[23] Rockefeller was also thwarted in his 1903 attempt to buy the influential *Ohio State Journal* in Columbus, the state's capital. At his request, John D. Archbold, vice-president of Standard Oil, gave Senator Joseph B. Foraker (R-Ohio) $50,000 to buy stock in the newspaper. Foraker approached the publisher who refused to sell and then returned the money to Archbold. Standard Oil, however, was reportedly successful in gaining control over one of the leading dailies in Florida.[24]

The Rockefeller dynasty also secretly financed magazines, including *Outlook*, *Gunton's Magazine*, *Fra*, and *Manufacturers Record*, a specialized journal for business leaders and industrialists. In addition, one of Rockefeller's associates, Alfred C. Bedlord, invested in *Leslie's Weekly* for a while. When Bedlord withdrew $300,000 of support, the magazine ceased publication. Unconfirmed rumors circulated that Rockefeller also owned stock in *World's Work*, but editor Walter Hines Page denied the allegation."[25] Critics nevertheless maintained that the editorial content of these magazines reflected the hidden ownership. For instance, when James Stillman, president of Rockefeller's National City Bank of New York, secretly bought stock in *Outlook*, the magazine reversed its pro-women and reform stances and began running articles promoting Standard Oil and opposing women's suffrage and public ownership of utilities.[26] *Gunton's Magazine*, infamous for its depiction of an insane President Theodore Roosevelt, became known as "the 'organ' of special privilege" because of its heavy-handed boosterism of Rockefeller's interests.[27]

J. P. Morgan was another industrial giant who secretly bought stock or outright ownership in various publications, many of them previously engaged in exposing business corruption. *Century*, *Scribner's*, *North American Review*, *American Magazine*, and *Harper's* allegedly fell under the control of Morgan or his associate Thomas W. Lamont, known as the "brains of the House of Morgan."[28] Immediately afterwards, according to critics George Seldes and Ben Bagdikian, these publications stopped printing critical articles about corporate America. Take the *Harper's* acquisition as an example. In 1910, Morgan's bank bought majority interest in the magazine. Within one week, all the editors and writers identified with *Harper's* exposés had been fired.[29] *Arena*, known for its progressive editorial policies, pronounced, "[T]here can be no shadow of doubt but what the same silent, determined and systemic agency that is seeking to bulwark the feudalism of privileged wealth in other directions, is at work to gain mastership of the opinion-forming magazines of the country."[30]

Morgan was also interested in newspapers. Some people believed that he loaned William Laffan money in 1887 to establish the *New York Evening Sun* and again ten years later to purchase the *New York Morning Sun*. Will Irwin, however, doubted the rumor. He speculated that Laffan's devotion to Morgan could be better explained by the fact that Laffan was a member of Morgan's social circle—not his indebted servant.[31] But the rumor continued.

Frank A. Munsey, publisher of *Munsey's* and the largest stockholder in the Morgan-controlled United States Steel Corporation, also was suspected of being Morgan's tool. According to a biographer, Munsey "preached with apostolic fervor—the greatness of United States Steel, the grandeur of Morgan."[32] He excelled in buying, selling, creating, and suppressing newspapers for Morgan, one of his critics charged. At one time or another, Munsey owned the *New York Telegram* and the *Daily News*, the *Washington Times*, the *Baltimore News*, the *Philadel-*

phia Times, the *Boston Journal*, the *New York Sun*, and the *Globe*. These newspapers, in turn, supported Morgan. Another of Morgan's banking associates, George W. Perkins, was widely thought to hold financial interest in the *New York Evening Mail*.[33]

While J. P. Morgan concentrated his acquisitions in the East, the copper barons were suspected of buying the press in the copper-rich areas of Montana, Arizona, and the Upper Peninsula of Michigan. In Montana, Democratic Senator William A. Clark and rival industrialist Marcus Daly of Amalgamated Copper owned most of the state's copper companies in the early 1900s and secretly controlled a string of newspapers that they used to slander each other. The two waged their feud in such newspapers as the *Montana Standard* and *Daily Post* in Butte, the *Independent* and *Record-Herald* in Helena, the *Missoulian* and *Sentinel* in Missoula, the *Anaconda Standard*, the *Billings Gazette*, and the *Livingston Enterprise*. Almost all of these newspapers lost thousands of dollars each year, but they provided the copper kings with mouthpieces to wage a public opinion war.[34]

Much of the public's distrust of the press manifested itself in vague accusations and innuendo. Department stores, farm implement firms, banks, insurance companies, baking-powder trusts, shoe manufacturers, breweries, and coal and timber companies all were accused of secret acquisitions. Coal companies, for instance, reportedly owned papers in southern and northern Colorado; steel bought publications in western Pennsylvania and Illinois; milling invested in papers in North Dakota and Minnesota; railroad, timber, and real estate subsidized papers in Washington state; sugar acquired two newspapers in San Diego; and brewing and distilling interests took over many Texas papers.[35]

Specific rumors also persisted. The *New York Times*' ownership, for example, came under suspicion. Norman Hapgood, editor of *Collier's*, and publisher William R. Hearst accused the newspaper of being secretly owned by August Belmont, a millionaire New York banker.[36] But editor Elmer Davis refuted the rumors and pledged that "the *Times* is not owned or controlled by Lord Northcliffe or Wall Street bankers or traction interests or the owners of department stores."[37] Sometimes, rumors involved financiers' and politicians' unsuccessful attempts to take over a publication. In 1906, for instance, New Jersey Senator John F. Dryden, also president of the Prudential Insurance Company, secretly tried to buy stock in *McClure's Magazine*. He allegedly asked J. Walter Thompson, head of the advertising agency representing Prudential, to act as an intermediary in the transaction. Thompson offered Curtis Brady, a loyal *McClure's* associate, $25,000 to buy stock for Dryden. After Brady's refusal, Dryden increased the offer to $100,000. But Brady still refused. *McClure's*, nevertheless, ended up the property of the West Virginia Pulp and Paper Company a few years later.[38]

Senator Dryden was one of many federal lawmakers who sought the political advantages of secretly owning a "juggernaut of publicity." While the 1906 *Congressional Digest* noted that twenty-one senators and representatives admitted that they were in the newspaper business, many others hid their ownership ties. Senator Nelson Aldrich, a powerful Republican from New Jersey considered by many to be antireform, anonymously owned the *Providence Journal* and was rumored to control the *Pawtucket Times* and *New York Sun*. He also helped other conservative Republicans purchase influential publications on the sly. Democrats likewise engaged in the covert practice. For example, Senator Isaac Stephenson invested in the *Milwaukee Free Press*; Senator Thomas Carter owned publications throughout Montana (as did Senator William Clark, a Republican); and Senator Joseph Bailey invested in several Texas papers that routinely supported his proposals. A lawmaker's affiliation with a publication, however, often would not be discovered until after his death. Such was the case of Indiana Republican Charles Fairbanks, whose three-fourths interest in the *Indianapolis News* and fourth-fifths interest in the *Indianapolis Journal* first came to light at the reading of his will.[39]

Ownership secrecy—whether perpetrated by a business or a politician—troubled Progressive reformers who counted on the press to expose corruption, change public opinion, and help bring about their social reforms. Interconnections, even when not secret, inevitably promoted "a tenderness . . . likely to affect the news columns," Edward Alsworth Ross, a leading sociologist at the University of Wisconsin, wrote in 1910.[40] When they remained hidden, Ross warned, there was an additional temptation "to make [the publication]—on the sly—an instrument for coloring certain kinds of news, diffusing certain misinformation, or fostering certain impressions or prejudices in its clientele." This subtle, yet potentially dangerous, effect on news content and editorial policy was precisely what troubled many reformers in the early years of the twentieth century.

Manufacturers Masquerade as Publishers

As reformers worried about big business secretly taking over the press, publishers and advertisers fretted about a more mundane but pragmatic business problem—advertising sheets masquerading as "legitimate" periodicals and unfairly competing for advertising dollars and for the second-class mail subsidy. Many manufacturers and wholesalers surreptitiously created these "illegitimate" publications, as postal authorities called them, solely to send advertisements for their products and services through the mail at the highly subsidized postal rate of two cents per pound. The circulars, however, belonged in the much more expensive third-class mail category established by Congress in 1879 for material "designed primarily for advertising purposes." Postage for these materials was eight cents per pound, but, in reality, it was much higher because the second-class rate was calculated by bulk, while third-class mail was assessed by piece, making actual postage as high as 14.7 cents per pound.[41]

From a business perspective, circulars disguised as newspapers or magazines made excellent sense. Not only did the company keep the advertising in-house, as it were, it also profited immensely from having the government subsidize the distribution costs of reaching a mass audience. Furthermore, consumers were more likely to be influenced by this type of advertising than by obvious display ads, handbooks asserted.

Fowler's Publicity, a 1,016-page encyclopedia on advertising published by a former Boston reporter, encouraged businesses to design advertising circulars that "look like a paper, not a collection of advertisements."[42] These publications should have titles that sound like legitimate papers, Fowler advised. "If the name is 'Smith,' call the paper 'Smith's Weekly,' or 'Smith's Monthly,' or 'Smith's Ladies' Companion,' or 'Smith's Magazine'," he suggested. "General names may be preferable, like the 'Ladies' Bulletin,' 'The Woman's Paper,' 'The Household Gazette,' the 'Family Fireside'."[43]

Businesses took Fowler's advice, and myriad company-created publications flooded the mails. The insurance industry, for instance, created twenty to thirty of these circulars to advertise the benefits of insurance.[44] Commenting on this marketing technique in 1892, the *National Advertiser*, a trade journal, noted, "It's a poor house nowadays that does not issue a paper of its own. We have bichloride of gold, varnish, typewriter, wagon, food and drug journals, and the end is not yet."[45] Owners of these papers "are engaged in the kind of business their publications represent," another trade journal observed. Some "put their own imprint upon the editorial page; others conduct their papers in the name of the editor, or some other unimportant individual, and still others stand behind incorporated companies."[46] These "illegitimate" papers surfaced everywhere. "The latest addition to fake journalism here [Seattle, Wash.] is the *Daily Evening Reporter*, a sheet made up principally of plate [advertising] matter and stolen dispatches and edited by nobody-knows who," the *Journalist* noted in 1891.[47] These publications favored "high-sounding title[s]," the *National Advertiser* observed, but they were "merely a cover for a swindling business" that had fraudulently qualified for the subsidized second-class mail rate in order to inexpensively "advertise the trash which the firm sells through the mails under different names."[48]

"Legitimate" publishers and advertisers were understandably angry when these "fake" publications intruded on their turf and unfairly took away advertising business. One way of fighting back was to support the Post Office Department in its persistent battle to purge the second-class mail of illegal advertising circulars, which were costing the department thousands of dollars each year. In 1891, a number of Chicago publishers launched a campaign to persuade Congress to change the postal laws to restrict the "increasing number of 'fake' advertising sheets that seek admission through the mails under the guise of being reputable publications."[49] To join the Chicago Publishers' Association, a publisher had to verify that he or she:

- had published regularly for at least one year;
- had a bona fide paid subscription list;
- accepted advertising from reputable businesses at equal rates;
- published for profit, not solely for postal privileges;
- did not publish house price lists longer than one page;
- was not devoted to furthering one advertiser's interests.[50]

These qualifications matched some of the Post Office Department's criteria for deciding which periodicals qualified for the second-class subsidy.

One year later the National Editorial Association, a group of weekly publishers, voted to work for legislation proposed by the post office to tighten entry requirements for the second-class mail subsidy.[51] The NEA, now the National Newspaper Association, reiterated the need to rid the second-class mail of advertising sheets at its eleventh annual convention in 1895. Members resolved that "[i]t is the duty of this association to assist in finding a remedy to safeguard the interests of legitimate newspapers and periodicals."[52] In 1904 the NEA again urged the Post Office Department to exercise greater care in discriminating between "legitimate" and "illegitimate" publications when deciding second-class mail eligibility.[53]

The American Newspaper Publishers Association joined the fight to purge the second-class mail of "illegitimate" publications in 1896 when it unanimously supported legislation to tighten entry requirements. " 'Whipper snappers' that issue [publications] for advertising purposes only must die," a speaker told publishers attending the association's tenth annual convention. "In this way the legitimate publishers again reap the benefits."[54] Representative Eugene F. Loud, a Republican from California and sponsor of the legislation, assured publishers that his bill would get rid of the "illegitimate" papers fraudulently using the subsidy "in order to protect a privilege that you now enjoy."[55] Although the bill ultimately died in the Senate, Representative Loud thanked members the next year for their lobbying efforts that at least helped to ensure House passage. State press associations also endorsed the post office's attempts to purify the second-class mail.[56]

"Legitimate" advertisers likewise urged Congress to tighten the eligibility requirements for the subsidy. Artemus Ward, publisher and editor of *Fame: A Journal for Advertisers*, led the crusade, asserting that he had suffered unfair competition from advertising sheets for more than sixteen years.[57] He urged advertisers, publishers, commercial organizations, wholesalers, and individuals to join the fight to persuade Congress to stop the "great injustice" and "fraud" perpetrated by "illegitimate" publishers illegally qualifying for the subsidy. Second-class mail privileges "have been so grossly misused that hundreds of houses [businesses] avail of them to float their own private circulars under the guise of newspapers, to the great injury of the established press," Ward wrote. "Such journals have no place in journalism, and should have no standing in the Post Office."[58] They unfairly diverted business away from legitimate publishers and advertisers, he continued, and were bankrupting the Post Office Department.[59]

While publishers and advertisers fretted about the unfair business practices of manufacturers and retailers secretly publishing advertising circulars disguised as legitimate newspapers and magazines, Progressive reformers began marshalling their efforts into legislation to prevent "legitimate" publications from becoming secret public opinion tools of unscrupulous financiers and politicians. Hidden press ownership—whether to manipulate public opinion or to qualify illegally for a postal subsidy—continued to be a public concern well into the twentieth century. However, another press abuse—disguised advertisements—was even more pervasive and insidious, as chapter 3 indicates.

CHAPTER THREE

Disguised Advertisements

In the summer of 1990, *Ms.* magazine was reincarnated as an adless publication. After almost twenty years of trying to court advertisers while denying them the customary "complementary copy" or "supportive editorial atmosphere" that women's magazines traditionally bestow on businesses, *Ms.* editors decided to convert the magazine into a periodical financed solely by subscriptions and contributions. In the first issue of the new *Ms.*, Gloria Steinem, the magazine's founding editor, described how advertisers typically try to assert control over editorial content.

> Food advertisers have always demanded that women's magazines publish recipes and articles on entertaining (preferably ones that name their products) in return for their ads; clothing advertisers expect to be surrounded by fashion spreads (especially ones that credit their designers); and shampoo, fragrance, and beauty products in general usually insist on positive editorial coverage of beauty subjects, plus photo credits besides.[1]

Steinem and other critics lament advertisers' seemingly increasing control over today's media as advertorials become common in news magazines, program-length commercials fill television programming, and brand-name products appear in movies.[2]

Advertisers' influence over editorial content is nothing new, of course. Reading notices—disguised paid advertisements—infested publications' news and editorial columns in the latter half of the nineteenth century.[3] Calling them "the worst fea-

25

ture" of the commercial press, historian James M. Lee asserted that "it was possible to insert at a higher cost almost any advertisement disguised as a bit of news."[4] The notices served the financial interests of businesses, advertising agencies, and the press. Business owners and advertising agents believed that they were more effective than display advertisements in attracting consumers' attention, while publishers accepted them as a lucrative means of generating revenues. Their popularity, however, declined during the Progressive years when "legitimate" advertisers and publishers, worried about unfair competition and their public images, campaigned against their use. This internal opposition coincided with policymakers' efforts to purify the news and editorial columns of periodicals using the highly subsidized second-class mail privilege.

Reading Notices Sell Products

As the business world turned to advertising in its quest to establish national markets for mass-produced merchandise during the late 1800s, the creators of advertisements began looking for more effective selling techniques.[5] Seeking to capitalize on the growing perception that the press could influence public opinion, they devised the reading notice premised on the belief that consumers would more likely read—and act on—messages disguised as news stories and editorials than ones presented as display advertisements. Many publishers, eager for advertising revenues, willingly printed these notices at a much more lucrative rate than they normally received for display ads.[6]

A patent medicine seller—"Dr." Warner—wrote the first reading notice, according to *Printers' Ink*, an influential trade journal for advertisers. Beginning with a headline set in newspaper type, the advertisement read like a regular news story but buried within it was the product's name, Warner's Safe Cure.[7] Thus marked the beginning of a marketing technique that became common in the press around the turn of the century. At first, the half-hearted disguise was apparent to readers. A headline such as "Havana in Ashes," for example, introduced a story about the pleasures of smoking Cuban cigars.[8] "The Capture of Sebastopol" publicized a store owner who was declaring war on high prices and "selling onion seed for two bits a quart cheaper than his next-door neighbor." A merchant selling products at cost created more excitement than the "Ass-ass-ination of Louis Napoleon," another notice proclaimed.[9] Patent medicine firms, in particular, flooded publications with these mock stories, often crudely written as testimonials. "Few people were so credulous as not to recognize these paragraphs for what they were," an observer wrote.[10] Businesspeople complained that the notices cluttered the paper and asked "if such a practice is not an injury to the substantial advertisers who pay for a neat display?"[11] Some readers even canceled subscriptions because "there were too many traps for compelling them to read what they cared nothing about."[12]

Advertising handbooks came on the market to instruct businesses on how to use reading notices more effectively. *Fowler's Publicity*, for instance, promoted the strategy of cleverly disguising promotions as news stories. "The direct puff, which everybody knows is a puff, has value," Nathaniel Fowler wrote, "but not so much as the puff so mixed with news and information as to appear to be genuine reading matter."[13] Advertisers were told to use several techniques when writing and displaying reading notices: connect prominent names with goods and sellers, use statistical information such as the sales volume of the advertised product, and demand that the reading notice look just like the publication's news columns. Fowler also urged businesses to avoid expressions such as "best," "unequaled," and "unapproached" because "[m]odesty in puff writing is absolutely essential, for anything which is disguised must be more carefully written than that which is not."[14] To illustrate, Fowler included six pages of advertisements disguised as news. Examples ranged from using a weather story to advertise thermometers to writing about a death to promote a particular insurance company.[15]

Advertising trade journals also offered suggestions on how to make reading notices more attractive and profitable. One innovation was to encourage several businesses to prepare a composite reading notice, promoting different products. *Fame* demonstrated how one notice could advertise twelve businesses.

Accident to a Well-Known Citizen

Last evening, while our esteemed fellow townsman Mr. Crossgrain, the well-to-do corn-dealer—who has the best goods for the lowest price in miles around—was walking through the busiest part of Main street, intent on viewing the great bargain display at Tape Bros.' big dry goods store, he accidentally slipped on the sidewalk, and fell with such force that he was picked up in a fainting condition. He was carried into Cabinet's well known furniture store, and gently laid upon one of their new air-spring $10 reclining couches, while a messenger ran to the next corner for Mr. Squills, the celebrated druggist, who, seizing a bottle of Plonk's Quick Reviver from a shelf at hand, threw around him the handsome overcoat he bought at Seam's last week, and hurried to the scene of the accident. He immediately felt the stricken man's pulse, timing it by the Jones split-second chronometer which he held in his hand. He then administered some of the Reviver, and sent around to Smith's Reliable Livery Stable for a carriage, in which he conveyed Mr. Crossgrain to his elegant residence on the healthy, dry, sandy-soil property of Emanuel Huggins (who has houses to rent in that salubrious locality from $40 a month up). It was found, on removing the sufferer's right shoe (one of Last's famous $6 Razor Toes), that his ankle had been sprained, so Dr. Splint, the eminent surgeon, was sent for, and he promptly used Lalley's Liniment with good effects. Mr. Crossgrain is said to be rapidly improving, and his chief regret is that during the accident he lost his silk hat—one of Tox's—which he says he would not have parted with for $10.

Fame's editor then asked, "Would it not pay to adopt the composite reading notice, so that many might be lightly assessed instead of one paying the whole bill?"[16]

At first, most reading notices involved nonpolitical advertising—theatre and book reviews, and ordinary products and services such as "cigars, candy, cocktails, or cabbage," the *Amer-*

ican Newspaper Reporter noted in 1875.[17] Sometimes publishers received little money for printing them. A business, for example, wanted newspapers in Richmond, Virginia, to print one display advertisement and one reading notice each week for three weeks in return for a free copy of "our magnificent book, History of the French Revolution; or, a Country without a God."[18] Some advertisers also expected reading notices to supplement their display advertisements. A headstone monument company, advertising for salespeople, told a publisher, "Should we decide to place this ad. in your paper, we would expect you, in your local news column, to give us a boost and do your best to help our ad. secure the man we want."[19]

By the late 1870s, N. W. Ayer & Son and Geo. P. Rowell & Co., two of the nation's first advertising agencies, were encouraging businesses and publishers to use subtle reading notices to make advertising more effective.[20] Noting that "advertising by reading notices has come greatly into fashion," Rowell also urged publishers to standardize their rates. After surveying dozens of weekly publishers across the country in 1872, he reported that papers charged anywhere from $5 to $140 to print an eighteen-line reading notice weekly for one year.[21]

Publishers, eager to please advertisers, usually cooperated with the agent for, after all, accepting "canned" editorials and news stories generated much more revenue than printing display ads.[22] An official of the Southern Pacific Railroad bragged to members of the California Press Association in 1894 that every paper in New York accepted reading notices.[23] William Randolph Hearst's *New York Journal*, for example, openly solicited notices from theatre companies. "Every [theatre] manager knew that the *Journal* offered a page advertisement and a Brisbane editorial for a thousand dollars," one of Hearst's biographers wrote. A history of the *New York Tribune* reported that the newspaper frequently promoted railroads, mines, and real estate in its news columns. Similarly, the *New York Post* carried reading notices on its news pages, but not as editorials, historian Allan Nevins observed. And the *New York World* had a reading notice department with "a commodious suite of offices" on the eleventh floor of the World Building "for the use of this important branch of great modern newspapers," the *Journalist* reported in 1892.[24] Even the *New York Times*, eventually a sharp critic of this advertising technique, accepted $1,200 from Bell Telephone in 1886 for publishing a four-column "industrial article" provided by the company. Testifying before a congressional committee, editor George Jones admitted the inclusion of the reading notice in the *Times'* news columns but justified the practice because three stars appeared by the company's name, indicating that it was an advertisement. Another *Times* article, "New York City's Growth and Commercial Development of the American Metropolis," Jones told Congress was actually an advertisement for ninety-six different businesses, all marked with stars.[25]

Likewise, midwestern newspapers typically blurred the distinction between editorial content and advertisements, sometimes to a reporter's embarrassment. Take the case of Mr. Barron, theatre critic for the *Chicago Inter-Ocean*. After attending Harrison and Gourlay's farce, *Skipped by the Light of the Moon*, he wrote a lukewarm review of the performance. Fearing that would be the case, the troupe's business manager had already paid the paper's business office 75 cents a line to print a raving review directly underneath Barron's column. The day after the performance the critic's tepid comments appeared, "but right underneath his notice, and with a big black heading, there was a glowing notice of Skipped, which said that it was the greatest success of the century and the funniest performance and most popular piece that had ever been seen in any age." The next day theatre critic Barron wrote another column, explaining that a gross mistake had been made, that the glowing notice was intended for the advertising pages, and that his opinion of the play remained unchanged. But "to his dismay in the same issue in which his protest was printed was still another notice of Skipped, . . . advising everyone to go and see it," the *Journalist* reported.[26] Such was the power of the business office.

In the late 1800s, few newspapers in the Midwest were immune to advertisers' pressures. William Allen White's *Emporia Gazette* even ran reading notices disguised as news stories.

The Royal Baking Powder Company, the country's largest advertiser in the 1890s, paid White to run front-page stories on the dangers of alum in certain baking products without revealing that the stories were actually ads for alum-free Royal Baking Powder.[27] Some midwestern papers printed so many of these ads that trade journals took notice. The *Journalist* worried about the widespread proliferation of reading notices, even though it continued to accept them. In 1891 the journal criticized the *Cleveland Plain Dealer* for putting "so many advertisements and paid reading matter in its news columns" that the paper looked like a "mess of hash."[28] One month later, another columnist for the *Journalist* lamented, "Last week all the editorials for the *Grass Valley Tidings* were patent medicine 'ads.' What are we coming to?"[29]

As this marketing technique gained in popularity, writers began to satirize the practice. A *Chicago News* reporter, for example, poked fun at reading notices prepared for railroads:

1. For the setting forth of virtues (actual or alleged) of presidents, general managers, or directors, $2 per line for the first insertion and $1 each for subsequent insertion.

2. For puffs expressed in choice English, with occasional French phrases or poetical extracts (the whole with a palpable motive of honest enthusiasm), $2.50 per line; 50 per cent reduction on each subsequent insertion.

3. General passenger agents and division superintendents will be accorded half rates on the terms offered in rule No. 1. But in all cases where the title of Colonel is used, regular first-class rates will be demanded.

4. Thousand-mile tickets on the basis of two cents per mile will be received in exchange for advertising done at our card rates, but these tickets must hold good on passenger as well as on freight trains.

5. No deviation from the card rates can be made in favor of parties handing us five-cent cigars with the puffs they desire published.

6. For complimentary notices of the wives and children of railroad officials, we demand $1.50 per line. We have on hand, ready for immediate use, a splendid assortment of this literature.

7. Poetry will be made to order at $3 per inch, agate
measure. We are prepared to supply a fine line of heptameter
puffs, also a limited number of sonnets and triolets, in exchange for 1,000 mile tickets. Epic poems, containing de-
scriptions of scenery, dining cars, etc., will be published at
special rates.

8. General superintendents sending requests for the suppression of news must accompany their request with $10
bills—not necessarily for publication, but as a guarantee of
good health.[30]

But many publishers openly continued to applaud the practice.
S. F. Whipple of the *Lowell* (Mass.) *Daily Citizen* noted that
reading notices furnished valuable information and were
"much more profitable than any other class of matter that we
run."[31] Others used the technique in promotional campaigns,
filling their news and editorial columns with copy extolling
their circulations, reporting expertise, advertising successes,
and facilities. The *St. Paul Globe*, in an 1890 issue of *Printers'
Ink*, asserted that reading notices were perfectly legitimate—
and successful. "It appears as pure reading matter and will be
noticed in preference to display advertisements, and very often
read by persons that do not intentionally peruse advertising,"
the newspaper claimed. "It is insidious, attractive and inter-
esting."[32]

As advertisers became more sophisticated around the turn
of the century, they designed the notices in the form of tele-
grams. News bureaus formed to write and market these special
advertisements.[33] Telegraphic reading notices quickly became
"one of the latest and most effective methods used for certain
lines of advertising," the *Journalist* noted. "Everybody who
reads a paper reads the telegraphic news. . . . The leading
editorial may be skipped, but the telegraph never."[34] A managing editor described how these notices were craftily integrated
into the news columns.

As we know it, in the editorial room, a reading notice is an
advertisement cloaked in the ordinary type of the news, and
it is printed in the news columns. How can one tell the
difference? In our paper there is no way of telling.

So it happens that a certain reading notice in the paper at hand is, to all intents and purposes, a telegraph news item. It is dated Arizona, with an ordinary news heading, etc. . . . It tells of the discovery of a new gold mine, which gives promise of a wonderful vein. That is all. Still, that is enough. The seed is planted. Next Sunday our advertising manager will carry half a page devoted to this gold mine in Arizona, with shares offered to the public—shares promising to pay anywhere from 20 per cent to 100 per cent within a year, and after that untold wealth—I fancy, for the boomers!

Does the tale of the gold mine end here? Not quite. If you read the half-page advertisement carefully, you will see it tells the reader to keep in touch with the gold-mine stock by reading the financial news column. A few days later there will be an item in the financial column booming Arizona mine stock. The item will have all the earmarks of bona fide news. It will be in the regular column signed Observer. Observer? Who is he? I don't know myself. All I know is the Observer is sent to us daily by our special advertising agent.[35]

Businesses also saw new opportunities for reading notices. No longer satisfied with simply promoting merchandise, manufacturers began using mock news stories and editorials to create markets for new products and services. Procter and Gamble Co., for example, introduced Crisco, the first solid vegetable shortening, through reading notices in the *Ladies' Home Journal* and at least four other national magazines. And Sears, Roebuck and Co. used reading notices "extolling the wealth and generosity" of its mail-order business in its first endeavor into newspaper advertising.[36]

Reading Notices Promote Ideas

Corporate interests also wanted to shape public policy through the press. Some paid publishers large sums of money for the use of their news and editorial columns, while others hired moonlighting reporters or contracted with newly created publicity bureaus to furnish newspapers and magazines with prepared articles, editorials, interviews, letters, and news items.[37] "These appear in the public press without a suggestion of their real purpose," a critic observed. "They are not accompanied by any of the marks of advertising matter."[38]

Patent medicine interests were perhaps the most blatant in their attempts to control the press through advertising pressures, but insurance companies, Standard Oil, and the railroads were not far behind. In the years before Congress passed the Pure Food and Drug Act in 1906, patent medicine advertisements disguised as editorials flooded publications with one message: no government regulation. Most publishers printed them wholesale.[39] Not only were they financially compensated for running the reading notices, the publishers were also motivated by fear. Many had signed the "contract of silence," an agreement, written in red ink, that revoked a publication's advertising contract if "any law is enacted by your State restricting or prohibiting the manufacture or sale of proprietary medicines." An official of the Proprietary Association of America boasted that he had contracts with fifteen to sixteen thousand newspapers and had never been refused by a publisher.[40] In fact, publisher William Allen White, reportedly the person who gave copies of the contract to muckrakers Samuel Hopkins Adams and Mark Sullivan, had signed the agreement.[41] The patent medicine lobby was so powerful that most publications, according to a Hearst biographer, printed as news "advertising matter that made the most arrantly [sic] false claims of cures . . . under news heads with no indication that it was advertising."[42]

The insurance industry also undertook a massive public opinion campaign through the press during the 1905 Armstrong Commission's investigation into its business practices. Charles Evans Hughes, head of the investigation and future chief justice of the United States, concluded that several insurance companies paid newspapers one dollar a line to print disguised advertisements as news stories. Upton Sinclair, however, suggested that the newspapers received up to five dollars a line.[43] The Mutual Life Insurance Company, for instance, spent between $5,000 and $6,000 for one item carried in one hundred newspapers from New York to Minnesota in October

1905. The same company paid about $11,000 for six articles published as telegraphic news on October 25, 1905, at the "solicitation largely of the newspapers themselves."[44] One year later, *Cosmopolitan,* a Hearst magazine, suppressed highly critical information about New Jersey Senator John Dryden's ties with the insurance industry after Prudential Insurance bought an additional $5,000 worth of advertising in the form of a reading notice.[45] Prudential's "An Aid to Business" praised Senator Dryden and his association with the company. It looked identical to the magazine's regular articles. The only clue to its origin was a small line at the end: "When you write please mention the *Cosmopolitan.*"[46] Prudential Insurance and Senator Dryden sent many periodicals similar reading notices, including the *Independent, World's Work, New England Magazine, North American Review,* and *Leslie's Weekly.* Prudential then used these "news stories" in promotional materials without disclosing they were paid advertisements.[47]

Standard Oil Company began buying news and editorial space in publications west of Pennsylvania in 1898. It sent two employees to Kansas in 1905 to convince the state's press to print long reading notices "bristling with tables and calculations . . . admirably calculated to bewilder and mislead."[48] The manager of the *Kansas City Journal* admitted that his paper received $3,340 for eight such articles. Upton Sinclair claimed that many newspapers received from $500 to $1,000 from printing one Standard Oil reading notice.[49] The oil company was similarly successful in Ohio, where the state's attorney general found that the company had hired the Malcolm Jennings News Bureau and Advertising Agency to place reading notices in about 150 Ohio and Indiana newspapers in support of Standard Oil's political agenda. The *Lima* (Ohio) *Times-Democrat,* for instance, ran the following notice:

> Whether the Standard Oil Company of Ohio is in trust or out of a trust is a question for the courts to decide, and whether the consumers of oil are getting a better quality at less cost, and handled with greater safety than formerly, is a question for the people to decide. In the commercial affairs

of life it is things, not words, that count in making up the balance sheet of loss or gain, of benefit or injury. Monopoly and octopus, combines and trusts are haughty words, but the best goods at lower prices are beneficial things. It is much easier to say harsh words than it is to make things cheap.[50]

In 1907 the Interstate Commerce Commission concluded that "Standard Oil Company buys advertising space in many newspapers, which it fills, not with advertisements, but with reading matter prepared by agents kept for that purpose, and paid for at advertising rates as ordinary news."[51]

Railroad companies also engaged in this practice to influence policy making. Take, for example, the Alabama railroads. In the late 1800s, several lawmakers tried to pass legislation to strengthen the state railroad commission's regulatory authority after several hundred petitioners asked for the increased control. Immediately, railroad companies initiated a successful public relations campaign to get voters to sign petitions against the legislation. The *Montgomery Advertiser* and possibly other newspapers published the petitions without identifying them as paid advertisements.[52] A few years later, the railroads conducted another massive advertising campaign in the state's weekly press to influence the election of railroad commissioners. As part of the campaign, they also convinced a few publishers to write editorials attacking the candidate they opposed and then paid other weeklies to publish portions of those attacks. The editor of the *Daphne Standard* revealed that the railroads offered him $100 for his editorial space in the three weeks before the 1904 election. He said the press agent told him that no editor had refused the offer. Nevertheless, the railroads' candidate was soundly defeated.[53] In Wisconsin, railroad interests also successfully infiltrated the state's press, paying editors from $200 to $1,000 to campaign against Senator Robert La Follette and his railroad reforms.[54]

Other legislative proposals prompted flurries of reading notices. When the Aldrich currency bill was pending before Congress in March 1908, one businessman candidly approached publishers: "I wish to have published in as many papers as possible, opinions of prominent business men and bankers of your district favorable to the Aldrich Currency Bill now before the Senate."[55] Leading dailies that ran the notice received ten dollars; weeklies got two. During attempts to reform the meat-packing industry, Upton Sinclair accused Armour & Company of "paying over two thousand dollars a page to all the farm publications of the country—and this not for advertisements, but for 'special articles.' "[56] Corporations also bought news space to influence state legislatures. In Massachusetts, for example, the United Shoe Machinery Corporation paid a large number of dailies to print reading notices implying that it would leave the state if certain legislation were enacted. One editor testified in court that he received $40 a week from the Shoe Machinery Trust for printing editorials opposing the bill. Three Boston newspapers—the *American*, *Post*, and *Traveler*—exposed the arrangement; the legislation was enacted, and the corporation remained in the state.[57] One unidentified midwestern university even used reading notices to influence the state legislature to give it a larger appropriation. As journalist Hamilton Holt observed, university authorities "took money forced from a reluctant legislature to make the legislature give them still more money."[58]

Private utility companies similarly used disguised ads to oppose campaigns for municipal ownership of utilities. Boston newspapers were particularly guilty of accepting reading notices from the Boston Elevated Railroad Company, much to the disgust of the Boston-based *Arena*'s editors and a few local publishers.[59] Press critic George Seldes also accused the National Electric Light Association of deceiving the public through "canned" editorials and news items. "[T]he American people were fooled—not a few all the time, or all a part of the time, but all the people all the time," Seldes wrote.[60] Some editors, of course, refused to print the fake utility stories. Fremont Older, editor of the *San Francisco Bulletin*, said no to the Home Telephone Company, even though the company already had signed a contract with the paper's business department.[61] In Seattle, E. H. Wells, editor of the *Star*, wrote publisher E. W. Scripps in 1903 about an attempt by the president of a local bank and utility company to convince him to accept reading notices as other Seattle newspapers were doing. Wells refused.[62]

Industry Opposition Mounts

Even when reading notices were in their infancy and primarily devoted to selling merchandise and not politics, a vocal group of publishers and journalists condemned their use. Some advertisers pushed to abolish them too, stating that they undermined efforts to promote integrity in advertising. Ethics certainly motivated some to oppose their use, but competing financial interests played the dominant role in campaigns against this type of advertising.

As early as the 1870s, several prominent journalists came out against using news and editorial columns for paid advertisements. One even refused to work for a publication that carried reading notices. In 1871 Washington Gladden resigned as religious editor of the *Independent*, the leading religious weekly, because three of its columns—insurance, finance, and publisher's notes—were, as historian Allan Nevins noted, "so edited and printed that, though pure advertising at $1 a line, they appeared to a majority of readers as editorial matter."[63] Likewise, Richard W. Gilder, editor of *Scribner's*, was offended by his magazine's policy of accepting disguised ads. After complaining to publisher Josiah G. Holland in 1878, Gilder wrote, "There were no more paid-for or assisted articles in the magazine."[64]

In the latter half of the nineteenth century, publishers and editors began organizing trade associations to discuss common business concerns, as so many other businesses were doing at that time. Advertising issues, including the legitimacy of reading notices, soon became the focus of discussion. The Wisconsin Editorial Association, as early as 1858, resolved that "we condemn the system, becoming too general, of indiscriminate 'puffing'—gratuitously or for pay—such notices being often at the expense of truth, and unjust to the public."[65] Murat Halstead of the *Cincinnati Commercial* chastised publishers at the 1874 Kentucky State Press Association convention for printing disguised ads. "Paid matter shall be published so that the fact will not be concealed," Halstead said. "If this could be declared and established by the press as an invariable rule, an immense and perplexing embarrassment would be removed."[66] Seven years later at the South Carolina State Press Association convention, a speaker blasted publishers for printing patent medicine notices as news. The practice "has about the same effect in deceiving the public, as though the editor in solemn form had signed a certificate as to the efficacy of the medicine about which in reality he knows nothing."[67] The Minnesota Editors' and Publishers' Association took on the issue in 1885 when a participant urged members to develop a "clear distinction" between editorial space and advertising to help improve the industry's image.[68] Charles A. Dana, owner of the *New York Sun*, reiterated this plea before the Wisconsin Editorial Association in 1888. He urged journalists to "[n]ever print a paid advertisement as news matter." No advertisement should sail "under false colors."[69] Ironically, a columnist for the *Journalist*, a trade journal that accepted reading notices, urged publishers to follow Dana's maxim but doubted that many would willingly. "Progressive [*sic*] as it claims to be, there is no institution more conservative than the newspaper," Stephen Fiske wrote. "It retains all the faults of the past and makes room slowly for reforms and improvements."[70]

National trade associations proved Fiske right. Even though the American Newspaper Publishers Association and the National Editorial Association discussed the issue of reading notices, they took no formal action on their use. In 1891 the NEA president sharply criticized the practice for committing "fraud upon the reader by insertions of more or less lengthy and prominent articles which are merely and only advertising in attempted disguise."[71] But members, mostly publishers of weeklies, did not vote to condemn the practice. ANPA leadership, on the other hand, seemed not so adamantly opposed to reading notices. Throughout the 1890s, the association, whose members were publishers of daily newspapers, debated the merits of this type of advertisement, usually in the context of other advertising problems. At the 1890 convention, for example, a member asked for suggestions on how to handle advertisers who demanded certain page positions and news type but refused to pay the higher rate.[72] Evidently, he was concerned about financial compensation, not the ethical questions involved with running advertisements as news stories or editorials. Victor Lawson of the *Chicago Daily News* responded with his paper's policy:

> We don't publish anything as advertising that looks like reading matter. . . . A man sends us an advertisement to be set in the body type of the paper so it shall look like reading matter: There is only one step for us to take; that is, offer him "adv." after it, $1.75 a line, and it goes in. If it is over forty lines deep, instead of following, "Advertisement" precedes it. If he doesn't want it so, very good. If he says "I will take display columns but want it set in reading matter type," very good; but the foreman's rule is to put display type on each side of it, so it is understood that it is an advertisement, and there isn't any genuine reading matter within one column of it. It doesn't deceive the general public and everybody is pleased except the advertiser.[73]

Lawson often had to explain this policy to businesses not used to having to identify the notices as advertisements. But his resolve to keep "an absolute separation . . . between the editorial and business departments of the paper" never wavered, he said.[74] Convention participants, however, did not share Lawson's stance, and the issue was dropped. Four years later, ANPA members discussed whether reading notices appearing as telegraphic stories should be inserted in publications without marking them as advertisements.[75] The year before, Geo. P. Rowell & Co. had asked publishers whether they would be interested in "short items of information and reading notices to be published . . . as telegraphic news or special dispatches from us as your correspondent, and in the same form, style of type and position as your general news matter, and without any designating marks whatever to indicate their nature."[76] The agency enclosed a contract, a stamped return envelope, and the following sample reading notice.

> New York, July 10th.—Mr. . . . President of the . . . Fire
> Insurance Company, of this city, stated to-day that, in view
> of the financial stringency at present prevailing throughout
> the country, his company was taking special measures to
> settle all claims for losses with the greatest possible dispatch,
> waiving the time limit allowed, and seeking to relieve the
> insured with the least delay. Such a policy is to be com-
> mended, and will, no doubt, be appreciated by many.[77]

Editors of the *New York Herald* and *New York Evening Post*, in
particular, ridiculed Rowell and any publisher willing to sign
the contract. "We cannot repress a feeling of humiliation that
the methods resorted to by would-be successful newspapers
have so lowered the commercial honesty of journalism that the
circulation of such an insulting offer is possible," the *Herald*
editorialized.[78] Although participants at the 1894 convention
debated the issue, the association adopted no position on the
practice. Three years later, ANPA decided to appoint a five-
member committee to work with advertising agents to establish
guidelines for reading notices, including uniform definitions
for such terms as "reading matter," "pure reading matter,"
"absolutely pure reading matter," and "news matter."[79]

While state and national associations deliberated, individual publishers like Lawson implemented their own policies.
Several publications, earlier willing to print reading notices,
now condemned them. Cyrus Curtis of Curtis Publishing
Company announced in November 1894 that the *Ladies' Home
Journal* would no longer accept ads disguised as news. "The
special rate of eight dollars per line for such advertising has
been withdrawn," Curtis said. "All advertising hereafter found
in the *Journal* will be of the regular display nature, in the regular
places assigned it, and no artifice will be allowed to deceive the
reader that it is anything else. This rule has been made by the
Journal entirely for the protection of its readers."[80] Others
were not so altruistic. Whitelaw Reid, editor of the *New York
Tribune*, stressed the business advantages of getting rid of
reading notices. "Too many newspapers depreciate the value
of their own wares by admitting that it is necessary to give
editorial notice to an advertisement to make people see it. . . .

It would be better for journalists if every newspaper utterly refused to permit any single line of reading matter to be shaped by any advertising interest."[81]

Nevertheless, advertising agencies continued to claim that they could place reading notices in most of the country's publications. The *New York Times*, under the leadership of Adolph S. Ochs, angrily attacked an advertising agency in 1899 for claiming that it had the power to place advertisements as telegraphic news in many leading dailies. The "agency's offer is simply absurd—or it would be were it not also reprehensible from every point of view," the paper editorialized.[82] One year later, the *Times* again lambasted the practice when another advertising agency released a thirteen-page brochure listing newspapers throughout the country that accepted reading notices. Calling the brochure "[q]uite the most saddening, discouraging and humiliating piece of printed matter," a *Times* editorial berated the publications that "are willing, for a consideration, to enter into the miserable conspiracy."[83]

Editorial writers and columnists in other publications also decried the reading notice as "an insidious attempt" to dupe the public that was "worthy of aught but contempt."[84] Enterprisingly, some touted their refusal to accept reading notices in promotional campaigns. The editor of the *Boston Post*, for example, bragged about his newspaper's refusal to be "muzzled" by a street railway that offered $100 for each advertisement printed as news. "His paper is getting a good advertisement out of it," the *Journalist* noted.[85]

As the twentieth century began, there emerged a concerted effort from within the press to purge news and editorial columns of reading notices. Some journalists, such as Lawson and Ochs, explained their actions in ethical terms: disguised advertisements violated the public trust. Others, such as Scripps and Reid, talked about pecuniary interests. In any event, more publishers and editors began to advocate the clear labeling of advertisements that resembled news or opinion columns.[86] Even newspaper guides published in the early 1900s warned editors not to accept reading notices "unless run with some distinguishing mark—it does not pay to deceive your readers."

Handbooks also praised publications that had begun to label notices "by the abbreviation 'adv.' or some symbol such as a star or a dagger."[87] The Kansas Editorial Association sounded another death knell for the practice in 1910 when it approved the industry's first code of ethics, which stated, "[u]nsigned advertisements in the news columns should either be preceded or followed by the word 'advertisement' or its abbreviation."[88]

During this time, some advertising agencies and businesses were also reevaluating the legitimacy of reading notices. Once considered the most effective type of advertisement, the reading notice had lost favor by the early 1900s. Reformers attacked it as the epitome of what was wrong with advertising—fraudulent, misleading, deceitful, and dishonest. Recognizing the validity of these accusations, advertisers began discussing the deleterious effects of reading notices. Self-policing groups were organized in major cities to publicize fraudulent advertisements, and *Printers' Ink* lobbied state legislatures to enact legislation it helped to draft in 1911 to make deceptive advertisements illegal.[89] As early as 1892, in fact, one advertiser condemned the printing of lottery advertisements as news stories even before the Supreme Court forbade any type of lottery advertisement later that year. Calling reading notices "the most deceptive of guises," the author wrote that using them to promote lotteries was "unconscionable."[90] Another advertiser took a more pragmatic approach when dismissing the value of disguised ads. "Advertising that is not labeled advertising loses much of its force," he observed. "In business, things which are not what they appear to be, lose favor."[91]

More important to the reading notice's decline in popularity within the business community, however, was the rise of public relations. Businesses were beginning to learn how to convince publications to advertise their products and services in bona fide news stories. Reading notices—*paid* disguised advertisements—naturally lost their appeal when the same message could be conveyed more authentically and with no extra expense.

Nevertheless, this form of advertising continued to be promoted in handbooks and to appear in the press well into the

twentieth century.[92] An experiment conducted on the West
Virginia press in 1912 testified to its prevalence. Posing as a
liquor agent, William E. Johnson, press secretary of a temperance organization, offered the state's editors $1,000 or more
if they would print anti-Prohibition editorials in their papers.
More than sixty out of seventy editors accepted the bait. According to *Collier's*, Johnson

> was trying to separate the sheep from the goats in the edito-
> rial sanctums of West Virginia. Ten years ago he had trapped
> with the same bait 168 Texas newspapers whose editors were
> willing to poison the sources of public information for a
> price. Referring to his "catch" of West Virginia editors, and
> holding up a batch of letters, Johnson said: "These were the
> rascals I was after. I have no apologies to make. I went out
> after scamps and got them. It is not the first time I have set
> bear traps for crooks."[93]

Nor would it be the last time publications accepted reading
notices at their readers' expense. Reformers believed disguised
advertisements deceived consumers of the press. The next chapter examines another common deception—publishers who lied
about their circulations.

CHAPTER FOUR

Circulation Liars

The editor was dying, but when the doctor placed his ear to the patient's heart and muttered sadly, "Poor fellow—circulation almost gone!" he raised himself up and gasped, "Tis false! We have the largest circulation in the country!" Then he sank back on his pillow and died, consistent to the end—lying about his circulation.[1]

This vignette circulated among newsrooms and advertising offices in the late 1800s, illustrating the absurdity of many publications' circulation statements. A claimed circulation of twenty thousand, according to *Printers' Ink*, "might mean a print order of 2,000 and a paying clientele which can be detected only under a magnifying glass."[2]

Historians have aptly noted the late nineteenth-century press's habit of flagrantly lying about circulation. The practice, advertising historian Daniel Pope asserts, made no aspect of advertising "more mysterious than the circulations of the publications that sold advertising space." Daniel Boorstin amplifies this uncertainty in his comparison of buying advertising space where one "had only the vaguest notice even of how many subscribers or purchasers or readers there were" to purchasing a lottery ticket.[3]

Advertisers naturally resented the obfuscation. To them, a publication's paid circulation was a commodity—one that should be measured and assessed openly and accurately before purchase just like any other service or product. Publishers who refused to reveal circulation figures or who greatly exaggerated them were thieves and frauds, robbing not only advertisers and

45

honest publishers but also the federal government in its efforts to weed out "illegitimate" publications from the highly subsidized second-class mail privilege.

This chapter describes the dimensions of the problem and highlights the publishing and advertising industries' largely unsuccessful attempts to handle circulation liars before they turned to Congress and the post office for relief.

Circulation Fraud Common

The emergence of the penny press in the mid-1800s signified a fundamental change in the economic structure of the American press. While before newspapers relied on political subsidies for their financial base, publishers now needed large circulations—not for subscription revenues but for the advertising dollars they attracted. The larger the circulation, publishers reasoned, the more businesses would want to advertise and the higher the profits would be, particularly since the advent of inexpensive wood-pulp paper made mass production economical.[4] Vigorous competition naturally existed within this factious industry as publishers vied with one another—the penny-press publishers against the more traditional ones, daily against weekly, urban against rural, popular against trade, and, perhaps most ruthless of all, newspaper against magazine.

Thus, the mad scramble for readers began. Publishers sponsored contests, gave away premiums and sample copies, organized publicity stunts, ran sensational stories, and even paid life insurance policies to readers' survivors—all to become an area's circulation leader.[5] And if they did not succeed? Publishers would just continue to trumpet wildly exaggerated circulation claims in the leading trade journals.[6]

Some publishers publicly challenged competitors to prove their claims, while others offered money to anyone able to discredit their own circulation statements. In the 1860s, Henry J. Raymond, publisher of the *New York Times*, placed $2,500 on the line when he challenged the *New York Herald* to prove its claim that the *Herald*'s daily sales were higher than the *Times*'. The paper with fewer subscribers would have to give the money to families of volunteer soldiers. The *Herald* refused the challenge, stating that "betting is immoral," but continued to claim circulation supremacy.[7] The *Chicago Daily News*, on the other hand, offered $1,000 to anyone able to prove that the paper's stated circulation of 8,365 in the mid-1870s was not 3,000 more than any other afternoon paper in Chicago.[8] Other publishers provided sworn affidavits as proof that they were not inflating their circulations or used, perhaps more convincingly, second-class postage receipts to show their postal expenses in relation to other local publications.[9]

Still, circulation battles raged in every region of the country. In New York City, for instance, the *New York Morning Journal* claimed that it had the "largest local circulation of any paper published in New York City" at the same time the *New York Daily News* was boasting the "biggest number of readers in North America," causing *Newspaper Maker* to observe: "Really, now, it *does* puzzle one at times as to who's who and what's what."[10] No war, however, was more bloody than the Chicago fight between Robert R. McCormick's *Tribune* and William Randolph Hearst's *Examiner* and *American*, which lasted roughly from 1910 to 1914. News carriers were murdered and circulation routes sabotaged. Many observers, in fact, regarded this struggle as the impetus behind Chicago's notorious gang wars in the 1920s.[11] Milwaukee was the scene of another circulation battle, one so fierce that the U.S. Supreme Court ultimately had to settle it in 1904. The high court ruled that three Milwaukee newspapers—the *Wisconsin, Sentinel,* and *Daily News*—had illegally conspired to undercut the *Journal*'s circulation and advertising efforts, after the paper launched a campaign to clean up circulation abuses in the city's press.[12] Circulation scrimmages also erupted in Providence, Rhode Island, with the *Telegram* claiming the lead; in Minneapolis, with the *Times* and the *Tribune* vying for the top spot; in Omaha, between the *World-Herald* and *Bee*; and in Indianapolis, where the *Star* and the *News* exchanged barbs over each other's circulation claims.[13] Other battles occurred in California between Sacramento's *Bee* and *Record-Union* and San Francisco's *Chronicle* and *Examiner*; in Rochester, New York, between the *Post-*

Express and the *Union and Advertiser*, and in Cincinnati, between the *Times-Star* and the *Post* with two other city papers
(the *Gazette* and the *Tribune*) mediating the dispute.[14]

The press's incessant bickering over circulation data partly
stemmed from historically different ways of defining what constituted circulation. In the mid-1800s, publishers of urban
dailies could basically choose between two types of circulation
systems—the London "wholesale" plan, where the papers were
sold to carriers who in turn sold them to readers, or the Philadelphia "retail" plan, where the papers were sold directly to the
public.[15] The London plan was certainly more economical and
efficient for big-city publishers but provided little readership
information or accurate circulation data for advertisers. By the
late 1800s, these publishers were contracting with distribution
companies to deliver their papers to carriers and retail outlets.
To inquiries about circulation and readership, they often responded in generalities: "everybody takes it" or "it covers the
community."[16] Publishers outside the big-city markets, however, preferred the Philadelphia plan even though, in many
cases, it meant hiring a special circulation manager to handle
the additional paperwork.[17] With these systems came different
definitions as to what circulation actually represented. Was
circulation the total number of copies printed, sold, delivered,
or subscribed to? What about copies returned unsold by carriers? And how about copies given away or accompanied by
premiums worth more than the subscription? Should they be
counted as circulation? Individual publishers, advertisers, and
eventually trade associations debated these questions for years,
but it was not until the Post Office Department in the early
1900s developed administrative rules to curb abuses in second-
class mail did a standardized system of evaluating circulation
emerge.[18]

Nevertheless, many publishers continued to exaggerate or
lie blatantly about their circulations, often in sworn statements
or affidavits. One observer speculated, "For years they [publish-
ers] have been making false claims, and now when asked to
'prove up' they cannot do so without revealing the past as well
as present discrepancies in their circulation. Therefore they

continue to conceal."[19] Recognizing this propensity, "[a]dvertisers frequently divide by four the amount of circulation claimed by many publishers," the *National Advertiser* observed in 1892, even when "[t]here is usually an affidavit from the publisher, one from the mailing department and another from the printer, all sworn and subscribed to before some notary."[20] A popular story mocked the legitimacy of these affidavits.

> A Missouri man says that he recently went into the woods, painted a black circle on the end of a log, and when he went back to the log an hour later he found 300 dead rabbits there, the animals having mistaken the circle for a hole in the log and dashed themselves to death against it. Since his story has appeared in print he has received letters from the publishers of several New York dailies offering him the position of affidavit clerk, his duties being to swear to the circulation. But he says that he cannot tell a lie.[21]

Skepticism was justified, many thought, considering most publishers' outrageous claims. As evidence, the *New York Recorder* reported that some papers, swearing to circulations from 100,000 to 150,000 in affidavits, did not even have presses that enabled them to print more than 50,000 copies of an issue.[22] Other publishers set the counters of their printing presses forward thousands of copies before they began their press runs. Still others kept two sets of books—one for internal use and the other for auditing purposes. And yet others bribed their newsprint manufacturers and freight agents to submit bogus receipts for paper not delivered and shipments not made.[23] So, while a few publications, such as the *Detroit Free Press, Chicago Daily News, Washington* (D.C.) *Star, Indianapolis Star*, and the *Ladies' Home Journal*, won the favor of advertisers for regularly printing "verified" circulation figures that went up *and* down dependent on subscribers, most were regarded with suspicion.[24]

Advertisers Seek Disclosure

Advertisers were understandably reluctant to do business with publishers who routinely inflated their publications' circulation. At first, some simply refused to advertise in newspapers and magazines, according to a marketing professor at the Harvard Business School.[25] But, in the late 1800s, national advertisers, in particular, needed to reach mass audiences, and they turned to the media. By 1897, at least 150 companies were advertising more than 2,500 products nationally—and they wanted accurate, verifiable circulation data.[26] Advertisers developed various strategies to deal with chronic circulation liars. First, they approached publishers individually to resolve the problem; second, entrepreneurs published directories that listed publications' claimed circulations; third, advertisers joined with colleagues to form auditing associations to verify circulations; and, finally, they pressured lawmakers to require truthful disclosure of circulation figures.[27] Some publishers and various press associations also formed alliances with advertisers to combat circulation fraud.

Individual advertisers were advised to approach publishers as if they were conducting any other business transaction. "When an advertiser buys coal to make steam for his factory, he presumes and admits that the coal dealer is honest, but he weighs the coal just the same, and sees to it that the dealer's bill agrees with the scale," Bert M. Moses, president of the Association of American Advertisers, wrote in 1912. Similarly, when an advertiser buys newspaper space, he or she should not be embarrassed to ask publishers about their circulations before agreeing to advertise with them. "[I]t is the way business men do business," Moses asserted.[28] "If the publishers object to showing you, then they're not playing fair," an advertising handbook concurred.[29] Nathaniel Fowler, in *Fowler's Publicity*, went a step further: "[N]o man of common sense can see any reason why advertising should be purchased by the bag without knowing the size of the bag when that method of buying anything else would land every buyer in the poorhouse and keep him there."[30] Consequently, advertisers should "[a]sk the publisher what the circulation is and if it is not reasonable to believe his statement, ask him to prove it. If he refuses, drop him and his paper. He is unworthy of respect, and has no right to the advertiser's money." Besides, Fowler estimated that "[n]inety-nine percent of the publishers who refuse to state and prove circulation do so because they have little circulation."[31]

Patent medicine advertisers, who led the fight against circulation liars, took a more innovative approach. They trained salespeople to place an ear on the print shop's outside wall and to listen to the printing press's vibrations. Once they learned the rhythm of the machine, they could count the press's revolutions and then estimate the number of copies printed. Other advertisers followed newspaper carriers and counted the copies they distributed, compared circulation figures with population statistics, or tried to ascertain how much newsprint and ink were used on a press run.[32] Such individual investigations, however, were time-consuming, expensive, and piecemeal. And advertisers constantly had to counter publishers' efforts to keep circulations secret. A printing supply company, for example, in 1894 advertised an invention to help maintain secrecy—a press counter with a lock and key so only the publisher "need know for sure the number of impressions obtained."[33]

Some enterprising advertisers thought annual directories would be a good way to monitor circulation claims and advertising rates. The first—J. C. B. Kennedy's *Directory of Publications in the United States*—was published in 1852. It listed publications' titles, frequency, classification, and circulation, but no one believed the circulation data.[34] Other directories followed, but they seldom contained circulation information. Samuel Pettingill, for instance, decided not to include circulation data in his *Advertiser's Hand-book* because he did not want to penalize people who told the truth.[35]

Advertising agent George Rowell, however, took on the circulation riddle in his *American Newspaper Directory*, first published in 1869. In the beginning, Rowell used the word "claimed" to describe the circulation, but publishers objected. Then he changed it to "estimated," but they were still offended.[36] In 1888, he started guaranteeing certain publications' circulation figures and offering $100 to any person who could prove the data listed in his directory were inaccurate. "One Hundred Dollars Reward Offered for the Discovery of A Lying Circulation Report," Rowell advertised in his directory.[37]

Printers' Ink, founded by Rowell in 1888, not surprisingly, heralded the innovative approach to circulation verification.[38] After paying out three to four thousand dollars over a few years, however, Rowell discontinued the practice. In 1900 he renewed the challenge but required publishers to deposit $100 when they filed their circulation statements as their own guarantee of accuracy in case anyone successfully challenged their data.[39]

But Rowell's efforts did not yield truthful circulation figures. Adolph S. Ochs, publisher of the *Chattanooga* (Tenn.) *Times*, investigated Rowell's 1890 circulation data and reported his findings the next year at the National Editorial Association's convention.

> The total issue, according to the Directory, of all publications for one year was 4,020,425,000 copies, which would give 300 issues in a year to every family. Of this number, 140,817,000 are credited to monthlies, giving nearly eleven copies of a monthly every year to a family; 26,638,250 copies are credited to the weekly publications, nearly two weekly papers every issue for a year to a family. About the only conclusion that one can arrive at from a study of these figures is that a great number of the publishers have done some colossal lying about the circulation of their paper.[40]

Even Rowell admitted in 1900 that "no more than one newspaper in four . . . is willing to tell what its circulation is."[41]

Some publishers resented Rowell's meddling in their business affairs. "[T]here is no more reason why the publishers of newspapers should give away their own private affairs, than should Rowell and Co. give away the exact amount of their bank account," one person wrote in 1891. "I think his [Rowell's] informal directory is a nuisance with its bulldozing tactics regarding circulation," another observer concluded.[42] In 1895, the *Spokane* (Wash.) *Spokesman-Review*'s business manager wrote publisher W. H. Cowles that he considered Rowell's attempts to monitor circulations "a species of blackmail that should not be tolerated." Cowles nevertheless decided to comply with Rowell's request for circulation information.[43] The publisher of *Harper's Weekly*, however, refused to do business with Rowell because he thought the advertising agent was a prying busybody for asking about a publication's circulation. Likewise, the business manager of the *Baltimore Sun* believed it was immoral to ask a newspaper to broadcast exact circulation figures.[44]

Allan Forman, editor of the *Journalist*, went further and accused Rowell of coercing publishers to buy advertising in the directory in exchange for a favorable circulation rating. Rowell, in fact, did lose a few court cases for listing erroneous circulation figures for certain papers, but supporters vehemently denied that he had maliciously assigned low circulations to publications not advertising in his directory.[45] By 1891, fourteen national and regional publications were compiling information on periodicals; most listed circulations. This duplication allowed publishers to court another directory if unhappy with Rowell's evaluation. William Allen White, publisher of the *Emporia Gazette*, for instance, went to the Lord & Thomas agency in 1901 after Rowell's directory consistently underestimated the *Gazette's* circulation. Sending along copies of his paper and the competitor's, White wrote the agency, "You can see at once by comparing the two papers which paper is the popular paper. . . . I do not like to be put in the light of questioning the affidavits of anybody, but neither do I like to be put in the position of playing second fiddle to a paper that has less than one third the circulation of the *Gazette*."[46] While White was able to verify his paper's circulation, truthful statements remained rare, and publishers continued to challenge the directories' accuracy when their publications were listed with smaller circulations than their competitors' papers.

Since individual efforts and directory listings did not faze the circulation liar, several national advertisers met in New York City in 1898 to discuss other alternatives. They decided to form their own auditing organization united behind one principle: "any publisher refusing to open to them the way for a thorough and free examination of his claims concerning circulation, would be refused the business of the advertiser." One year later with the blessing of trade journals, the Association of American Advertisers (AAA) began its first audit on Frank A. Munsey's magazines in New York. Within three years, the association had audited four hundred publications in more than fifty cities.[47]

Many publishers, however, refused AAA's request for an audit. Even if they did allow one, the investigations revealed only limited information, for the organization did not use a standardized audit form and never precisely defined the term *circulation*. By 1912, after 1,058 investigations, AAA ran out of money; in 1913, the organization died. In the meantime, at least five other groups, including the *Mail Order Journal*, were auditing circulation records, but abuses continued.[48] James Keeley of the *Chicago Tribune* attempted to explain to AAA members in 1913 why the audits were not successful. Circulation statements were meaningless, Keeley maintained, and

> entitled to the place of honor in any joke book. Certificates and circulation examinations only promoted fraud and chicanery because one never knew whether to trust the methods used in securing these assertations. I say to you that the accountant does not live who can go into the office of a publication and come away with the positive and absolute knowledge that he has obtained the facts. What these accountants certify to are merely totals of figures furnished to them by the publications themselves.[49]

Needless to say, Keeley hastened to add, all publishers were not liars nor did they approve of their colleagues' deception.

An Alliance Forms

By the late 1800s, circulation liars had become a major embarrassment for honest newspaper publishers looking for legitimacy and increased advertising revenues. These publishers particularly worried about how to stop national advertisers from flocking to popular magazines, such as the *Ladies' Home Journal* and the *Saturday Evening Post*, with circulations nearing one million subscribers and reputations for honesty. By 1900, mass-circulated magazines had secured 60 percent or more of the national advertising market.[50] Alarmed by this trend, newspaper owners recognized that they had to make a concerted effort with advertisers to drive the circulation liars from their ranks.

A few publishers had long been fighting the battle. Horace Greeley, E. W. Scripps, Victor Lawson, and Cyrus Curtis, for instance, established early policies of providing truthful circulation information to advertisers. In Scripps's words, "Either lying or white lying about circulation is dishonest and disastrous to prestige." He advocated a policy of disclosure. "Circulation books must be kept open to all advertisers. They shall be informed that they are welcome to examine them at any time. Every advertiser shall be given what information he wants, accurately and truthfully."[51] Judge Lynn J. Arnold, president of the *Albany* (N.Y.) *Knickerbocker Press*, was more insistent. "There can be nothing more reprehensible than a publication which deliberately deceives as to the quantity and quality of its circulation. It is simply selling an article, and the day is coming when it can no more succeed by deception than can any merchant."[52]

Agreeing with advertisers, these publishers considered a publication's circulation statement a commodity—a product to be bought and sold like any other product. Victor Lawson, editor of the *Chicago Daily News*, compared it to a bolt of cloth.

> The advertiser should not be asked to take the publisher's word that the bolt of circulation cloth he buys is worth the money. . . . As to the quality of the circulation sold, the advertiser's personal inspection of the yard-wide cloth should enable him to judge intelligently as to whether or not it is "all wool." That must always be a matter of opinion, but the number of yards should always be a definitely ascertained matter of fact.[53]

Speaking before the Southern Newspaper Publishers Association (SNPA) in 1911, George C. Hitt of the *Indianapolis Star* reenforced the consumer-transaction concept. "The man who tells an untruth about the circulation of a newspaper is no better than the man who uses shortweight scales," he asserted.[54]

The SNPA was a good audience for Hitt's message. Made up of southern newspaper owners whose publications were smaller than the northern metros, the association was sensitive to the problems of competing with large-circulation papers, particularly ones that might be lying about their circulations. In 1909, members spent one afternoon during their annual convention discussing circulation problems, including how to compete against liars.[55] The National Editorial Association, a group of weekly publishers, shared SNPA's concern about unfair competition. As early as 1891, some members were calling for legislation to require publishers to open their circulation records for public inspection just like banks and insurance companies were forced to make certain documents available to the public. Publishers who refused should be punished, in the words of one participant, "as any other thief."[56]

Some trade journals picked up on this idea and published a flurry of articles calling for the government to legislate the circulation liar into well-deserved oblivion. The *Kings' Jester*, an advertising journal, editorialized, "Insurance companies, banks and other corporations must file statements and be subject to rigid inspection besides. Why should not newspapers, in respect to their circulations, be under the same law?"[57] One writer for the *Newspaper Maker* argued for a regulation to make circulation liars criminals because honest newspapers "suffer from the action of such scoundrels, just as a church suffers from the ferine action of a scamp in its fold."[58] Mandatory circulation disclosure would particularly help small, relatively obscure, newspapers, the *Journalist* stated. "The big, powerful, far-reaching metropolitan dailies and weeklies, whose circulation figures are glibly given as the regular output, will very surely be found wanting when weighed in the scales of Truth," the trade journal predicted, "while papers that are so little . . . will, from the necessity of just claims, be forced to the front."[59]

Even before 1891, several publishers were suggesting that legislation was needed to curb widespread circulation abuse. Horace Greeley of the *New York Tribune*, for example, argued in the 1860s that every publisher should be required by law to publish a detailed circulation statement. Similar to other weights-and-measures regulations, such a law would be a simple act of justice to advertisers, Greeley thought. At that time, the New York legislature was considering a bill to protect advertisers from circulation liars by compelling publishers to disclose each issue's press run. Opponents, however, feared dishonest publishers would use the affidavit to give "an air of formality and solemnity to assertions which would otherwise be treated as loose or doubtful."[60] Instead of enacting new legislation, the *Nation* suggested that the legislature appoint independent officers to investigate claims of circulation fraud. Neither proposal became law in New York, but they demonstrated early industry support for certain types of press regulation.[61]

The Minnesota Editorial Association also discussed the prospect of government regulation in 1885 after one participant spoke on publishers' rights and responsibilities. In order to force publishers to "be fair and honorable towards the public," a speaker suggested, "Every newspaper publisher should be required by law to publish as often as once a quarter, a verified statement of the circulation of his paper, and this should be the basis of his price for advertisements." The remarks generated debate but no consensus.[62]

Three years later, W. H. Brearley of the *Detroit Evening News* broached the subject before the American Newspaper Publishers Association at its second annual convention. He suggested a law to require publishers to file circulation statements with the clerk's office in the county where the paper was published.[63] The association did not vote on his proposal. At its fourth convention in 1890, ANPA downplayed the problem when someone from the audience asked how a truthful publisher should compete with a liar. Charles W. Knapp of the *St. Louis Republic* jokingly responded, "I think the liar ought to respond to that." The ANPA president retorted, "I believe there are no such papers in the Association." The association's secretary then said, "I don't think it is a matter that concerns this Association. The liars are all outside—all of us tell the truth."[64] Of course, the problem did affect ANPA membership, mostly owners of large dailies. In fact, two years later, the editor of the *Omaha* (Neb.) *Bee* urged the association to prepare its own directory of members' circulation figures.[65]

Indeed, no publisher remained unaffected by the circulation problem; either they were victims or perpetrators of the fraud. The circulation liar stung some publishers unexpectedly. New management at the *Kalamazoo* (Mich.) *Telegraph*, for example, discovered that the former owner's sworn affidavits verifying 13,000 subscribers were fraudulent; the paper only had a circulation of 5,958. Similarly, a Duluth, Minnesota, publisher bought his rival's paper believing that it had a circulation of 4,600—what his competitor claimed. In reality, it was 1,700.[66] And the new business manager of the *Cleveland* (Ohio) *Plain Dealer* had the embarrassing task in 1898 of squeezing the excess out of the paper's claimed circulation. The year before his predecessor had told advertisers that the *Plain Dealer* had two times its actual circulation; the new manager publicly apologized for the lie. [67]

By the time the Newspaper Publicity Act became law, an alliance had formed between advertisers and some publishers with a common objective: to run the circulation liars—"that hoary evil of the counting room"—out of business.[68] In the meantime, the Post Office Department had decided how to administratively handle the circulation liars who were flooding the second-class mail with "illegitimate" publications. Congress, however, was still concerned with the press's deception in the areas of circulation, disguised advertisements, and hidden ownership. Part 2 discusses how the federal government became involved in regulating these unsavory business practices and the consequences of the regulations.

PART TWO

Progressive-Era Regulations on the Press

Deeply entrenched in traditional journalism history is the assumption that the government and the American press are natural adversaries—the press, a vigilant "watchdog"; the government, needful of watching. Coupled with this supposition is another naive belief—that the First Amendment guarantees the preservation of this adversarial relationship by prohibiting Congress from regulating the press.

Contrary to this idealistic portrayal, the federal government has been intricately involved in the day-to-day workings of the press since the beginning of the Republic. The early Congresses, eager to unify the new nation, recognized the nation-building potential of newspapers and decided to encourage their widespread distribution. In 1792 lawmakers agreed to subsidize the mail delivery of newspapers, believing that a substantial subsidy would serve an important policy interest—that of uniting a literate population divided geographically, politically, and socially. Under the subsidy, newspaper postage was minimal—1 cent for papers sent up to one hundred miles and 1.5 cents for those mailed farther. Publishers could also mail their papers free to other editors. In contrast, letter postage ranged from 6 cents per sheet to 25 cents depending on the distance sent.[1]

Newspaper publishers, usually associated with a political party, eagerly accepted the postal subsidy without questioning the desirability of government intervention. Retailers and manufacturers soon took advantage of Congress's largess and began flooding the mail with advertising flyers and catalogs disguised as newspapers. Furious with "illegitimate" publications using their subsidy, publishers pushed lawmakers to tighten the qualifications. In 1876 Congress approved a much higher postal rate for "publications designed primarily for advertising purposes." Three years later, after intense lobbying from publishers, lawmakers designed the current four-tier postal rate structure that distinguished between news publications and advertising sheets. Without a doubt, the 1879 law was "passed chiefly for publishers' benefit," one historian has noted, considering that it allowed publishers to mail their publications for 2 cents per pound while charging advertising circulars 1 cent per ounce.[2]

Once again, regulatory action coincided with "legitimate" publishers' interests, and no one in the press questioned congressional authority to define what constituted a news publication in terms of content, size, shape, or frequency. But publishers, lawmakers, and postal officials were upset with "second-class matter fiends"—in the words of one former postal administrator—who continued to devise ingenious schemes to circumvent the classification system. Postmaster General Wilson S. Bissell estimated in 1897 that up to 85 percent of the publications in the second-class category did not deserve the subsidy.[3] The abuses fell within three areas: first, businesses hid their ownership ties with a publication; second, retailers and manufacturers used disguised advertisements that resembled news stories to make their publications appear newsworthy; and third, they devised schemes to inflate their circulations and mailed thousands of copies to nonsubscribers. When the post office discovered the deception, the publication was kicked out of the second-class category and charged the much higher third-class rate. Although disaffected mailers sometimes challenged these decisions, the post office routinely won the appeals, a fact that reflects the judiciary's ever-increasing willingness during the early twentieth century to rely on administrative discretion when deciding agency cases.[4]

Postal administrators, however, were forced to spend more and more time and the department's dwindling budget policing the application process for second-class mail permits. Meanwhile, legitimate publishers complained about advertising circulars fraudulently using their subsidy and stealing potential advertisers. Both groups joined forces and repeatedly asked Congress to tighten once again the subsidy's entry requirements. Lawmakers introduced numerous bills to curb the abuses, but Congress continued to postpone action, relying on the post office to handle the problems. Finally, after years of struggling, postal administrators arbitrarily tightened the application process and, consequently, took the privilege away from many advertising circulars and other illegitimate mailers. "Legitimate" publishers praised the department's efforts, as did the courts when a disaffected mailer protested the administrative action.[5] Ironically, by the time Congress was willing to take on the press in 1912, the post office no longer needed—or wanted—its help. Nevertheless, lawmakers used the publishers' postal privilege as the vehicle in which to impose regulations on the press's business practices.

Until 1912, Congress had left the press basically alone in terms of regulation except for the Alien and Sedition Acts of 1798, the 1873 Comstock law involving obscenity, and the 1890 legislation that barred publications carrying lottery advertisements from the mail.[6] Rarely was the First Amendment brought into the debate. The lottery law, for example, was narrowly intended to stop a powerful Louisiana business from using the mail to operate an illegal lottery. Most lawmakers dismissed the argument that it abridged press freedom as did the U.S. Supreme Court, when it affirmed congressional authority to exclude harmful material from the mail.[7] Similarly, the First Amendment was not of concern to reform-minded

Progressives looking to curb the press's business abuses. By using the postal privilege Congress had granted the press, lawmakers reasoned that the judiciary—if true to precedent— would probably uphold any new conditions they might impose on publications applying for the subsidy.

Congress was in turmoil in August 1912—the month the Newspaper Publicity Act became law—as lawmakers readied for the anticipated bloody November elections. The Republican Party had irreversibly split, divided between the conservative old guard and the insurgents, a term coined by journalist Mark Sullivan to describe progressive Republicans who disagreed with party leadership. The party regulars had nominated President William H. Taft for a second term, while Republican progressives, primarily from midwestern and western states, selected former president Theodore Roosevelt to head the Progressive (Bull Moose) Party. The Democrats had chosen Woodrow Wilson, governor of New Jersey, on the forty-sixth ballot to head their ticket. And Eugene Debs was again running for president on the Socialist ticket. Such was the highly volatile nature of American politics in 1912.[8]

Populist lawmakers, mostly Democrats, had long complained about the press's unhealthy alliance with the trusts that, they believed, controlled the nation. When the Democrats gained control of the House of Representatives in 1910 after eighteen years of being the minority party, reform-minded lawmakers began pushing for legislation to curb the excesses of business, including those of the press. Regulation was desperately needed, the House Pujo Committee investigating the "Money Trust" concluded in 1912, because "[t]he concentration of wealth, money and property in the United States under the control and in the hands of a few individuals or great corporations has grown to such an enormous extent that unless checked it will ultimately threaten the perpetuity of our institutions."[9]

Democratic initiatives, however, had often been squashed in the Senate, where the Republican Party still held a slight majority. The growing schism between mainstream Republicans and the insurgents, consequently, meant good news for the Democrats since the insurgents sometimes bolted their party and voted with the Democrats on reform legislation. Like many Democrats, the insurgents distrusted the press, often accusing it of unhealthy corporate alliances and unfriendly coverage of their proposals.[10] It was not surprising, then, that some of them joined forces with the Democrats in 1912 to enact the only Progressive-era federal regulations imposed on the press—the Newspaper Publicity Act.

The process by which the Newspaper Publicity Act became law bore many of the earmarks that characterized reform policy making in the Progressive era.[11] First, reformers from both political parties looked for models of state regulations that could be adapted for use by the federal government. Second, lawmakers looked to the "experts," in this case postal bureaucrats who had spent years finetuning administrative rules governing the second-class mail subsidy, for guidance as they crafted legislation. Third, although congressional debates showed some partisan cleavages, strict party affiliations only partly explained the voting. Fourth, people who championed the law did so for a spectrum of reasons; some acted on their beliefs about the role of untainted communication in the democratic process; others simply wanted to punish hated publications. And last, the object of the reforms—the press—did not uniformly oppose the law; some publishers and advertisers supported one or another of its provisions, reflecting intra-industry competition.

The second half of this study deals primarily with the regulators and the press's response to having its business practices supervised by the government. Chapter 5 explains the policy making that led to the press regulations and describes how Congress, the post office, and the courts reacted to the legal challenge brought by disgruntled publishers. Chapters 6, 7, and 8 take each of the three regulations that compose the law—ownership disclosure, advertisement identification, and circulation verification—and explain the regulatory circumstances that preceded congressional action. They also show how publishers and advertisers tried to use each of the regulations for their own interests. Chapter 9 analyzes the significance of the regulations and synthesizes the study's underlying themes of progressivism and publicity, government regulation and the press, and the increased reliance on professional administrators in the policy-making process during the early years of the twentieth century.

CHAPTER FIVE

The Press Examined

On Saturday morning, August 24, 1912, hours before the Sixty-Second Congress adjourned, members hurriedly approved a controversial postal appropriations bill. Buried within the legislation were the only federal regulations governing the press enacted during the Progressive years. The regulations, known as the Newspaper Publicity Act, required most publications using the highly subsidized second-class postal rate to identify their owners and to label advertisements resembling news or editorials. Dailies also were forced to publish accurate circulation figures. Several lawmakers admitted afterwards that their thoughts were elsewhere when the vote was called, most likely on the upcoming contentious election in November.

The act's opponents claimed that politicians' inattention allowed a few Populists angry with the press to push through legislation that threatened the First Amendment rights of all periodicals. Proponents, on the other hand, asserted that members of Congress knowingly voted for the regulations in order to curb abuses within the industry, abuses that harmed the credibility of legitimate publishers and advertisers. Not surprisingly, then, the Newspaper Publicity Act has been praised as a significant reform, condemned as insidious regulation of the press, and dismissed as a toothless nuisance.

This chapter explores how policy makers—in state legislatures, Congress, the post office, and the courts—took on the issue of press regulation, the First Amendment notwithstanding.

Precursors to Federal Regulation

Lawmakers have worried about corporate influences on the press since the advent of commercial journalism. The Populist Party's 1892 local party platform broadly asserted that "newspapers are subsidized or muzzled." Corporate corruption—in the press, in business, in the ballot box, in Congress—was bringing the nation "to the verge of moral, political and material ruin."[1] Republican insurgents and Democrats also blamed the press for falling under the influence of advertisers, sensationalizing the news, and catering to base human desires. In a speech before the Periodical Publishers' Association in 1912, presidential hopeful Senator Robert La Follette, one of the most vocal Republican insurgents and also a publisher, blasted the press for being controlled by the "money power."[2] Likewise, William Jennings Bryan, long-time Democratic leader and owner of the weekly *Commoner*, often discussed the need for federal legislation to require publishers to publicize their business interests and to purify their editorial and advertising columns.[3]

The states moved first to regulate some of the press's most egregious business practices, just as they had pioneered regulatory initiatives against other industries. In 1893, the California legislature enacted the nation's first circulation-disclosure law. At the urging of William Randolph Hearst, publisher of the *San Francisco Examiner*, legislators made it illegal for a publication in California to "willfully and knowingly misrepresent the circulation of such newspaper or periodical, for the purpose of securing advertising or other patronage."[4] Other states followed suit. The Colorado legislature prohibited a publication from using "untrue or misleading statements, as to its actual bona fide circulation." Kansas lawmakers went a step further and forbade publishers from lying about a publication's actual paid circulation defined in the statute as copies sold at the regular, advertised price. Copies distributed free or at a substantially reduced price, in other words, did not count as bona fide circulation.[5]

State legislatures also debated whether the public had the

right to know the names of persons responsible for a publication. Pennsylvania and New York legislators passed laws in 1907 to require publications to print in a prominent place their owners' names or, in the case of corporate ownership or partnership, to identify their officers. The Pennsylvania law also forced disclosure of managing editors' names, while the New York statute required owners' or officers' addresses.[6] By 1912, several states had enacted similar legislation.[7] California, in fact, went so far as to require authors to sign articles or editorials that might "blacken the memory of one who is dead, or to impeach the honesty, integrity, virtue or reputation . . . of one who is alive and thereby expose him or her to public hatred, contempt or ridicule."[8]

On the federal level, Congress considered placing restrictions on the press several years before passage of the Newspaper Publicity Act. In 1897 Representative Welsey Jones (R-Wash.) introduced a bill to require publications using the mail to identify their stockholders and editorial writers. "[T]he reading public has a right to know the sources of the editorial literature which they read and the influences that dictate such utterances," Jones said, but the bill died in committee.[9] Eleven years later, Texas Democrat Samuel B. Cooper sponsored similar legislation with the enthusiastic approval of President Theodore Roosevelt, but it never reached the House floor.[10] In 1910 Senator Robert L. Owen (D-Okla.), known for his allegiance to progressive causes, introduced legislation to require publishers to label advertisements that resembled reading matter—another precursor of one of the 1912 regulations. In a letter to a friend, the senator wrote that private monopolies "deceive the public by false news and by crafty articles in the press of the country, using intellectual mercenaries who make the worse appear the better reason."[11] Owen thought the mandatory advertising label would eliminate some of the deception, but it too died in committee, along with a hotly debated proposal to charge more postage on the advertising portion of a publication.

Congress also considered legislation that clearly went beyond regulating the press's business practices. The Sixtieth Congress, for example, rejected a bill that would have denied a publication mailing privileges if it carried stories about divorces, murders, or court proceedings regarding immoral activities. That same session two Pennsylvania representatives—Republican Ernest Acheson and Democrat Joseph D. Brodhead—sponsored separate legislation to prohibit publications from carrying liquor and divorce advertisements.[12] Neither bill was reported out of the House post office committee.

These state and federal attempts at legislating the press's business activities received little attention in the nation's major publications. Sometimes, certain elements of the industry actually pushed for their enactment, particularly the state laws requiring accurate circulation figures. By 1912, reformers intensified their campaign to encourage Congress to enact regulations to curb the press's excesses.[13] In one instance, the Right Reverend Henry A. Brann of St. Agnes Catholic Church in New York City aggressively lobbied for legislation to require editorial and column writers to sign their articles. "The paper is an impersonality," Brann said. "[S]ome one should be made to stand for what is in it. . . . Such a law would promote morality, honesty and manliness."[14] Accountability through publicity would help solve other press abuses too, reformers reasoned. If food must be labeled, milk certified, and banks regulated, then why should the press escape regulations to guarantee its stories and advertisements, and to reveal its owners and circulation?[15]

The time was ripe for Congress to enact press regulations in 1912. Because of the First Amendment, though, lawmakers had only one means of curbing the press—through its second-class postal subsidy—and that was the avenue they took in regulating the press's business activities.

Policy Making in the House of Representatives

The Newspaper Publicity Act began as an amendment to the 1913 postal appropriations bill. The original legislation, reported out of the House Post Office and Post Roads Committee in early March, contained no mention of the controversial press regulations.[16] Nor did it include a rate increase for second-class mail, an issue vigorously fought and defeated in the previous congressional session. Although President William Howard Taft still believed that publishers did not pay their fair share of postage, he had tempered his crusade to raise the second-class rate.[17] His 1909 proposal to increase publications' postage had been met with such hostility that the president wrote Herman Kohlsaat, publisher of the *Chicago Record-Herald*, "I have not been familiar myself with any situation politically where there has been so much hypocrisy, so much hysteria, so much misrepresentation by the press growing out of their own personal interest in legislation."[18] Taft's reluctance to take on the publishers again could have stemmed from a desperate, but futile, attempt to garner press support for his reelection, as a Republican congressman suggested.[19] But it could also be explained in part by his success at eliminating a $17.5 million postal deficit in his first three years as president— a feat considered to be one of his administration's greatest accomplishments.[20]

Whatever the reason, the press did not need to rally its forces against a proposed rate hike in the 1913 postal appropriations bill. Some publishers, however, were lobbying against the bill's parcel-post provisions. By lowering the postage on packages sent through the mail, parcel post would hurt local retailers and advertisers, these publishers believed, while benefiting mail-order companies. The editor of *Interstate Grocer* tried to frighten members to vote against the proposal by threatening to publish their positions on the issue. The ploy backfired when a Democratic congressman from Alabama angrily denounced the threat on the House floor and demanded that the editor publicly identify *Interstate Grocer's* owners, stockholders, subscribers, and circulation figures.[21] Lawmakers applauded.

The next day Democratic standard-bearer William Jennings Bryan again called for legislation to force publications to identify stockholders. Speaking before the National Democratic Club in New York City, Bryan said disclosure was the key since "[t]here is no greater menace than the predatory interests which own newspapers and employ brilliant editors to chloroform

their readers while the owners pick their pockets."[22] Behind
the scenes in the House of Representatives, action was already
taking place to make Bryan's proposal a reality.

Shortly after reporting the appropriations bill out of the
House post office committee, chairman John A. Moon (D-
Tenn.) asked members of the House Committee on Rules to
permit riders (proposals that bypass regular legislative action)
to be attached to the bill. Committee members agreed to the
request, an unusual concession that occurred only eleven times
in 1911 and 1912.[23] Democratic Congressman Henry Barnhart
then persuaded the rules committee to support a rider which
would require publications to print in a prominent place in
every issue the names of their owners, investors holding more
than $500 worth of stock, and managing editors. Barnhart,
a weekly newspaper publisher from Indiana, had introduced
similar legislation the routine way the previous year, but it
died in committee. In support of his request, the congressman
showed committee members copies of ten of the country's
leading newspapers. Two listed editors, one named its publisher, while the other seven circulated anonymously. The proposed rider would let Americans know "who controls and
directs editorial opinions," Barnhart said, and would "bring
the honest editor out from under the unfair suspicion that he
is controlled by evil influences." With chairman Robert L.
Henry's avid support, the rules committee quickly voted to
support Barnhart's rider and urged the full House to do the
same.[24]

Republicans, however, strenuously objected to the irregu-
lar procedure of adding riders to appropriations bills to expe-
dite legislation, and a long partisan debate ensued.[25] As the
House clerk read the rules committee's report into the record,
former Speaker of the House Joseph Cannon interrupted to
protest the procedural deviation. The riders—particularly Barnhart's amendment and the parcel-post proposal—circum-
vented the legislative process, bypassing appropriate House
committees, and subsequent hearings and reports, Cannon
complained. Such maneuvering was more czarlike than any of
Cannon's controversial actions as speaker that caused him to

lose political power in 1910, other Republicans contended. Democrats, delighted with being the majority party after so many years, defended the practice. "If you have a meritorious proposition that you can defend, that is just, that is in the interest of the American people," rules committee chairman Henry argued, "there is no better time to consider it than the first opportunity when you can get it before the legislative body." This way "no one can claim that they have been sent to a committee and there pigeonholed, nor can they charge that the Committee on Rules has been recreant to the trust reposed in them." A rider like the Barnhart amendment was especially important since it allowed the American people to "see the men who stand behind the guns trained against public officials," Henry added, amid applause.[26]

At this point, members began asking questions about the Barnhart rider. A Michigan Republican wanted to know why the amendment was limited to $500 worth of stock. The rules chairman responded that "we thought that when we can reach those who own as much as $500 worth of stock we could reach all worth considering to rectify the evils." But the rider could certainly be amended, he added.[27] Albert Burleson, Texas Democrat and future postmaster general, wondered why the amendment did not deal with a publication's indebtedness. Again, Henry, a fellow Texan, said that could be added during general House debate, and he would gladly vote for it. The rider at this point, Henry explained, primarily "establishes a principle that hereafter the newspapers and periodicals and the journals that form public opinion are not authorized to give expression of their views unless the American people know the ownership of those weapons of public expression."[28]

Representative Henry Barnhart also spoke briefly on behalf of his rider. Saying that he represented "the great and glorious profession of journalism," the *Rochester* (Ind.) *Sentinel* publisher declared that he would support amendments to make the legislation "as broad and effective as possible" to clean up the profession "that guides the world." When debate ended, House members overwhelmingly approved the addition of the Barnhart rider to the appropriations bill.[29]

As soon as the modified legislation came up for debate, Barnhart introduced two more amendments. The first incorporated Burleson's suggestion to include indebtedness of $500 or more to the ownership requirement, and the second one required the labeling of advertisements that resembled news stories or editorials. "If there be editors who sell their souls for a mess of pottage, their identity should be known," Barnhart said. "And if there be newspapers or other periodicals published to promote corrupt practices or prey upon the credulity of the people by covertly upholding avarice and greed, let the light of publicity shine fully upon them."[30]

On the House floor, the proposed press regulations received scant debate compared to the bill's provisions covering appropriations, Sunday mail service, parcel post, federal funds for post roads, and railroad express companies. When they were discussed, Democrats generally praised their intent and sought ways to broaden their scope, while a few Republicans tried unsuccessfully to dilute the legislation's impact, and Socialist Victor Berger denounced the regulations as "insane," though written with the best of intentions. Several Democrats saw Barnhart's amendments as an extension of other publicity laws. "If campaign committees and candidates for public office should disclose the source of the money for campaign expenses, why should not the newspapers and magazines, whose editorials have a greater influence over the campaign than the distribution of money?" a Wisconsin Democrat asked.[31] In keeping with the Democratic Party's emphasis on publicity as a cure for corporate corruption, others wanted them to go further in curbing press abuses. Asserting that the press had "fallen on evil days," Representative John A. Thayer (D-Mass.) thought publishers should also be required to publicize "the sums paid by the largest advertisers" quarterly or at least annually so that the "overt influences in the news and editorial columns might be revealed."[32] A Kentucky Democrat wanted to require identification of all editors, while a South Dakota lawmaker sought to strike out the $500 limit on ownership disclosure, believing that all owners should be identified. And a Georgia congressman saw the debate as an opportunity to introduce an amendment to bar publications in "dry" states from carrying liquor advertisements.[33] Although none of these proposals was approved, no one defended the press during the House debate.

Only a few representatives strongly opposed Barnhart's regulations and then usually not out of concern for the press but because of worry about implementation. Victor L. Berger, the first Socialist elected to Congress, said the "impossible and ridiculous" proposal was an example of how a "bill, introduced with the best of intentions, can be turned into an insane piece of legislation." The Wisconsin congressman feared that labor publications in particular would be damaged if they had to identify their owners and stockholders. For example, more than 8,700 people "owned" the Socialist *Milwaukee Leader*, Berger said, and many of them might be blacklisted if they were identified. Furthermore, if the paper had to list all of its investors, then "we could not print anything else. We could not even tell our people in Milwaukee that this is the only kind of reform they can expect from the Democratic side," Berger joked as Republican lawmakers laughed and applauded.[34] To address Berger's concerns, House members approved an amendment to exempt publications "published by or under the auspices of fraternal or benevolent societies or orders or trades-unions."[35]

Another opponent of the bill—J. Hampton Moore, a Pennsylvania Republican—believed that the regulations would unfairly require publications to reveal private business information and would become "an entering wedge to the throttling of a free press." He also worried that the press would attack any lawmaker who voted for the legislation.[36] Trying to reassure colleagues who feared such reprisals, Barnhart promised, "[E]very honest editor and every deserving periodical reader . . . will approve this method of compelling all editors and publishers to stand out in the broad sunlight of day. The reading public which pays for editorial enlightenment is entitled to know who's who in journalism before it decides what's what."[37] Another Democratic congressman-publisher agreed with Barnhart's observations but wondered whether any law could improve the press's public image. Barnhart countered Congressman James M. Cox's cynicism, asserting that "while the good editor will never be free from criticism, [he or she] can be made free from unjust accusations of being controlled by corrupt proprietary interests if this law is enacted." Likewise, the "bad editor will be exposed to public view by the same process of publicity."[38]

When debate ended on this section of the postal appropriations bill in late April, Barnhart's proposed press regulations remained intact with only minor content changes. On May 2, 1912, the Democratic-controlled House approved the entire appropriations bill.[39]

The Senate's Turn

As the House of Representatives debated the proposed regulations, some publishers were pressuring the Senate to protect their business interests and those of honest advertisers. The Chilton Company, publisher of many trade journals, led the fight for federal legislation to require publishers using the second-class mail subsidy to "print in a prominent position in each issue, statements under oath, showing in detail the exact circulation of the issue next preceding."[40] When the House of Representatives did not include such a requirement in the 1913 postal appropriations bill, the Chilton Company intensified its lobbying efforts in the Senate and urged other publishers and advertisers to do the same.

As chairman of the Senate Committee on Post Offices and Post Roads, Jonathan Bourne, Jr. (R-Ore.), was subject to much of the lobbying pressure. Bourne, often aligned with the Republican insurgents, was familiar with controversy. Once a golf companion of President Taft, the first-term senator from Portland quickly grew disenchanted with the Republican administration and became one of its chief critics. In 1911 he became the first president of the National Progressive Republican League, an organization designed to publicize progressive principles and indirectly to support Senator Robert La Follette's bid for the Republican presidential nomination.[41] Although quick to criticize the press, Bourne bragged that he was the only Republican on the Senate post office committee to vote against the president's proposals to increase the second-class postal rate. Despite this vote, the Oregon press did not support him, and he blamed it for his defeat in the April 1912 Republican senatorial primary.[42]

Still upset about his primary defeat, Bourne became immersed in the debate involving the press regulations as soon as the House bill was reported to his committee in early May. Postmaster General Frank H. Hitchcock, who ran President Taft's presidential campaign in 1908, immediately notified Bourne that he opposed the legislation. The "provision is not only needless but will be positively harmful as it will . . . be resented as a censorship of the press," Hitchcock wrote Bourne. Nevertheless, "[i]f the provision has merit at all, it would seem beyond controversy that its provisions should apply alike to all second-class publications, particularly since such insertion will be simple and require but little space," he continued, explaining his objection to the exclusion of benevolent, fraternal or trade-union organizations.[43] After this exchange, Hitchcock and the Post Office Department stayed out of the debate. In fact, one month later, a top postal official declined Bourne's request to draft an amendment to the legislation, explaining that Hitchcock had ordered his staff not to become involved in the negotiations.[44]

Publishers, however, did not share Hitchcock's reluctance to work with Bourne. The Chilton Company continued to press the senator to add a circulation requirement to the bill, and the editor of the *Wisconsin Equity News* urged Bourne to retain the "important and necessary" disclosure regulations. Several other publishers told Bourne to kill the legislation. Calling the regulations "immoral, wicked and unjust," the president of the Orange Judd and the Phelps Publishing Companies ordered Bourne to do "away with all these subterfuges—these unpatriotic, unwise, impracticable, demagogic schemes to fetter the press!"[45] The Butterick Company, whose magazines circulated 27 million copies in 1911, sent its attorney Herbert Noble to meet with Bourne on the impracticability of the proposals, particularly the ownership requirement. Noble followed up the meeting with a detailed letter, asserting that the legislation would cost the company $81,000 to publish the names of approximately nineteen thousand stockholders. The editor of the *Dakota Farmer* expressed similar concerns as did T. W. Doubleday, publisher of such publications as *World's Work* and *Nature Library*, and F. C. J. Tessaro, a lobbyist for the American Newspaper Publishers Association, the Trade Press Association, and the Periodical Publishers Association of America. Tessaro also asked the senator to hold hearings on the proposed regulations, but Bourne declined, explaining that "there are so many new provisions in the bill and only a limited time in which to consider same."[46]

After much behind-the-scenes lobbying and a visit from Representative Henry Barnhart, sponsor of the legislation, members of the Senate post office committee substituted a milder version of the bill, a move appreciated by some segments of the press but still criticized.[47] Instead of requiring the identification of every person investing $550 or more in a publication, the Senate version exempted people owning less than one percent. It also reduced the disclosure requirement to twice a year rather than once a week and sliced in half the penalty of $100 to $1,000 for failing to label disguised advertisements. Picking up on Postmaster General Hitchcock's comments, the committee also eliminated the House exemption for fraternal, benevolent, and trade-union publications.[48]

These changes provided "a more practical and more easily administered" way of achieving "accountability," Bourne told his colleagues as he presented the committee's report to the full Senate. Committee members were in "hearty accord" with the House's intent of letting the public "know to whom the paper is in any way obligated or may have a bias," Bourne said, but they believed the original legislation was "needlessly burdensome." Representative Barnhart, in fact, agreed that the Senate version retained his purpose—that of publicity, he added. Such publicity was necessary because of the "common belief that many periodicals are secretly owned or controlled, and that in reading such papers the public is deceived through ignorance of the interests the publication represents." Since the second-class mail privilege "gives these publications a circulation and

a corresponding influence unequaled in history," Bourne said
the committee concluded that "the public should know the
individuals who own or control them."[49]

Along with the committee report, Senator Bourne presented his colleagues with an information print describing each
provision of the appropriations bill. Common today, this hand-
out marked the first time legislation was systemically explained
in writing before members voted on it. Bourne also sent the
summary to several publishers, along with a letter stating that
he hoped the information would result "in more intelligent
legislation, preventing the enactment of 'jokers' through the
lack of information, and economizing the time of Senators and
Representatives." Although he received much public acclaim
for his efforts, ironically, some publishers later attacked him
for sneaking the press regulations through Congress.[50]

Senators needed the bulletin to sort through the myriad
amendments attached to the postal appropriations bill. What
came to be known as the Newspaper Publicity Act, in fact, was
one of the least debated features. Lawmakers were much more
interested in the provisions to create a parcel post (Bourne's
cause), to fund a roads program, and to change postal employees'
classifications. Nevertheless, debate over the press regulations
primarily divided along ideological lines. Several mainstream
Republicans vigorously opposed them, while Democrats and
insurgent Republicans generally endorsed them as a remedy—
albeit partial—for press abuses.

The opposition mounted an attack to gut the legislation
with little success. First, a few Republican senators introduced
amendments to exempt, in the words of Senator Jacob H.
Gallinger (R-N.H.), "all the little publications scattered all over
the country" from the regulations. Acknowledging that large
publications might be "controlled by some corporation or plu-
tocrat," Gallinger thought it was ridiculous to require ownership statements from weekly newspapers with less than five
thousand circulation and from innocuous publications, such as
"the Youth's Companion, the National Temperance Society
Magazine, the Humane Society Magazine, the church publications, and the Sabbath school publications." The majority of

senators accepted Gallinger's point about nonprofit publications but not about the weeklies. Kansas senator Joseph L.
Bristow, a well-known Republican insurgent, persuasively argued that the ownership requirement should apply to large and
small publications alike for it was probably more "injurious to
the public welfare for an influence to own a large number of
small papers as one large paper."[51]

Senator George T. Oliver, Pennsylvania Republican and
publisher of the *Pittsburgh Gazette-Times* and *Chronicle-Tele-
graph*, next took up the fight to weaken the press regulations.
First, he unsuccessfully fought to limit the number of people
associated with a publication who had to be identified under the
legislation. Instead of identifying "editors, publishers, business
managers, and owners" as the bill stated, Oliver suggested
that "editors" be switched to "managing editor," "publishers"
changed to "publisher," and "business managers" deleted alto-
gether. Democratic senator James A. Reed from Missouri vigorously objected to the proposed changes. "The principal purpose of this bill is to advise the public as to just who is owning
the paper," Reed asserted. "[A] newspaper that has but one
publisher will state that fact, but if the newspaper should hap-
pen to have two publishers [as in a partnership], then they will
be required to set forth their names" and not hide behind the
partnership's name. Likewise, editors needed to be identified,
Reed argued, because "[o]ne of the greatest evils, in my opinion, of the newspaper business . . . is the fact that the public
do not know, and can not find out, who is responsible for the
articles that appear." The amendment was defeated.[52]

Senator-publisher Oliver next unsuccessfully tried to convince his colleagues that the clause requiring publications to
disclose the names of investors invaded publishers' private business rights. Senator Reed again countered Oliver's arguments.
Wasn't every publication using the second-class mail privilege
"engaged in public business in one sense?," he asked. Exposing
financial indebtedness was one of the bill's fundamental goals,
Senator Bourne added, for how else could one "show what the
[publisher's] bias is or what the accountability may be"? Oliver
responded, "If [a publisher's] creditors aim to control his pol-

icy, his creditors can very readily conceal the act that they are his creditors." To that, Reed agreed, "but, because misstatements may be made in some instances is no reason for failing to require information to be given; and if misstatements are made, then somebody will have been guilty of bad faith and the remedy will be at hand."[53]

As the Senate debated the proposed press regulations, the University of Wisconsin hosted the first National Newspaper Conference where academicians, politicians, critics, editors, and publishers wrestled with the issues of secret ownership and disguised advertisements, much like the senators in Washington, D.C. Although some participants urged Congress and state legislatures to enact disclosure legislation to curb the abuses, no evidence suggests that they or other critics were influential in getting the press regulations enacted.[54] Nevertheless, the Senate approved the committee's substitute for Barnhart's House bill with a few minor changes soon after the conference.[55] One day later, the Senate passed the entire amended postal appropriations bill. After a brief procedural debate, a conference committee was appointed to resolve the differences between the House and Senate versions.[56] Committee members made only one change in the Senate substitute of the Barnhart bill—adding a circulation-disclosure requirement: "And also, in the case of daily newspapers, there shall be included in such statement the average of the number of copies of each issue of such publication sold or distributed to paid subscribers during the preceding six months."[57] With time running out before fall recess, the Senate and House quickly approved the conference report with no public debate on the new circulation requirement and sent the postal appropriations bill to President Taft for his signature.[58] The Chilton Company's lobbying efforts were finally successful.

As of October 1, 1912, most commercial publishers had to publicize twice a year heretofore private information about their businesses, including the names and addresses of their editors, managing editors, publishers, business managers, owners, and stockholders holding more than 1 percent of the stock. Daily newspapers had the additional requirement of disclosing their average circulations for the preceding six months. And all advertisements resembling stories or editorials had to be plainly marked "advertisement."[59]

Congress Stands Fast

While the press regulations had relatively smooth sailing through Congress, as soon as the bill became law a storm of controversy engulfed them. Outcries from publishers of daily newspapers predicting business ruin and government censorship drowned out the quiet acceptance of many weeklies and magazines, and the enthusiastic response of the trade press. Urged on by the American Newspaper Publishers Association, many dailies condemned the Newspaper Publicity Act and accused Congress of clandestinely giving in to a few Populists who hated the press.[60] Senator Bourne quickly refuted that argument. Although the legislation began as a rider to the House appropriations bill in early May, the Senate post office committee did not report it to the full Senate until late July, Bourne wrote the owner of the *Pittsburgh Post* and *Sun*, so "there can be no suspicion of hasty action."[61] Indeed, the press had reported on the proposed regulations while they were in committee and had also praised Bourne for preparing a detailed bulletin on the appropriations bill.[62]

By mid-September, the ANPA had launched a campaign to repeal the regulations at the same time it was trying to convince publishers to challenge the law's constitutionality in court. Congressional members who had voted for the regulations were depicted either as vindictive toward publications "which have had the audacity to criticize adversely their public record" or naively unaware of the law's dangerous, anti-press overtones.[63]

As the daily press intensified its attack, most lawmakers remained silent on the controversial law, an understandable strategy since many were campaigning in a turbulent election year. But Representative Henry Barnhart and Senator Jonathan Bourne, both running for reelection, went on the offensive after taking the brunt of press criticism for their prominent roles in the law's passage. Reminding a *New York Times* reporter that he, too, was a newspaperman, Barnhart denied that he had proposed the legislation out of vengeance or ill will. Rather, he drafted the bill

> to let the public know who owns, edits, and controls the periodicals which the public reads—to "smoke out" the secret owners and publishers of the publications owned and controlled for selfish or evil purposes, and to free legitimate and meritorious publishers from the unfair charges frequently made against their publications that they are under this or that baneful financial influence.

Eventually, responsible publishers and journalists would endorse the law, Barnhart predicted. Those who did not were probably owners of "certain big publications which do not want it known that trust magnates like Perkins, J. P. Morgan, and their kind own and influence them."[64] Already more than fifty publishers had contacted him in support of the regulations, Barnhart said; many of them, in fact, called for even more rigid requirements. "We newspapermen have for years been crying out for publicity—publicity as to corporations, etc.—and I think that it is high time we took our own medicine."[65] The congressman, who won reelection, did, however, try to distance himself from the "inconvenient" circulation requirement added in conference committee.

Senator Jonathan Bourne, who was running for reelection as an independent after losing the Republican primary, did not waver in his support of the press regulations. He considered them the best remedy for getting rid of "those irresponsible and dishonest publications which have been the greatest menace to the good standing and influence of the press."[66] Comparing the Newspaper Publicity Act to other public disclosure laws, Bourne said it was "just as important for the public to be protected from false news, as for it to be protected from impure foods, and there is just as much justification for requiring a paper to carry the names of its owners, as for requiring that a can of fruit shall bear the name of the concern that packed it."[67] The law "leaves every newspaper and magazine absolutely free to express its own opinions or the opinions of others and to publish any news or any facts," and it "gives no official the slightest inquisitorial or controlling power."[68] From Bourne's perspective, the press had no legitimate reason to oppose the regulations. Some publishers were "on the right side of the question," Senator Knute Nelson, a Republican insurgent from Minnesota, reassured his friend as he forwarded a favorable editorial to Bourne's office. Thanking Nelson for his support, Bourne predicted, "Within a very few years the newspapers themselves will be the strongest advocates of the law."[69] Indeed, his prediction came true within two years but not before he was voted out of office. Noting Bourne's defeat, Louis Wiley, business manager of the *New York Times*, gloated, "This action on the part of the electorate of Oregon may be regarded as typical of the feelings of the people of the United States for a measure which is repugnant to the civilization of the twentieth century."[70] Of course, he was referring to the Newspaper Publicity Act.

Opposition to the press regulations did not guarantee reelection, however, as a mainstream Republican congressman from New York discovered. Opposing the original bill, Representative Henry S. De Forest introduced legislation to repeal the regulations in a move to help his reelection campaign. It didn't, and he lost his House seat in the November election. Two other Republicans who had voted for the regulations also introduced bills to repeal or tone down the law. North Dakota Senator Porter McCumber—not up for reelection—offered an amendment to alleviate "unjust burdens upon the newspapers," after his state's publishers convinced him that the regulations were wrong. Likewise, New York publishers persuaded Representative Luther Mott to introduce legislation to weaken the ownership requirement.[71] When none of the bills got through committee, publishers speculated that Congress had decided to wait for the anticipated Supreme Court's decision striking down the press regulations. In the unlikely event that the High Court would affirm the law, Warren W. Bailey, the newly elected Democratic representative from Pennsylvania who owned the *Johnstown Daily Democrat*, vowed to fight for its repeal. The *New York Times* supported this strategy; the Supreme Court, after all, needed to decide "once for all, whether the guarantee of freedom of speech and the liberty of the press is to be destroyed."[72] Letting the Supreme Court decide, however, troubled Georgia representative Charles L. Bartlett, one of the few Democrats who voted against the "much too drastic" press regulations. "The Supreme Court has decided that Congress may prohibit anything from going through the mails and that, I fear, will govern the ruling," Bartlett correctly predicted.[73]

The Post Office Sputters into Action

President Taft's postmaster general Frank Hitchcock faced a dilemma. He had originally opposed the press regulations but now was legally bound to enforce them. And it could not have come at a worse time—the 1912 presidential election was less than three months away and President Taft was trailing in the three-way race. So, with "great reluctance," as noted in the press, Hitchcock began preparing to enforce the act. At every chance, he reminded publishers that the Post Office Department disliked the law but would administer it "faithfully and impartially."[74] Hitchcock had an enormous job on his hands. In less than two months, the department had to design a form eliciting the required information and then distribute it to most publications nationwide. Furthermore, local postmasters needed to be notified of the changes and instructed on how to administer the regulations. These tasks imposed "strange and arduous duties upon the department," officials complained.[75] In mid-September, the postmaster general reported that the new forms were in the mail to 28,144 publications using the mail subsidy—2,514 dailies, 17,217 weeklies, 5,277 monthlies, 1,351 quarterlies, and 1,785 miscellaneous periodicals. Only about 1,500 nonprofit publications did not have to file the statement.[76]

All the while, publishers kept contacting the department for clarification. Were free books and theatre passes considered "valuable considerations," requiring reviews to be labeled as

advertisements? Did listing only the names of trustees fulfill
the ownership requirement? How was the term "circulation"
defined? Postal officials hesitatingly answered the first two
questions. Yes, reviews generated from free books and theatre
passes should probably be labeled, though the courts would
ultimately have to decide the law's limits. No, identification of
trustees alone would not meet the ownership requirement at
least not until a court ruled otherwise.[77] The department, however, did not want to tackle the circulation inquiries. Instead,
Postmaster General Hitchcock—some said at the president's
urging—asked Attorney General George W. Wickersham to
interpret this provision of the Newspaper Publicity Act. In less
than two weeks, the attorney general issued an ambiguous
opinion that criticized the regulation but offered little legal
guidance on how to administer it.[78]

   Although the law specified October 1 as the deadline for
publishers' compliance, the post office ran into trouble deliv-
ering the required forms, especially on the Pacific Coast. Some
publications did not receive the forms until October 4, adding
fuel to the critics' complaints. But between 3,000 and 4,000
papers did meet the deadline, including 38 dailies. More than
18,000 publications, including 1,016 dailies, had filed by October 11, when Postmaster General Hitchcock announced that
the department would soon begin contacting publishers who
were in noncompliance. One month later, compliance stood at
83 percent with 23,500 publications, including 1,908 dailies
(76 percent), filing.[79] By this time, however, Hitchcock had
agreed to postpone enforcement until the Supreme Court's
decision.

   The post office's reluctance to enforce the law vanished
when Albert S. Burleson, former Democratic representative
from Texas, became President Woodrow Wilson's postmaster
general in March 1913. Burleson, along with most Democrats
in Congress, had voted for the Newspaper Publicity Act and
had even recommended strengthening its ownership requirement. Not surprisingly, then, the Post Office Department
moved to enforce the regulations as soon as Burleson was at
its helm. The first indication of this policy shift came in early

March, when the New York City postmaster notified the *Journal of Commerce*, one of the papers challenging the law's constitutionality, that its postal subsidy was in jeopardy unless it complied immediately with the law. Soon afterwards, Burleson announced that it was his duty "as an executive officer to enforce the law as I find it" until the Supreme Court ruled otherwise. Noting that nonenforcement "would be a discrimination to the 90 percent of newspapers that have complied," Burleson expressed no sympathy for the delinquent publications, including dailies in Boston, New York City, Philadelphia, Chicago, and St. Louis.[80] Attorneys challenging the law immediately asked the Supreme Court for a restraining order, which it quickly granted, much to the delight of some publishers who predicted that the Court would soon strike down the press regulations.[81] They were wrong.

The Supreme Court Upholds the Law

As publishers, editors, advertisers, politicians, and postal administrators grappled with the Newspaper Publicity Act, the judiciary controlled its fate. Only the Supreme Court could ultimately determine whether Congress had acted constitutionally in passing the press regulations and whether the Post Office Department had the administrative authority to enforce the law. The second decade of the twentieth century marked a transitional period on the High Court. Six of the justices were Taft appointees, including three Democrats—Horace H. Lurton, Joseph R. Lamar, and Chief Justice Edward D. White. The Court's caseload was at an all-time high, jumping from about 200 cases each term in the early 1900s to more than 290 cases in 1912 and 1913. Many of the cases involved the politically explosive question of the constitutionality of controversial state and federal laws. Critics, including former president Theodore Roosevelt, attacked the Court for its judicial activism when it overturned some of these laws. Under White's leadership, however, the Court usually showed a steadfast hesitation to second-guess Congress and the increasingly powerful administrative agencies, including the Post Office Department.[82]

Nevertheless, the American Newspaper Publishers Association was determined to fight the Newspaper Publicity Act, and offered the assistance of its attorneys to any publisher willing to mount a court challenge. At first, the association thought the publisher of the *Freie Press* in Brooklyn, New York, would test the law, but when he declined, it recruited the New York-based owner of the *Journal of Commerce & Commercial Bulletin* and *The Review*.[83] Lewis Publishing Company, publisher of the *New York Morning Telegraph*, also decided to challenge the law. In early October, both businesses asked the New York federal district court to enjoin the post office from enforcing the press regulations because they violated the First Amendment and would financially ruin the newspapers. Esteemed judge Learned Hand dismissed both cases, and, as expected, the attorneys immediately asked the High Court to decide "a public question of great importance."[84] Asserting that Congress wanted "to regulate the business of journalism, while pretending to regulate the transportation of the mails," James M. Beck, Lewis Publishing's attorney and former U.S. solicitor general, posed this "grave" constitutional question: "How far can Congress, under the pretext of exercising an unquestioned federal power, such as the power 'to establish post offices and post roads,' so use that power as to accomplish objects not within the scope of the Federal Government?"[85]

The Supreme Court immediately agreed to hear both cases concurrently, and attorneys filed written briefs in mid-October. Oral arguments followed in early December.[86] ANPA attorneys for the *Journal of Commerce* argued that the law set a dangerous precedent: "If this power exists what is to prevent Congress from further extending its power by the denial of the privileges of the mail or the imposition of a severe penalty with respect to any newspapers owned or financially influenced by individuals advocating certain public questions or the policies of political parties?" Rather, "[e]very newspaper, magazine or periodical has the right to express its opinion no matter who owns it or influences it and to deny it this right, either directly, or indirectly, by the use of a governmental department or by subjecting it to a heavy penalty, is in contravention of the Constitution," they asserted.[87]

In a separate brief, James Beck elaborated on his contention that Congress meant the law to regulate journalism, not help in the delivery of mail. First, the Post Office Department had opposed the legislation, fearing it would be seen as press censorship, he said. Second, the department already required similar information from publications seeking the second-class mail subsidy. Third, the *Congressional Record* indicated that members spent more time debating the merits of regulating the press than of helping the post office run more efficiently.[88] Since Congress could not enact the press regulations per se because of the First Amendment, Beck continued, members attached the requirements to a postal appropriations bill. "Can it be possible that what Congress could not do directly it may nevertheless accomplish indirectly by the pretense that such supervision is necessary in order that the Post Office Department may suitably carry on its important function?" The Supreme Court must throw out the Newspaper Publicity Act and reaffirm the "policy of our Constitution that no burden shall be imposed upon the press, no restriction upon its rights, no impairment of its influence," Beck argued, except in cases of libel and immorality.[89]

U.S. solicitor general William Marshall Bullitt took a different tack in his brief. Basing his argument on the assumption that noncompliance meant loss of the second-class subsidy—not all mail service as the newspapers had asserted—Bullitt reminded the justices that the Supreme Court had already ruled that "Congress can affix such conditions as it chooses to the right to be admitted to the second-class rate."[90] Congress was given this discretion because the Court saw the special mail rate as a privilege afforded to the press rather than a right. "Congress requires the individual to pay about eighty times as much per pound to get his letters carried as it requires a publisher to pay for sending newspapers through the mails," Bullitt explained. "The newspapers can comply and obtain the benefit or they can refuse to comply and use a less favored method of transmitting their papers." Either way, "there is no limitation on the power of the press to publish what and how it pleases, and to circulate as it pleases, save that it can not have the second-class postal rate unless it conforms to the statute." Likewise, Bullitt reasoned, the statute did not take away property without just compensation. A publication did not have to comply with the regulations, but if it did, "it receives its compensation a thousandfold in the almost nominal rate it pays for transmitting its papers."[91]

ANPA attorneys fired back a reply brief. The solicitor general's argument that the statute only applied to second-class mail was "wholly unexpected" and "without warrant," they said. The statute was clear. "It says unless the publisher does certain things, he shall be denied the privileges of the mail. It does not say he shall be denied the privileges of the second class mail."[92] In support of their position, the attorneys used Attorney General George Wickersham's opinion that the law was "highly penal" in excluding publications from "not merely the privilege of being carried in the mails as second-class mail matter, but the privilege of being carried in the mails at all." If the Court ruled in favor of the regulations, the justices would be practicing "judicial legislation," rewriting the law to make it constitutional—a serious accusation in those days of repeated challenges to the Supreme Court's authority.[93] In a separate brief, Lewis Publishing's attorney Beck also voiced his indignation to Bullitt's "ingenious" attempt to rewrite the statute and predicted that "[t]his Court will not construct a new statute to save the face of Congress." Nor would it allow Congress to use a special postal privilege to harass the press. Otherwise, lawmakers could "pass a law that no newspaper should be admitted to the privileges of second-class matter unless its editorial columns should support the views of the majority in the next Congress . . . [and] the judiciary would be powerless to prevent such a strangling of free discussion."[94]

The press followed the court case closely, often printing excerpts from the briefs.[95] When the Supreme Court heard oral arguments in early December, the *New York Times* praised the newspapers' attorneys for their "strong presentation" and asserted that the justices were "interested deeply" and paid "close attention." But some publications worriedly reported that several of the associate justices asked questions about congressional authority and that Chief Justice Edward D. White offhandedly remarked that newspapers vexed with the law might receive more relief from Congress than from the judiciary.[96]

Six months later, the Supreme Court unanimously affirmed that Congress had the authority to place conditions on publications accepting the highly prized second-class mail privilege. Thus, in one of the year's "most important cases," the Court ruled that the Newspaper Publicity Act was indeed constitutional.[97] According to Chief Justice White, known for his support of broad administrative latitude, the case rested on one question:

> Was the provision intended simply to supplement the existing legislation relative to second-class mail matter, or was it enacted as an exertion of legislative power to regulate the press, to curtail its freedom, and under the assumption that there was a right to compel obedience . . . to deprive one who refused to obey of all right to use the mail service?[98]

Accepting Solicitor General Bullitt's reasoning that the press regulations applied only to publications using the second-class mail rate, the Chief Justice wrote, "When the question is thus defined, its solution is free from difficulty."[99] Of course, Congress could legally impose such regulations on the press. Although the Court limited the opinion to a narrow legal question of congressional authority, as White was prone to do in order to get unanimous decisions, the justices nevertheless indicated that they agreed philosophically with the law's intent. "We believe that, since the general public bears a large portion of the expense of distribution of second-class matter, and since these publications wield a large influence because of their special concessions in the mails, it is not only equitable but highly desirable that the public should know the individuals who own or control them," the Chief Justice opined.[100] Publishers, however, should not conclude that Congress intended to violate press freedom when it enacted the Newspaper Publicity Act. After all, the Court asked, had not lawmakers favored the press with "great privileges and advantages at the public expense" for many years?[101]

The verdict was in. The Newspaper Publicity Act, though still controversial, was the law, and publishers who wanted to use the second-class mail subsidy had no choice but to comply with the regulations. The decision marked the first time the Supreme Court sanctioned federal controls aimed directly at the press's business activities and tied closely to the postal privilege. The next three chapters examine how the law affected each of the abuses it was intended to address—secret ownership, disguised advertisements, and false circulation figures. Central to these chapters is the underlying theme that once the industry realized that the press regulations would not go away, it quickly moved to embrace them.

CHAPTER SIX

Ownership Disclosed

Give Light and the People Will Find Their Own Way," reads the inscription on the masthead of E. W. Scripps' newspapers.[1] In passing the Newspaper Publicity Act more than seventy-five years ago, Congress wanted to force the press to shine a light on itself, informing the public about its owners and some of its business practices. The people needed this information, lawmakers believed, to "find their own way" through the editorials and news columns of a publication, aware of hidden agendas and special interests. Commercial publishers using the second-class mail today still must identify their publications' owners and any investors who hold more than 1 percent of the stock. This ownership statement appears once a year in publications ranging from the *New York Times* to *Journalism Quarterly* to *Playboy*.[2]

Public disclosure—not a desire to improve the post office's efficiency in determining mail classifications, as some have contended—was the congressional intent behind this regulation. Long before Congress enacted the Newspaper Publicity Act, the Post Office Department was requiring publications applying for a second-class permit to submit ownership information as one way of distinguishing between "legitimate" and "illegitimate" publications. The "legitimate" press supported the post office's administrative initiative in curbing what it perceived as unfair advertising competition. Only when disclosure became a statutory, public requirement did some publishers rebel and complain of government interference.

This chapter chronicles the post office's early administrative attempts to establish ownership criteria for admission to the second class, examines the press's reactions to administrative and statutory disclosure requirements, and looks at how the post office has enforced the regulation.

The Post Office Monitors Press Ownership

During the mid-nineteenth century, the post office wrestled with the thankless task of determining which publications qualified for the highly desirable second-class mail privilege. Since most periodicals carried advertising, it was up to a postal official to determine whether a publication was primarily or incidentally designed for advertising purposes. Initially, local postmasters made the decisions, and "[t]here were almost an endless variety of rulings," a former administrator admitted.[3] In one of the first cases appealed to the department's solicitor (also known as the assistant attorney general), ownership was the key question. After reviewing the case, it was "perfectly obvious" that *National Normal* was an advertising sheet for the National Normal University School of Lebanon, Ohio—not an independent newspaper, the solicitor decided.[4]

National Normal accepted the judgment, but other advertising circulars tried harder to hide their true owners from postal officials. In 1884, for instance, the Post Office Department battled a fashion publication whose owners repeatedly changed—at least on paper—in unsuccessful attempts to qualify for the subsidy. *Ehrich's Fashion Quarterly* first applied for a second-class permit in April 1884 under the ownership of the Fashion Publishing Company. The New York postmaster decided the periodical was an advertising circular and denied the request. The company resubmitted the application, after changing ownership to the company's president. Again, the post office denied the application. Two months later *Ehrich's Fashion Quarterly* reapplied for the subsidy, listing a Joseph H. Choate as the new owner. Choate turned out to be the company's attorney. This bureaucratic maneuvering compelled the department's solicitor to devise a standard form to help assess an applicant's intent and business practices. Out of eight questions, three dealt with ownership, including the names of for-

mer and present owners and investors.[5] Two years later the
post office's central classification office in Washington, D.C.,
expanded the application criteria to nineteen. Seven of the
questions addressed ownership and financial control:

> 5th. Are [the owners] in any way interested, pecuniarily,
> in any business or trade represented by the publication, either
> in the reading matter or in the advertisements; if so, what is
> the interest? 6th. Who are the editors of the publication, and
> how is their compensation determined? 7th. Have the editors
> any pecuniarily interest in any business or trade represented
> by the publication, either in the reading matter or in the
> advertisements; if so, what is the interest? 8th. Is your publi-
> cation regarded by the trade which it purports to represent
> as a general organ of the trade, or is it considered as represent-
> ing the business interest of a special house in that trade,
> whose price current or advertisements appear therein? 9th.
> As a result of the publication of your paper or magazine, is
> the interest of any business house in the trade especially
> advanced, notwithstanding your design of making the publi-
> cation a journal representing the trade? 10th. Can any house
> in good standing advertise in your publication at the regular
> published rates? 11th. Have any of the business houses which
> advertise in your publication any interest (either by past
> connection or special contract) therein respecting advertise-
> ments or subscriptions; and if so, what is that interest?[6]

In 1887 the Washington, D.C., Classification Division also
took on the task of overseeing the issuance of all second-
class permits. Local postmasters, often inexperienced political
appointees, were still responsible for collecting eligibility data
from publishers applying for the subsidy and for issuing provi-
sional second-class mailing permits. They then sent the applica-
tions, affidavits of ownership, sample copies, and other evidence to the Washington, D.C., office for final evaluation of
the publications' admissibility.[7] This change from a decentral-
ized to a highly centralized evaluation process was meant to
purify the second-class mail. Yet still the abuses continued. In
1897, postal administrators estimated that up to 85 percent of

the publications issued second-class mail permits should not have been receiving the subsidy. A decade later, the estimate was 60 to 80 percent.[8]

The post office continued to entreat Congress to tighten the subsidy's entry requirements, particularly when postal deficits skyrocketed in the early years of the twentieth century. Seeing more regulation as a means to curb competition, publishers and advertisers, including the American Newspaper Publishers Association and such trade journals as *Fame* and the *National Advertiser*, joined the post office in advocating stricter ownership restrictions. Yet lawmakers kept postponing action, until the department took the initiative and tightened the application process, kicking many advertising circulars and other mailers out of the second-class category.[9]

"Legitimate" publishers and advertisers praised the revised regulations for driving some of the "illegitimates" out of business.[10] Postal administrators, nevertheless, hastened to reassure the press that it had nothing to fear from the department's new aggressiveness. "Government is not seeking to attack legitimate newspapers, but aims to suppress 'fly-by-night' publications," the superintendent of the post office's classification department told the New York State Press Association in 1910.[11] In a speech before newspaper circulation managers the next year, James J. Britt, third assistant postmaster general, reiterated the promise. "No honest publisher has anything to fear at the hands of the Post Office Department. But no dishonest publisher has anything to hope for."[12]

By 1912, Congress was ready to demand ownership disclosure from the press and saw the second-class mail privilege as the vehicle in which to do so. For many years, lawmakers had listened to postal officials complain about how ownership secrecy interfered with the cost-efficient operation of their department. Now, a majority in Congress was also convinced that publishers should be required to publicize who controlled their publications. After all, Progressives believed, didn't the public deserve to know who owned the press—the lifeblood of a democratic society?

The Press Reacts to Ownership Disclosure

While most publishers approved of the post office's inquiries into the ownership of publications seeking the preferential second-class mail rate, many condemned the statutory requirement. Submitting ownership information to the post office was one thing; publicizing it was something else indeed. A vocal minority of publishers, however, saw the disclosure regulation as a necessary tool with which to improve the industry.

First, consider the publishers who called the ownership requirement an "ass" of a law and the "most preposterous," the most "silly," the most "ridiculous" statute ever enacted by Congress.[13] These publishers issued dire warnings about loss of press liberties. The *New York World* saw the "measure [as] a meddlesome, inquisitive, socialistic and unconstitutional attempt to bring newspapers under the control of the Government, just as the railroads are now under control."[14] The *New York Times*, supportive of public disclosure in other industries, complained that Congress had gone too far in mandating publicity in the press. "Is there any detail of private business as to which Congress may not decree publicity?," a *Times* editorial asked.[15] Louis Wiley, the *Times'* business manager, compared the law to the British Licensing Act of 1662 and predicted that Congress would soon "empower United States marshalls, backed by a corps of accountants to invade the offices of . . . publications to determine . . . whether or not the statements made are true and that no perjury has been committed."[16] Yet, in truth, the government was not "competent to dictate the size of type or the color of the paper," Wiley said.[17] George W. Ochs, publisher of the *Philadelphia Public Ledger*, also rejected the idea that Congress had the authority to dictate policies to the press. Besides, what was wrong with Standard Oil owning a newspaper, he asked.[18]

Similarly, press associations decried the federal government's intrusion into the suites of newspaper owners. The American Newspaper Publishers Association, the Western Iowa Editorial Association, the Massachusetts Press Association, and the Illinois Daily Newspaper Association, for example, adopted resolutions opposing the law. Illinois publishers criticized "the growing tendency of the United States Government toward paternalism in matters pertaining to the press" and condemned "the new law requiring publicity in matters in no wise concerning the general public."[19] The Farmers' National Congress also ridiculed the law's simplistic nature. "If unpatriotic men or corporations wish to control publications through either ownership or mortgage they will not proceed by such clumsy methods as will be revealed by the [law]," the farmers' organization stated in a letter to Senator Jonathan Bourne.[20]

The ownership requirement even became the butt of publishers' jokes. Albert W. Bitters, owner of the *Rochester* (Ind.) *Daily* and *Weekly Republican*, poked fun at its intrusiveness by adding the following question to the statement he submitted to the post office:

> In what bank does the editor deposit the funds of the office?
> Answer: In the southwest pocket of a pair of hand-me-down pants which are not all wool.[21]

Fred Newell, publisher of the *Canto* (Penn.) *Sentinel*, sarcastically disclosed that he owned a lawn mower, wore false teeth, was a Taft man, and used to go to Sunday school. An editorial in the *Bushnell* (Ill.) *Record* mocked:

> While Uncle Sam is prying into private affairs that are none of his business, perhaps it might be in order to inform him that the *Record* man is a brunette and a Republican; he has a pretty bad corn on his left foot and his hair shows signs of falling out; he has only one good eye and walks a little splay-footed; he has a wife, a daughter, a couple of grandchildren, an alleged automobile, a horse, a Jersey calf, and a peg-legged cat. . . . he is neither a criminal nor a dependent.[22]

And the editor of *Printers' Ink* chided the government for making the disclosure demands in the same issue that he printed the required information. "If the Government of the United

States would like to know what is our bank balance, how much we pay for white paper, and how much salary our editor draws, that information also shall be forthcoming," editor James I. Romer wrote. He was even willing to tell the government "whether we employ black or white scrub-ladies." In the next issue, Romer muted his sarcasm and admitted that the law's intent might be "laudable" but that "does not excuse looseness and ambiguity in carrying it out."[23]

Even while the American Newspaper Publishers Association was recruiting publishers to challenge the law's constitutionality, a few came out publicly for the ownership requirement. George G. Booth, publisher of the *Detroit Daily News*, said his colleagues should "bless the day the law was enacted" because of the need to raise "the standard of the publishing business." Honest publishers need not fear "giving to the public frankly the facts relating to ownership or financial backing that they may at least judge for themselves whether the newspaper is a public journal or a private organ or the organ of some special interest," Booth told colleagues. Otherwise, the government might impose more stringent regulations that really would interfere with press freedom, he added.[24] The *Albany* (New York) *Knickerbocker-Press* echoed Booth's sentiments: "Many newspapers are kicking like mad over this legislation, but newspapers are advocating publicity in all kinds of business, therefore it is no more than proper that they should begin to take their own medicine. The more publicity the better."[25] The publisher of the *New Orleans Item* gave pragmatic business reasons for his support. "The more the public knows about newspapers the more it is going to advertise," he asserted. "The more honest the newspapers are with the public in every direction, the greater their value as properties, and the more certain their prosperity."[26]

The *New York Globe, Chicago Tribune, Salt Lake Herald, Washington Star, Boston Post,* and the *Christian Science Monitor* also defended ownership disclosure. "A newspaper is a public institution, and in its relations to the Post-office Department it is in enjoyment virtually of a public franchise," the *Washington Star* stated. "There should be no secret as to ownership."

The *Chicago Tribune* believed that "[i]n this age of regulation of industry let the newspapers stand on an equality with other business. . . . it is good policy to compel publicity."[27] The *Boston Post* also saw disclosure as good public policy for "newspapers, which are so free to recommend publicity for everybody else, should be willing to submit themselves to the calcium light of publicity."[28] The law will "equip the people with information by which they may know the spurious from the genuine, the faker from the prophet, and the swindler from the seer," the *Christian Science Monitor* wrote.[29] Disclosure was also the "best way to answer the chief criticism made against the American press," the *New York Globe* asserted.[30] Jens Grondahl, publisher of the *Red Wing* (Minn.) *Republican*, described that criticism in Populist terms in an editorial defending the regulations:

> [P]oliticians, "big business" and special interests have ac-
> quired the control of a great many publications, large and
> small, which have been conducted, not for the welfare of
> their readers, but for the special benefit of their owners
> or promoters and oftentimes with the express purpose of
> confusing and misleading the public with regard to the vital
> issues. . . . [The law] compels the pirates of the newspaper
> world to be decent . . . [and is] the only safeguard to insure
> the continued integrity of the press.[31]

A few Socialist editors wanted Congress to go even further in ensuring ownership disclosure. The penalty for publicizing false ownership information should be perjury—a criminal offense, Livy S. Richard of the *Boston Common* suggested. Only then would a publisher escape the "conditions of 'making money' [that] require that he must somehow chloroform his soul."[32]

These statements of support from within the press helped to neutralize some of the attacks from publishers unhappy with the regulation. "[T]he harsh criticisms of the bill in its first days have sobered down considerably," the *Fourth Estate* reported in early October 1912, "and now many of the biggest publishers and newspapers are looking upon it as the opening wedge to a rejuvenation of the business ethics of the country's newspaper industry."[33]

Once the Supreme Court ruled in favor of the law in June 1913, most members of the press quickly saw the public-relations value of supporting the ownership regulation. After all, as the bill's sponsors repeatedly forecasted, what honest publisher could object to having his or her readers know a publication's owners and stockholders? The *New York Times*, in fact, reported that it was going to publish an ownership statement regardless of the Supreme Court decision since the paper had "nothing to conceal."[34] Even the ANPA became an ardent supporter of the regulation, within one year of the court decision. At its annual convention in 1914, members approved a resolution urging vigorous enforcement of the law's "truth-in-publishing" requirements.[35] Trade journals routinely reported on how most publishers believed the press regulations were a "good thing for the entire industry."[36] Postmaster General Albert S. Burleson applauded the success of the Newspaper Publicity Act, which, he stated in 1919, was welcomed by the "vast majority of publishers who were glad to be relieved of the unfair competition which formerly existed."[37] Not surprisingly, then, the movement to repeal or at least weaken the ownership requirement—much discussed in the press before the Supreme Court's decision—never materialized in Congress. Although two bills were introduced in the years immediately following the court decision, they received little support from lawmakers or in the press and eventually died in committee. A 1915 proposal by Secretary of State William Jennings Bryan to require journalists to sign their stories and editorials met a similar fate.[38]

The Post Office Enforces the Regulation

Though reluctant, the Post Office Department was responsible for ensuring that publishers file and then publicize sworn ownership statements. As postal administrators began reviewing hundreds of statements shortly after the law went into effect, they soon came across a significant number that violated

the ownership requirement. Instead of listing all investors holding at least 1 percent stock in the publication, as the law
required, some publishers identified only one or two trustees
who held stocks for unnamed owners. In a press release shortly
after the law took effect, Postmaster General Hitchcock notified
publishers that all beneficiaries must be named because "otherwise a loophole would be left for an evasive report, thus de-
feating the purpose of the law."[39] Other top administrators also
reminded publishers that incomplete ownership disclosures
violated the law. Warning publishers that statements filed with
the post office were "scrutinized very closely," Third Assistant
Postmaster General James Britt said that those who were not
forthcoming with complete ownership information would
have to file accurate amended statements or lose their mailing
privileges.[40] Soon afterwards, however, the postmaster general
decided to postpone enforcement until the Supreme Court
ruled on the law.

Some publishers persisted in listing only corporations'
names on their ownership statements after the Supreme Court's
decision. The *New York American*, for example, listed its publisher, owners, and stockholders as the Star Company of New
York City and Jersey City. A 1914 administrative ruling determined that the newspaper had "utterly defeated the purpose
and intent of Congress" by disclosing only the corporation's
name and not the names of individual stockholders. The *New
York American* had to disclose the required names, the solicitor
ruled, or the post office would take away its mail subsidy.[41]
More mundane inquiries also occupied the bureaucrats' time
as publishers sought direction. Someone, for example, wanted
to know if farm, agricultural, and poultry magazines needed to
file ownership statements. Yes, as long as they used the second-
class mail subsidy and were for-profit publications, a postal
official responded.[42]

Publishers who refused to file ownership statements or
who submitted false or incomplete ones faced losing their
second-class mail privileges and being criminally prosecuted in
court for perjury. Prosecutions were rare. "We learn from
unofficial sources that prosecutions under the law have been

delayed because of the pressure of other and more important matters," *Editor and Publisher* reported in 1914.[43] Outside pressures on the Post Office Department to prosecute suspected violators intensified during World War I as public attention focused on the loyalty of the foreign-language press. Many people believed that pro-German elements secretly owned or financially supported most of the nation's German papers and some of the other periodicals that carried critical stories about the U.S. war effort. At first, they thought the postal ownership requirement might be used to investigate these publications but later decided that the 1917 Trading-with-the-Enemies Act, which required foreign-language papers to submit translations before publication, would be more effective in determining a publication's loyalty.[44]

One prosecution involving the ownership regulation, however, did finally go to federal court in 1920 after a grand jury issued a twenty-count indictment against Delavan Smith, an Indianapolis publisher, for filing four affidavits with the post office which contained false ownership information. Smith had signed the false statements before a notary public, an action that the federal district court judge found made the statements legally binding. Nevertheless, the judge ruled against the prosecutor's attempt to charge Smith with a more serious crime—violating Section 28 of the Criminal Code that prohibited "falsely making, altering or counterfeiting affidavits."[45] Smith's publication could be kicked out of the second-class mail, the judge determined, but Smith himself could not be prosecuted under the federal criminal code. The post office's solicitor, however, reevaluated that decision four years later and concluded that a person knowingly falsifying an ownership statement could be criminally prosecuted for perjury.[46] Yet, it rarely happened.

The absence of tough criminal penalties disappointed reformers who had hoped the regulation would fundamentally change the way the press did business. Like many other laws enacted in the Progressive years, the Newspaper Publicity Act—including the ownership disclosure provision—fell far short of its original intent, critics complained. Less than one year after the Post Office Department began enforcing the law, the president of the National Municipal League was disillusioned. "The public [still] does not know who is really in control" of the press, he said, because the required ownership statement "does not prove that the owners of this newspaper stock have no investment in the Steel Trust, the Oil Trust, in the Beef Trust."[47] Press critic George Seldes elaborated on this concern more than thirty years later in *One Thousand Americans*. While the law required publications to reveal their owners and stockholders, Seldes maintained that some continued to "conceal their real backers . . . [with] controls [that] are invisible to the inquiring mind."[48] For example, the "topmost ranks of Big Business and Big Banking are represented in the control of the weeklies and monthlies," he wrote. This control is "partly open, partly secret, but whether open or secret, it is not known to the millions."[49]

Secrecy was possible, according to Seldes, for two reasons. First, the law did not require publications to reveal their debts. When Frank E. Gannett, publisher of the *Brooklyn Gazette*, borrowed heavily from the International Power and Paper Company, he did not disclose the debt even though 40 percent of the newspaper was mortgaged. Likewise, S. E. Thomason of the *Chicago Journal* did not reveal similar indebtedness.[50] Second, although the regulation required disclosure of owners' and stockholders' names, most people did not realize, for example, that A. K. Lockett represented J. P. Morgan's interests or J. Howard Pew was also the president of Sun Oil.[51] This subterfuge became an issue to *Time Magazine*'s readers in the 1930s, Seldes wrote. *Time*'s ownership statement in 1935 listed several individuals who held more than 1 percent stock. Rumors began to circulate that these individuals were really representing the Morgan interests. Scores of letters flooded the magazine's office until in 1937 *Time* responded to the inquiries in its letters-to-the-editor column.

In 1922 (before *Time* was published) and in 1925, Time Inc. raised a total of $148,000 by the sale of preferred and

common stock. Of this amount Mr. Harry P. Davison subscribed something less than $10,000. Since then the pre-
ferred shares in question have been retired, Mr. Davison has
become a Morgan partner and his common shares have been
registered in the name of J. P. Morgan & Co. for the account
of Henry P. Davison [one of the individuals listed in the
1937 statement]. His holdings amount to less than 3% of
Time, Inc. stock now outstanding. Some 54% is owned
by its editors, writers, business staff and their immediate
families.—Ed.[52]

Time's next ownership statement identified one of its stockholders as "J. P. Morgan & Co. (account of Henry P. Davison)." But most corporate interests were obscured under the
names of faceless individuals, Seldes believed. Anaconda's control of much of Montana's press certainly remained "shrouded
in mystery," until 1951, several decades after Congress enacted
the law to unveil the secrecy.[53]

At the first inkling that the ownership regulation was not
working as intended, some Progressive reformers, including
William Jennings Bryan and Walter Lippmann, immediately
began pushing for more accountability in the press. In 1915,
Bryan, then Secretary of State, called on Congress to require
publishers to identify the authors of all stories and editorials.
This idea dated back to Civil War days when General Joseph
Hooker in 1863 temporarily required stories published in the
North to carry bylines as a means of attributing responsibility
and blame. Discrediting the proposal, the *New York Times*
noted that reporters had refused to sign their real names to
stories when a New York City paper tried to require bylines.
Nevertheless, Walter Lippmann championed Bryan's campaign
for more press accountability. "We ought to know the names
of the whole staff of every periodical," Lippmann wrote in his
1920 book, *Liberty and the News*. "[E]ach article should be
documented, and false documentation should be illegal."[54]

Interest in identifying the names of editorial writers has
continued into the 1980s. Some think it should be voluntary,
while legislators in South Carolina proposed legislation in 1987

to prohibit unsigned editorials.[55] First Amendment experts, however, question the constitutionality of mandatory disclosure of authorship, citing a 1960 U.S. Supreme Court decision that struck down a Los Angeles ordinance requiring that authors and sponsors of handbills be identified. "There can be no doubt that such an identification requirement would tend to restrict freedom to distribute information and thereby freedom of expression," the Court stated. "Anonymous pamphlets, leaflets, brochures and even books have played an important role in the progress of mankind. Persecuted groups and sects . . . have been able to criticize oppressive practices and laws either anonymously or not at all." Nevertheless, the opinion was a narrow one; the Court did not consider whether other authorship disclosure laws designed to prevent fraud, false advertising, libel, or "any other supposed evils" would also be unconstitutional.[56]

Questions remain about the effectiveness of the ownership provision of the Newspaper Publicity Act. Did it achieve the publicity goals of its Progressive sponsors? Are readers better able to evaluate a publication's news columns and editorials because of the disclosure? Even among supporters of public disclosure, few think readers actually read the ownership statements or, for that matter, wonder much about who owns the press in America. But people who want "to strain [their] eyes on the small print" of the statement should be given that opportunity, Congressman Morris Udall (D-Utah) said during a 1962 congressional hearing.[57] Others continue to call for even more public disclosure of the press's ownership ties and special interests.[58] Publicity is one solution to the troublesome ethical problem of newspaper publishers and stockholders sitting on boards of directors of various institutions and corporations, two authors argued in a 1979 *Columbia Journalism Review* article. "[M]aking public the names and ties of all directors would at least make these facts a matter of public record," they concluded.[59] For some, that's reason enough for the regulation.

The next chapter takes on the advertising provision of the Newspaper Publicity Act. Like ownership disclosure, the regulation was a product of the Progressive mind that valued publicity as an antidote to corporate abuses. In this case, the abuse involved advertising deception—businesses and publishers deliberately disguising advertisements to resemble news stories and editorials.

CHAPTER SEVEN

Advertisements Identified

Dear Ann Landers—I just read a news story in our local paper about a pill for people who hate to diet and exercise and want to lose weight.

This miraculous pill was developed by two prominent doctors at a world-famous hospital. It is sold with a guarantee that you can eat anything you want and as much as you want. No calorie counting or exercise. Also there are not hunger pangs.

It is 100 percent safe. All you have to do is take one pill with a glass of water before each meal. It breaks the fat into particles while you sleep. . . .

These pills sound like exactly what I've been looking for. They cost $35 for 180 plus $3 for handling, which is expensive for me, but worth it if they work. What can you tell me about this discovery?

—Excited Michiganer

Ann Landers' response:

Dear Ex.—What you read wasn't a news story but an advertisement. . . . In my opinion, such ads should not be permitted. How these charlatans get away with this stuff is beyond me.[1]

Advice columnist Ann Landers apparently did not know that such practices have been illegal since 1912. Neither do some publishers.[2] Not surprisingly, then, disguised advertisements, or reading notices as they used to be called, are flourishing in some periodicals, even though historian Edwin Emery concluded years ago that the advertising provision of

106

the Newspaper Publicity Act "corrected a long-standing but dubious practice of newspaper publishing."[3]

Progressive-era lawmakers saw the regulation as a consumer-protection measure designed to disinfect a publication's news and editorial pages long tainted by disguised advertisements from special interests. In the process, they thought that it might also help postal administrators in their difficult task of distinguishing between "illegitimate" advertising sheets and "legitimate" publications deserving of the highly favorable second-class mail subsidy. As with the ownership regulation, however, the post office had already acted administratively to handle the problem of reading notices after numerous appeals to Congress had fallen on deaf ears. Ironically, by the time Congress was ready to expose the reading-notice abuse, the department no longer wanted lawmakers' help. But Congress acted anyway, believing that disclosure would help the public better evaluate the information presented in the press. In the decade following the 1913 Supreme Court decision affirming the law, the regulation received much attention—and support—from the press besieged with demands for "free publicity" from businesses and organizations. Advertisers also supported the regulation as a way to clean up their industry and to curb unfair competition from press agents. But the regulation's enforcement mechanisms were weak, and supporters soon concluded that the law had no teeth.

This chapter shows how the post office administratively handled the reading-notice problem before Congress intervened in 1912, describes how publishers and advertisers reacted to government interference with this business practice, and examines the regulation's effects on the press.

The Post Office Struggles with Reading Notices

When Congress relegated "publications designed primarily for advertising purposes" to a much more expensive mail rate in 1879, postal bureaucrats breathed a sigh of relief.[4] At last, there was a clear congressional mandate to exclude publications of manufacturers and retailers advertising their goods and services from the subsidy intended for "legitimate" periodicals. The post office had been struggling to distinguish deserving publications from self-serving ones for years without direct statutory authority.[5] With the 1879 law, postal officials thought the classification battle was nearly won. But, in reality, the struggle intensified. Tempted by the prospect of saving thousands of dollars in postage if they could qualify as second-class mail, some businesses became even more adept at hiding their publications' intent. Camouflaging advertisements as news stories was a favorite technique. Not only did businesses try to pass off advertising circulars as "newspapers" this way, they also benefited from what many considered a highly effective marketing strategy.

With increased statutory authority, postal administrators became more aggressive in scrutinizing advertising content in order to determine whether a publication deserved the subsidy. As more circulars were denied the second-class privilege, unhappy businesses challenged the department's authority. In one of the first appeals, the publisher of *Citizen Soldier* asked the solicitor (also known as the assistant attorney general) for the post office to overturn a departmental decision that his publication was an advertising sheet even though it met the congressional definition of a newspaper. The solicitor, however, concurred with postal officials, concluding that *Citizen Soldier* was "so apparently, palpably, and notoriously devoted to forwarding the private interests of the proprietor . . . that I can not see how we can avoid the conclusion that the paper is devoted, primarily, to advertising [the publisher's] business." The determination, he said, rested on the publication's use of reading notices for "by far the most valuable advertisements are those which, in the nature of editorials, call particular attention to that character of business in which the advertiser is engaged."[6]

Disgruntled mailers continued to appeal classification decisions, but the post office's top lawyer and the courts routinely sided with the department. The challenges did, however, motivate postal administrators to establish uniform guidelines to use in determining a publication's intent. In 1887, they devised

a list of nineteen questions that a publisher applying for the
second-class privilege had to answer. Five of the criteria dealt
with advertising policies, including:

> 7th. Have the editors any pecuniary interest in any busi-
> ness or trade represented by the publication, either in the
> reading matter or in the advertisements; if so, what is the
> interest? 8th. Is your publication regarded by the trade which
> it purports to represent as a general organ of the trade, or is
> it considered as representing the business interest of a special
> house in that trade, whose price current or advertisements
> appear therein? 9th. As a result of the publication of your
> paper or magazine, is the interest of any business house in
> the trade especially advanced, notwithstanding your design
> of making the publication a journal representing the trade?
> 10th. Can any house in good standing advertise in your
> publication at the regular published rates? 11th. Have any
> of the business houses which advertise in your publication
> any interest (either by past connection or special contract)
> therein respecting advertisements or subscriptions; and if so,
> what is that interest?[7]

At the same time, the department attempted to clarify the
congressional definition of what constituted an advertising
sheet. "A publication may be largely engaged in advertising,
and still not be published primarily for that purpose," Postmaster General William F. Vilas said. But if the advertisements
form "the principal part of the reading matter, and the other
matter appears to be put in merely to attract attention to the
advertisements," then "it may reasonably be deemed to be
designed for advertising purposes."[8] Still, the decision ultimately rested with postal bureaucrats being able to decipher a
publication's intent.

With more businesses trying to pass off advertising sheets
as newspapers, the Post Office Department had to devote an
increasing amount of time, energy, and financial resources to
monitoring the application process. In 1905, forty clerks at the
department's headquarters in Washington, D.C., spent their
time answering from 300 to 500 inquiries daily about mail

classification. Even so, their supervisor, Third Assistant Postmaster General Edwin C. Madden, told members of the Penrose-Overstreet Commission in 1906 that more than 60 percent of newspapers and up to 80 percent of magazines receiving
the subsidy were not entitled to it.[9] The proliferation of advertisements in all publications complicated the post office's task,
Madden explained, testifying that some "legitimate" publications ran more than 70 percent advertisements, not counting
the reading notices.[10] This observation, along with other testi-
mony, led the commission to conclude that "every periodical
is designed for advertising purposes or no periodical is so
designed."[11]

So what was the solution? Commissioners urged lawmakers
to change the way the post office administered the second-class
privilege. First, publications carrying more than 50 percent
advertising should not receive the subsidy.[12] Second, Congress
should adopt an advertising/news ratio to be used in determining a publication's postage. A publication's reading matter
would be assessed at the subsidized rate, the commission recommended, while its advertisements would be charged higher
postage.[13] This idea met with much press opposition. One
publisher, representing the Periodical Publishers Association,
warned commissioners that "[a] great many [more] periodicals
would be strongly tempted to run disguised advertising matter,
to run 'write ups' [reading notices], and it would be a constant
question for the Post Office Department to determine whether
a certain article in praise of the Prudential Insurance Company,
for instance, was an advertisement or a contributed article."[14]

Congress did not act on the commission's recommenda-
tions, leaving the post office to continue to manage the administrative headache of the second-class mail. The summer after the
release of the commission's report found the post office still
struggling over reading notices. In this case, postal officials
suspected *The Booster* of Kelso, Washington, used reading notices to hide its advertising intent. Indicating that he could not
tell whether the descriptive articles were "paid advertisements
or information of a public character," the solicitor recommended that "the publishers be required to furnish full informa-

tion as to the character of these descriptive articles, whether or not a valuable consideration is received for their publication, and if so, from whom, and whether . . . [the publishers] are financially interested" in the items advertised.[15] This ruling gave postal bureaucrats additional administrative authority to require publishers to disclose certain business practices when applying for a second-class permit. It also led to the department's 1910 decision to take the privilege away from the *Jersey Bulletin and Dairy World* after determining that the publication devoted "a large percentage of its text to 'writeups' (textual advertising) of the [live]stock advertised."[16]

Once again, the Post Office Department had administratively usurped Congress by implementing rules to curb the use of reading notices *before* lawmakers got around to dealing with the problem in 1912. As was the case with ownership disclosure, members of Congress were more concerned about purifying the press than helping the post office administer the second-class subsidy. Even though the postmaster general came out against the advertising regulation, lawmakers acted anyway, believing that disclosure would help the public better evaluate the information presented in the press.

The Industry Reacts to Labeling Disguised Ads

The press reacted to the advertising regulation in much the same way as it did to mandatory ownership disclosure. Most dailies initially opposed it, while a few mainstream publications and the trade press immediately recognized the public-relations value of such disclosure. After the Supreme Court decision in 1913, many publishers changed their minds about the regulation and openly tried to use it to get around businesses' demands for "free publicity." Leaders in the advertising industry, on the other hand, applauded the regulation from the start, speaking about "its far-reaching importance" and "immense value" to the advertising world.[17]

Dailies such as the *New York Times*, *New York World*, *New York Herald*, the *Syracuse Post-Standard*, and the *Boston Post* highhandedly dismissed the regulation as superfluous and unnecessary. Newspapers had long ago abandoned the dishonest practice of printing disguised advertisements as news, they asserted.[18] The *Chicago Tribune* worried that small papers would no longer receive "minor perquisites . . . such as free theater tickets and free books" because the resultant reviews would have to be marked as advertising.[19] Other publishers doubted that the post office would show common sense in administering the law. Mockingly describing the potential for lunacy, one publication ran a fictionalized short story about a small-town editor who marked everything in his newspaper "advertisement"—including anniversary announcements, church notices, obituaries, and school activities—for fear of losing his highly prized second-class mail permit.[20] Another publication, the German-language *Philadelphia Tageblatt*, protested the law by labeling every item in the newspaper "advertisement," including its masthead.[21]

To counter the naysaying, a few mainstream publications went on record in support of identifying disguised advertisements. The *Washington Star* expressed the firm belief "that all paid advertising printed as reading matter should be plainly marked 'advertisement.' "[22] Likewise, the *Chicago Tribune* concluded that if the government were going to regulate businesses, then it would be "good policy to compel publicity" in the press "to show up purchased news and editorials."[23] In explaining his support for the regulation, George G. Booth, publisher of the *Detroit Daily News*, asked his colleagues: "What possible objection can there be to ridding the papers of the intolerable nuisance of tricky reading notices, notices written by the greatest advertising writers whose sole aim is to cause the public to feel that they are reading something disinterestedly published by the editor?"[24] The editor of *Newspaperdom*, a monthly trade journal, dismissed claims that the regulation was not necessary because reading notices had long ago disappeared. Private advertising agencies such as Thompson-Koch Co. continued to insist that their advertisements for Neuralgyline and other home-cure concoctions be printed as news, he said. "Such nice little papers as the *Herald* of Huntington, Indiana; the *Chronicle*, of Marion, Indiana; the *Herald* of Anderson, Indiana, and a lot of others, have yielded to this demand of the Thompson-Koch Co. and blushes diffuse me as I gaze upon indisputable evidence of their prostitution."[25] The Chilton Publishing Company, influential in getting the circulation requirement inserted in the law, also supported the advertising provision. "There is no possible excuse for the publication, disguised as news, of advertising matter furnished by some interested person," the trade publisher wrote. "The reader is entitled to know whether what he is asked to read as news is real news . . . or merely the biased opinion of those having something to dispose of. This law should guarantee that knowledge."[26]

Advertising leaders agreed with this assessment. Legitimate advertisers no longer disguised advertisements, they said. Consequently, the regulation would help the industry by penalizing those who still did. "From the standpoint of the fair and square advertiser," one trade journal proclaimed, "the innovation created by the new law is only a decided advance in publishing and advertising ethics."[27]

Still, the advertising regulation came under special attack in the court cases before the Supreme Court. Attorneys for the *Journal of Commerce* and the Lewis Publishing Company argued that the labeling requirement, in particular, was ambiguously worded and implied that publications found in violation of the regulation would lose all mail service, not just the second-class subsidy.[28] Countering that claim, Solicitor General William Marshall Bullitt argued that Congress intended the advertising regulation to apply only to periodicals using the subsidy like the other two regulations in the Newspaper Publicity Act. He admitted, however, that the statute "might have readily expressed this idea in a more apt form." If the Court could not agree with this interpretation, Bullitt said, then the justices should consider the constitutionality of each of the three regulations separately. That way, the justices could decide that the advertising clause was unconstitutional "without affecting the validity of the prior provision[s]."[29]

The Supreme Court unanimously accepted Bullitt's explanation of congressional intent and ruled that the advertising regulation was not "a censorship and control over the press that is directly contrary to the Constitution."[30] In fact, the Post Office Department had the administrative right to determine the advertising status of a periodical for many years, the Court stated. "[I]t is impossible in reason to perceive why the new condition as to marking matter which is paid for as an advertisement is not equally incidental to the [post office's] right to classify" publications according to second-class eligibility requirements.[31]

Publishers quickly adapted the Supreme Court decision to their advantage. "Free publicity" and "free write-ups" had become major problems in the industry during the early decades of the twentieth century. As reading notices fell out of favor, businesses began employing press agents to garner free space in the nation's publications—either by convincing editors that the publicity was newsworthy or tying it to purchased advertising. The latter ploy was reprehensible to the editors of the *St. Petersburg* (Fla.) *Daily Times*: "A merchant would not expect a newspaper to purchase from him a suit of clothes and ask that he give it a pair of shoes or a hat. He would not sell to the newspaper a bolt of cloth and expect to give it a pair of shears. And yet his request for free space is just as unseeming as any of these things."[32]

In 1916, the American Newspaper Publishers Association launched a major campaign to discourage papers from "giving away" space that should be charged as advertising. Joining the crusade, the *Fourth Estate* challenged publishers to "Say NO to free publicity requests and stop the abuse entirely."[33] Many advertisers supported the press's campaign to eliminate free publicity, believing that the trend was "stealing" advertising revenues. Businesses that could get publicity in the press without paying for it would no longer need to buy advertising, they feared.[34] Take, for example, the case of a public utility company ready to spend $20,000 on newspaper advertising. A press agent convinced the company to hire him for the same money to place free publicity in the area's media. Such an arrangement harmed publishers and advertisers alike, a trade journal observed.[35] Consequently, the two industries needed to work together to eliminate all unmarked free publicity, said the chairman of the National Newspaper Committee of the American Association of Advertising Agencies.[36]

One way to stop the trend toward free publicity, publishers and advertisers thought, was through the advertising provision of the Newspaper Publicity Act. Louis Wiley, business manager of the *New York Times*, who once ridiculed the regulation, now heartily embraced it. "Free publicity is not only illegal but a deception upon the readers of a newspaper," Wiley told participants at the thirteenth annual convention of the Associated Advertising Clubs of the World. "To print advertisements, puffs, statements which are not news, under the guise of news, unless they are labeled as advertisements as required by law, is deceit. Newspapers which practice imposition of this kind always are punished."[37] An editorial in the *Fourth Estate* advised publishers to use the regulation against businesses pestering them for free space. "When a publisher is asked to give free publicity, let him send the party requesting it a copy of the clause of the law printed herewith, and he will not have any further worry. It isn't necessary to write long, explanatory letters. Just say NO and the law will back you up."[38] The regulation should be particularly helpful to "weak publishers [who] should certainly welcome such steps because they haven't the backbone, or cannot afford at present, to say 'No!' to a request for free space," the president of the Moses Advertising Service in Baltimore predicted.[39]

Strict enforcement was the key, however, and that was up to the post office.

The Post Office Enforces the Regulation

The Post Office Department was ambivalent about the advertising provision of the Newspaper Publicity Act. The department "had not asked for the law and did not want it,—in fact [it] had the responsibility shoved upon it by Congress," *Printers' Ink* reported.[40] Indeed, Postmaster General Frank H. Hitchcock came out against the legislation when it was before Congress. Under the new leadership of Postmaster General

Albert Burleson, however, administrators announced that the department was going to enforce the regulation governing "editorials, textual business write-ups, descriptive news stories, etc. which have for their purpose the calling of public attention to the merits of something in which the undisclosed advertisers are interested."[41] It appears that Representative Henry Barnhart (D-Ind.), the regulation's sponsor, may have leaked the first report of a postal investigation to *Fourth Estate* reporters in 1914. According to the trade journal, Barnhart said that Postmaster General Burleson "has information that certain newspapers, some of them among the largest and most influential in large cities from coast to coast, are printing articles for the 'shipping trust' against the tolls and are accepting payment therefor. Those articles, the department is informed, are printed as news and editorial matter without being designated as advertising."[42]

Two years later, the post office also reprimanded twenty-five to thirty publishers for printing the article, "Chevrolet Car Wins Contest," without marking it an advertisement, even though the article had been "published under an understanding that automobile manufacturers and dealers will be given reading notices when they advertise in a publication."[43] Although the publishers were not paid for carrying the story, postal officials concluded that "valuable consideration" was promised in the form of future advertising.[44] Mocking the ruling, a silk manufacturer from Connecticut said, "[I]ts logical conclusion would be that all mention of members of Congress should be marked 'Advertisement' on the ground that it was publicity for the Congressmen and assisted them in reelection to their position."[45] But publishers welcomed the decision, believing that they could use it to dissuade businesses and organizations from demanding free publicity or write-ups as a condition for advertising contracts. "It is just as dishonorable to graft space as it is to promote fake mines, and while the Government is cleaning out the scallywags, it is good to know that the press agent is 'getting his,' " *Newspaperdom* gloated.[46] Another trade journal noted that publishers now had the perfect answer to press agents or advertisers harassing them for free space. "Uncle Sam thereby puts publishers in the position where they must say to the advertiser, 'Much as I would like to do this for you, I cannot. Surely you would not expect me to jeopardize my publication by doing as you ask?' "[47]

The post office, however, refused to issue any blanket rules outlawing the use of free publicity, much to the disappointment of publishers and advertisers who wanted to tell publicity seekers that the federal government prohibited them from printing their releases.[48] Rather, postal officials said they needed to look at each case individually, weighing all of the minor differences and consulting with the publisher, before making an enforcement decision. *Printers' Ink* observed that most complaints were resolved with a warning "not to do it again." Trade journals also realistically concluded that the post office had "no time to search America's 26,000 newspapers and periodicals for reading notices." Consequently, someone had to complain about a particular story or editorial before the department investigated.[49]

Even though Congress intended the regulation to help better inform the public, most of the complaints came from business competitors—publishers, advertisers, or businesspeople who wanted to punish a rival.[50] The business manager of the *Nashville Banner*, for instance, complained to postal officials about a special "Stand by the President" edition that the *Tennessean* and *American* printed in 1918.[51] The feature, made up of more than seven hundred reading notices, ran five and one-half pages. Each notice cost from two to ten dollars depending on its length, but the section was not labeled an advertisement. In a letter to the local postmaster, the business manager asked for an investigation after citing a few examples of the notices.

CHOOSE CHERO-COLA!

Both "over here" and "over there" Chero-Cola is the favorite. It has the pep and the zip and zest and it satisfies. 5 cents the bottle and worth a million pleasures. CHERO-COLA BOTTLING CO., 110 Woodland St.

CLEANLINESS IS A VIRTUE!

And in laundry it is a certainty if you send it to McEwen's Steam Laundry. Known to the Nashville people as the laun-

dry of supreme satisfaction. No scarred edges or half-way
work if it comes from McEwen's. Only the BEST is allowed
to go out of this good laundry. Yes, we are doing all we can
to aid Uncle Sam and help win the war. Phone Main 2780.
Put that down—2-7-8-0.[52]

When investigating a complaint, postal officials tried to
ascertain the "news value" of the article in question. If there
were "news value" in a given piece, then it would be considered
a bona fide news or informational article or editorial. If there
were not, then the story should be labeled an advertisement.
According to *Printers' Ink*, "news value is the acid test, and
unless that element is present it is held that reading notices
must be marked."[53] But judging news value proved to be a
burdensome, virtually impossible, task for the post office—one
that was often ironically delegated to the publisher of the story
in question. Consequently, the publisher many times had the
last word in a reading-notice investigation, at least until 1917.

What is news? What is advertising? These questions, long
troublesome, became even more important to publishers and
postal officials after Congress enacted the War Revenue Act in
1917. First discussed during the Penrose-Overstreet Commission in 1907, the new law charged two types of postal rates for
publications qualifying for the second-class subsidy—a low, flat
rate on a publication's editorial content and a higher, distance-
based rate on its advertising content.[54] In other words, a publication's postage increased with distance and advertising volume. Each issue of a publication had to be marked as to editorial
and advertising copy and then submitted to the local postmaster, who would assess the correct postage. The Classification
Division in Washington, D.C., stood ready to answer questions
or to settle disputes.

Congress expected publishers to comply with the law and
to identify all advertisements—disguised or not—so they could
be assessed the higher postal rate. To encourage compliance
and to reassure publishers, high-ranking postal administrators
attended press meetings where they were interrogated about
the advertising regulation and the zone law. At the Interna-

tional Circulation Managers' Association convention in 1918, for example, Third Assistant Postmaster General A. M. Dockery tried to reassure the audience that the post office appreciated the press and was trying "to smooth out, so far as we can, all the 'wrinkles' that may develop in the administration of this [zone] law, and we want the cordial, hearty, and patriotic cooperation of the newspapers, and I am sure we will have it."[55] Accompanying Dockery was General Counsel W. C. Wood who faced the most questions about the department's definition of an advertisement. What about "office ads?," A. E. MacKinnon of the *Philadelphia North American* asked. The "office ad" itself was not an advertisement if it only listed an issue's contents by page number, Wood responded. However, "[i]f you are outlining there something to induce those readers who get that issue to subscribe to future issues, it would appear to be in the line of an advertisement, to obtain subscriptions."[56]

How about statements of ownership and circulation, J. M. Schmid of the *Indianapolis News* asked? Information required by the law would certainly not be classified as an advertisement, Wood said. "[B]ut if there is added something to the effect, that 'This publication has the largest circulation of any in the city' and other statements, this effect being to have the advertiser come to this publisher instead of going to another, it would appear to be advertising."[57] Then how about free publicity for such patriotic activities as Liberty Loans, war stamps, and the like? "[I]f the insertion . . . is paid for, then it would be advertising, without question," Wood responded. "[I]f it is published in any matter to let the people know what's being done, to invite them to join in these activities, and nothing is paid for its insertion, it would not be advertising."[58] What about local charities, McKernan of the *New York World* asked? Consistent with the Liberty Loan answer, Wood answered: "I believe that if a church was holding some kind of a festival and a free notice to that effect was given in the newspaper, such notice would not be considered an advertisement, but if the church inserted and paid for the publicity, certainly it would come under the head of advertising."[59]

Confusion continued to exist over what items in a publication should be counted as advertising. Even critic H. L. Mencken wondered if his book reviews would be considered advertisements. After hearing from the post office, he concluded: "I don't think there will ever be much chance of mistaking my own reviews for advertisements. The publishers commonly regard them as the very opposite, and even refuse to give regular advertisements to the publications in which they are printed."[60] Attempting to clear up more of the confusion, the post office printed a series of circulars, clarifying the difference between an advertisement and a news item. First and foremost, the post office considered any reading matter that could benefit the makers or sellers of a named item an advertisement, subject to the higher zone postal rates. But what about stories on new products or inventions? Couldn't these stories have "news value" in addition to their promotional value? In the fall of 1920, the post office released another circular trying to clarify the distinction once again:

> Matter descriptive of an article or product that is in fact new is not regarded as advertising, provided no advertisements of the manufacturers or other persons with respect to the sale thereof are carried in the publication. In all cases, however, where an article or product is advertised in a publication, any matter appearing in the reading columns with reference thereof is regarded as advertising regardless of whether or not the product is new.[61]

This clarification relieved a publisher from having to pay extra postage on, for example, an "editorial describing the joys of army life," while running an advertisement for recruits in the same issue of the publication.[62] It also signaled publishers that the post office was not going to actively pursue some types of free publicity as a form of advertising.

The industry battle over free publicity abated somewhat in the mid-1920s. Although press associations still debated the issue, few publishers or advertisers mentioned the post office or the Newspaper Publicity Act as remedies to the problem.[63] The nature of free publicity was also becoming more insidious. Initially, businesses sought free publicity for such commercial purposes as store openings and automobile contests; more recently, however, organizations representing corporate America coveted editorial space for political ideas and business policy. In some cases, they paid for the space as long as the copy was not identified as an advertisement, a practice reminiscent of the days preceding the Newspaper Publicity Act and now blatantly illegal. Ninety percent of Alabama's newspapers in 1925, for instance, editorialized in favor of Alabama Power Company. Only later was it discovered that the publications received money for printing the "canned" editorials from E. Hofer and Sons, a publicity bureau located in Salem, Oregon, that had contracted with Alabama Power Company.[64]

Press critics have reported more recent instances of publications disguising advertisements as news stories and editorials.[65] Ben Bagdikian, for example, exposed the rural press's pervasive practice in the early 1960s of using "canned" editorials representing such conservative interests as the National Association of Manufacturers, the American Bankers Association, the American Petroleum Institute, the Bourbon Institute, and the American Legion. In one case, newspapers in South Carolina, Montana, and Michigan ran editorials in May and June 1963, all starting with the phrase, "Remember the Medicare proposal of the Kennedy Administration? It got nowhere . . ."[66] The editorials, not labeled advertisements, came indirectly from the American Medical Association. Likewise, "canned" editorials praising the steel industry were traced to a publicity bureau representing U.S. Steel and the American Iron and Steel Institute.[67] While acknowledging that the rural editors may have agreed with the canned editorials and might not have been paid to run them, Bagdikian asserted, "[T]here is a profound difference between the identical NAM [National Association of Manufacturers] editorial appearing in six hundred newspapers and six hundred local editors thinking and writing about what the NAM has to say."[68] Some lawmakers agreed and, in 1966, proposed legislation, similar to the already existing advertising regulation, that would have required "canned" editorials to be labeled and identified as to the special interest behind them.[69] Robert U. Brown, editor of *Editor and Publisher* at that time,

urged the press to police itself in order to forestall more government regulation. "A grass roots condemnation of the practice
would have a lot of influence on editors, even the smallest
ones," Brown asserted, as he encouraged "every state publishers' and press association to take a public stand on the issue."[70]
Although Brown's campaign never materialized, the legislative
proposal died without much debate.

Some publishers continue to engage in the dubious practice
of disguising advertisements as news stories and editorials.
Columbia Journalism Review regularly "darts" publications, associations, and individuals suspected of misleading their readers this way. In 1988, for example, darts went to *Spy*, *Interview*,
Details, *Paper*, *Hollywood Reporter*, *Chicago Metro*, and *L. A.
Style* for "running individually designed ads [for Dom Ruinart
champagne] that cleverly mimic their own particular editorial
content, layout, and tone."[71] Another dart went to the Michigan Press Association in 1985 for a "singularly inappropriate"
item in its confidential newsletter that offered advice on how
to make an advertisement look like a news article or column.[72]
On the other hand, *Editor and Publisher* praised a workshop at
the 1990 Associated Press Managing Editors convention in
which participants learned how to produce special advertorial
sections in cooperation with a paper's advertising department.
While labeled advertising, these sections should "not be placed
where an ad is expected to be seen," Mac Tully, advertising
director of the *Fort Worth* (Texas) *Star-Telegram*, advised. They
are particularly effective marketing tools for grand openings,
he added, where many businesses could advertise their involve-
ment in the project.[73]

Other publications, however, received kudos for their handling of the ongoing problem of free publicity and canned
copy. The *Los Angeles Times*, for instance, in 1988 started
identifying news releases as paid advertisements in its business
section under the heading "Corporate News." The newspaper
already was charging for promotional releases printed in its
Saturday advertising supplement, "Weekend Getaway." The
Toronto Globe and Mail, however, stopped a similar policy in
1986, after determining it was not profitable.[74]

Disguised advertisements still exist in the press long after the enactment of the Newspaper Publicity Act. Reformers thought the regulation would purify the news and editorial columns. After initial resistance, publishers tried to use the law as an excuse for refusing businesses free publicity—much to the delight of advertisers. But the law's enforcement mechanisms were weak, and publications soon stopped nagging the post office to enforce the regulation. Advertisers and publishers, nevertheless, were also deeply interested in the third component of the Newspaper Publicity Act—the public disclosure of daily newspapers' circulation data. The next chapter shows how some embraced the law, then became disillusioned and established their own bureau to certify circulation statistics. Other publishers and advertisers successfully lobbied Congress in the 1940s and again in the early 1960s to extend the regulation to all commercial periodicals.

CHAPTER EIGHT

Circulation Revealed

The Newspaper Publicity Act's circulation regulation demonstrated that the Progressive-era Congress was willing to intervene in the business activities of a long-sacrosanct industry, the press, in order to help another, advertisers. Circulation liars had long plagued advertisers and honest publishers, who viewed them as thieves and frauds. After intense lobbying, Congress approved a limited remedy for the problem—daily newspapers had to publish accurate circulation figures twice a year. Although it affected a minority of publications, sociologist Alfred M. Lee credited the regulation with finally convincing publishers that they needed to give advertisers "a believable statement of the commodity [circulation] offered them."[1]

Advertisers and publishers soon became disenchanted with the post office's enforcement efforts, however. Officials refused to initiate investigations, to audit circulation statements regularly, or to release data on more than one or two papers at a time because of staff limitations. Critics also claimed that the government statement itself was a misnomer. In reality, it was merely a circulation report from the dailies to the government, not "an official statement based on official sources or one that has official sanctions," a newspaper management text noted.[2] Despite these criticisms, publishers and advertisers used the statements in promotional campaigns, recognizing that the regulation—which many considered toothless—still served the public relations' interests of each industry.

This chapter examines the post office's role in verifying circulation claims before 1912, describes how publishers and advertisers reacted to the regulation, including why they estab-

124

lished the Audit Bureau of Circulations in 1914, and explains why decades later weekly and magazine publishers asked Congress to be covered by the same regulation.

The Post Office Scrutinizes Subscriber Lists

The Post Office Department became involved in monitoring newspaper and magazine circulations in 1879 when Congress created the second-class mail subsidy and made "a legitimate list of subscribers" one of the criteria for the privilege. The law also specifically barred publications designed "for free circulation, or for circulation at nominal rates" from the subsidy. Lawmakers intended these conditions to help the post office keep advertising circulars out of the second-class mail. To assist local postmasters in determining which publications belonged in the second class and which did not, postal administrators designed regulations that, among other things, defined the law's terms. A subscriber was "a person who has actually paid, or undertaken to pay, a subscription price for a newspaper, magazine or other periodical, or for whom such payment has been made, or undertaken to be made, by some other person."[3] In other words, a subscriber had to want the publication enough to pay for it.

Publishers legitimately receiving the second-class privilege, at first, praised the post office for tightening the entry requirements. But they soon protested the department's implementation. One of the ways publishers inflated their circulation figures was by giving away sample copies. Naturally, they wanted to mail these "free" copies at the highly subsidized rate, but postal officials believed that the practice violated the "legitimate list of subscribers" provision of the 1879 law. The publisher of the weekly *Appleton* (Wisc.) *Post*, for example, ran into trouble when he tried to send a large quantity of papers at the second-class mail rate to nonsubscribers after an advertiser asked him to do so.[4] Although Congress did not specify how many sample copies could be sent through the mail without abusing the privilege, the department determined "that the regular circulation of a number of sample copies largely disproportionate to the number of copies sent to actual subscribers necessarily raises the inference that the paper is designed for free circulation, or circulation at nominal rates." Another publication with fewer than twelve subscribers unsuccessfully tried to circulate five thousand copies through the mail.[5] After years of frustration, the post office in 1887 came up with a standardized list of questions that all publishers applying for the second-class subsidy had to answer truthfully. Eight questions involved circulation:

> 12th. What is the greatest number of copies furnished to any person or firm who advertise in your publication? 13th. On what terms are these papers furnished? 14th. What number of papers do you print of each issue? 15th. About what number of *bona fide* subscribers (that is, subscribers who pay their own money for the publication and receive it regularly) have you to the next issue of your paper? 16th. What is the subscription price of your publication per annum? 17th. How many pounds weight will cover the papers furnished to regular subscribers? 18th. What average number of sample copies with each issue do you desire to send through the mails at pound rates? 19th. How are the names of the persons to whom you wish to send sample copies obtained by you?[6]

In addition, the department encouraged local postmasters to contact some of a publication's subscribers to see if they were really paying for the paper. An ambitious Chicago postmaster, for example, randomly contacted seventeen of the listed subscribers for *Cupid's Quiver*; only two met the legal definition.[7] The publication lost its subsidized mailing privilege.

With deficits plaguing the Post Office Department, lawmakers and postal administrators began to pay more attention to abuses within the second-class mail subsidy, including the sample-copy and paid-subscriber rules.[8] Although Congress declined to act on the second-class question, the public debate provided impetus for the department to further define the term "subscriber" and to refine its administrative rules. One of the most important changes involving circulation occurred in 1907 when postal administrators established a rule that limited a publication's sample copies mailed at the second-class rate to 10 percent of its total mailing weight.[9] This "regulation has taken out of the mails since January 1 [1908] millions of copies of publications whose 'circulation,' for advertising purposes, was swelled to the limit," officials boasted to Congress.[10] Heartily endorsing these rules, advertisers and some publishers encouraged the post office to enforce them as vigorously as possible in order to get rid of circulation liars.

As with the other two provisions of the Newspaper Publicity Act, the Post Office Department had already implemented administrative procedures to deal with circulation abuses involving *all* publications entered as second-class mail years before Congress required *dailies* to disclose their circulations in 1912. Although the circulation regulation was couched in terms of postal policy, lawmakers—particularly those who added the amendment to a last-minute conference committee report—certainly pleased advertisers and some publishers who had long wanted a federal law requiring truthful circulation disclosure.

Publishers and Advertisers React to Circulation Disclosure

At the beginning, the Newspaper Publicity Act's circulation requirement divided the press more than the other two regulations. Publishers of daily newspapers fiercely objected to its discriminatory nature—only they were forced to disclose circulation data. Seizing on this supposed discrimination, the American Newspaper Publishers Association claimed the regulation was blatantly unconstitutional. Meanwhile, some magazine and weekly publishers voluntarily published circulation statements to attract advertisers. The trade press also praised the regulation as the first step toward mandatory circulation disclosure of all publications. Similarly, advertisers applauded the requirement, seeing it as an important remedy for one of the industry's most vexing problems.

Many daily publishers, led by the ANPA, criticized the circulation requirement for being "perniciously inquisitorial," unfairly discriminatory, and "constitut[ing] an unwarranted interference with private business."[11] Surely the courts would overturn the regulation on constitutional grounds, these publishers believed, as they refused to comply with the law's October 1, 1912, deadline.[12]

A few dailies, however, came out publicly in support of circulation disclosure. The *Washington Star*, for example, editorialized that it believed "all facts regarding circulation should be public property."[13] In a letter to *Editor and Publisher*, the publisher of the *New London* (Conn.) *Evening Day* wrote that the regulation would "smoke-out" frauds. "A newspaper has no more right to conceal its circulation than a merchant has to conceal the number of yards in a roll of cloth," publisher Theodore Bodenwein stated. In an editorial printed on the same page as Bodenwein's letter, the trade journal concurred. Publishers who objected to the circulation requirement "are afraid to tell the truth because of the effect it will have upon their advertising receipts."[14] The *Chicago Tribune*, in fact, used its enthusiastic compliance with the regulation in promotional campaigns comparing its circulation with other dailies. In explaining why the paper supported the regulation, James Keeley, the *Tribune*'s business manager, said, "These men who lie about their circulation, who defraud the advertiser, are just as guilty of obtaining money under false pretenses, as is the cheap swindler who palms off a brass watch on a farmer under the pretension that it is gold. . . . I hope that the law is held constitutional. I hope that the Government will not hesitate to prosecute for perjury every publisher, be he big or little, who makes a false statement regarding circulation."[15]

Another sector of the press—trade publishers who were instrumental in getting the regulation passed in the first place—immediately resumed lobbying Congress to extend the requirement to all publications. Two weeks after the regulation became law, the Philadelphia Trade Press Association passed a resolution to that effect.[16] George Glavis, former postal administrator and current lobbyist and circulation manager for the Philadelphia-based Chilton Company, used the resolution to encourage members of the national trade press association to join the campaign to extend the law. Such a comprehensive regulation was needed, Glavis said, to help trade publishers gain national recognition and the advertising they deserved. The president of the Federation of Trade Press Associations joined Glavis's lobbying efforts and also convinced his organization to approve a resolution requiring members to publish their sworn circulation figures.[17] The New York Trade Press Association also voted to require similar circulation statements from its members as did the Grocery and Allied Trade Press Association, after one member threatened to resign if the resolution were not approved.[18] These organizations believed voluntary disclosure of circulation data would enhance the trade press's stature in the publishing world, particularly when many dailies were still protesting the mandatory requirement.

Lobbyist George Glavis, who worked closely with Senator Jonathan Bourne when the regulation was first being considered, again approached the senator to support new legislation to strengthen the law. Specifically, Glavis wanted Congress to force publishers to print detailed circulation figures in every issue of their publications and to require the post office to verify these statements at least twice a year. Before agreeing to do so, Bourne asked Glavis to identify some of the offending publications. Glavis declined, though he offered to accompany Bourne on an investigatory trip to the post office's headquarters. Bourne never introduced the legislation.[19]

Advertisers, not surprisingly, immediately endorsed the circulation regulation, heralding it as a long-awaited, albeit partial, remedy to one of the press's major abuses. In their eyes, this national recognition of a persistent advertising problem—publishers who lied about circulation data—was cause for celebration. "The principle of the new law follows out the ancient principles of weights and measures," the president of a New York City advertising agency stated. "[W]e believe most heartily in its enforcement in every way possible," a Boston agency concurred.[20] Indeed, some advertisers credited themselves with convincing members of the conference committee during last-minute deliberations to impose the requirement on daily newspapers. Yet they were not content to rest on their laurels.[21]

Following the lead of the Federation of Trade Press Associations, advertising organizations such as the Technical Publicity Association approved resolutions that encouraged Congress to extend the circulation regulation to all publications. The Advertising Club of Denver went further, recommending "to all advertisers in the United States that on and after December 1, 1912, no contracts for or purchases of advertising space be made with any publication . . . unless said publication has complied with the clause of this law relating to circulation statements."[22] Serving as a model of compliance, *Printers' Ink* had already voluntarily disclosed its circulation figures the first week of October 1912. "*Printers' Ink* has always advocated publicity in business," Editor James I. Romer explained. "There is no reason why what we advocate for others should not apply to ourselves."[23]

Most publishers, however, waited until the Supreme Court affirmed the regulation's constitutionality before jumping on the disclosure bandwagon. Shortly after the decision, advertisements began appearing in trade journals that trumpeted publications' circulation statements filed with the post office. The *Richmond* (Va.) *News-Leader*, for example, bragged that it "has more circulation in Virginia than any other paper, and has more paid circulation in Richmond than all the other Richmond papers combined." As proof, the advertisement listed the lower circulation figures the other city papers gave the post office.[24] The *New York Times* also regularly touted its circulation statements as well as carried "news" stories about circulation figures of other New York dailies.[25] *Editor and Publisher* summed up the good feelings about this regulation: "It is undeniably true that the present law has been a great boon to the advertiser and the advertising agent, and a blessing in disguise to the publisher."[26]

Many publishers and advertisers, however, soon became disenchanted with the post office's weak enforcement. Unscrupulous publishers of daily newspapers still lied about their circulation figures, critics said, but they now had a government-certified statement to make their lies more convincing.

The Post Office Enforces the Regulation

As with the other two regulations, postal administrators did not want the additional administrative responsibility of monitoring daily newspapers' sworn circulation figures. Shortly after the regulation became law, they fielded hundreds of inquiries from publishers and business managers of dailies asking about the circulation requirement. Most questions involved the definition of circulation. Uncomfortable second-guessing lawmakers in this controversial area, Postmaster General Hitchcock asked Attorney General George Wickersham to interpret the congressional intent behind the regulation. Attorney General Wickersham, known for his aggressive enforcement of antitrust laws, shifted the responsibility back to the post office, stating that the department must follow its own administrative precedents. He observed, however, that the law was "highly penal" by punishing publishers who did not submit accurate circulation figures with loss of all mailing privileges. Noncomplying publishers leaped on Wickersham's interpretation as justification for not filing the statements. The protest helped convince the postmaster general to delay enforcing the law until after the Supreme Court ruled on its constitutionality.[27]

Defining what constituted circulation continued to pose problems for the post office after the Supreme Court's decision. At first, the department told publishers that they should disclose the same circulation information they provided when applying for a second-class permit. Third Assistant Postmaster General A. M. Dockery told Don C. Seitz, chairman of the ANPA committee on second-class postage, that publications only needed to disclose their average number of copies distributed to regular paid subscribers.[28] A few months later, Attorney General J. C. McReynolds issued a new opinion on the circulation regulation. Disagreeing with the former attorney general's deference to administrative precedent, McReynolds thought Congress intended the regulation sweepingly to apply to all circulation. Consequently, circulation went beyond copies

"sold or distributed to paid subscribers" to "cover the whole
bona fide paid circulation of daily newspapers, however at-
tained, whether sold over the counter, distributed through
news agencies and news routes, or disposed of in any way."
The post office mailed copies of this opinion to 2,554 dailies.[29]
After initial confusion, publishers complied with the revised
interpretation, leading the Post Office Department to note in
its 1914 annual report that the attorney general's clarification
"has greatly simplified [the regulation's] administration and
assures uniformity and completeness in the statements filed
thereunder."[30] Some publishers and advertisers, however, continued to complain that the regulation distorted circulation
averages, benefiting newspapers with Sunday issues since they
were not required to file separate statements distinguishing
between Sunday and weekday circulation. "Under the government ruling a paper with a large Sunday circulation can include
that in its total and show an average daily issue which is misleading to the advertiser who used the week-day issues," a 1914
advertising text noted.[31]

Advertisers were also unhappy with the lack of access to
the circulation statements filed with the post office. Even before
the Supreme Court came down with its decision, advertisers
had asked postal administrators for access to the dailies' statements. But the bureaucrats delayed answering their requests
because the law did not expressly direct the department to
compile and release information.[32] Hence, any access policy
would be up to Postmaster General Hitchcock, who remained
undecided. Once the High Court affirmed the law, advertisers
again swamped the department with requests to see the statements filed at the department's headquarters in Washington,
D.C.[33] A postal official complained, "It seems to me that almost
every advertising agency in the country must have sent in a
request for the circulation figures on all or a large share of the
important newspapers of the country." The quantity of requests
made full disclosure impossible, Third Assistant Postmaster
General A. M. Dockery said. Individual requests for circulation
data on a particular publication were generally answered, Dock-

ery explained, but there was a "distinct disposition to regard unfavorably requests of wider scope."[34] The unidentified official was more blunt. "To comply with these requests is simply out of the question. Naturally we cannot give the information to one if we do not give it to all, and to answer the inquiries of this kind which have poured in would require the services of one hundred clerks in addition to our present overworked force." Advertisers should get the circulation data from the publications themselves, he added.[35]

Since the post office would not answer inquiries about multiple publications because of staff constraints, some advertisers went to Washington, D.C., to personally review the statements. Postal officials quickly blocked this practice by requiring that every request for circulation information be made in writing. Again, the post office urged advertisers to go directly to the publications. As one postal employee said, "Every time we give out a circulation statement we deprive the publisher of an opportunity to sell a copy of his newspaper."[36] Advertising agents, however, complained that publishers sometimes buried the statements in their publications, forcing them to check six to ten issues before finding the information. Since the post office had the data readily available, it should provide the statements on request. When this argument failed to convince administrators to change the policy, advertisers unsuccessfully lobbied Congress to amend the law to provide for such disclosure or to at least require publications to publish the statements in the same place each time. In the meantime, there was a "noticeable falling off in the volume" of advertisers' inquiries, a trade journal noted, because of "despair over attitudes of the postal officials."[37]

Advertisers were not the only ones upset about the lack of access to the circulation statements. Publishers wanted to see how they ranked among their competitors, and *Editor and Publisher* asked the post office for copies of all of the statements filed so it could compile them in a special issue to give to every advertising agent or space buyer in the country. When Dockery refused to provide the statements, the trade journal contacted the dailies and offered to reprint their statements as display advertisements for $25 each.[38] The *Mail Order Journal* also compiled the statements as a service to its readers.[39]

Some publishers and advertisers complained bitterly about the post office's failure to enforce the law aggressively. "The Postoffice [*sic*] Department has yet offered no valid excuse for not putting the law into general practice," *Editor and Publisher* editorialized in 1914. "It is time for someone in that department to get very busy in the interests of the army of publishers and advertising men to whom honesty in business is something more than an empty phrase."[40] Admitting that the department had overlooked some offenses at first, Third Assistant Postmaster General Dockery said the post office was now promptly investigating all complaints. Several publishers, in fact, had been forced to amend their original circulation statements, he said. While no statement was reflexively accepted, Dockery asserted, "it is not fair to proceed on the assumption that every publisher is guilty of misrepresentation unless proved innocent." Indeed, many complaints came from competing publishers who accused their rivals of filing false statements but did not provide any evidence to support their allegations.[41]

A few more favorably disposed toward the post office and the press thought the lack of prosecutions "shows how truthful publishers are and that none of them has a desire to trifle with Uncle Sam."[42] But the vast majority of publishers and advertisers remained dissatisfied with the post office's actions. At the 1915 convention of the American Newspaper Publishers Association, President Herbert L. Bridgman lamented, "[T]he conservatism, not to say indifference, of the postal officials at the intimation of investigation of the sworn semi-annual reports of circulation."[43] Participants discussed ways to amend the law to require vigorous enforcement and stiff penalties.

Advertisers also wanted to put teeth into the regulation by requiring the post office to send a corps of inspectors out in the field to audit circulation statements, similar to what the Treasury Department did when investigating income tax returns.[44] Another wanted the post office to jail "[p]ublishers who lie about circulation and thus use the mails to swindle advertisers."[45] These proposals, while appealing, seemed impractical to the editor of *Printers' Ink*, who estimated that at least 250 trained inspectors would be needed to verify each statement filed with the post office. "If such men can be had for $30 a week, Uncle Sam will have to foot the bill—something like half a million dollars a year. Granting that honest publishers and advertisers will be benefited, how is the public at large going to get that amount of value out of the law?" Rather than relying on the government to "solve the old abuse of fraudulent circulation statements," the editor reasoned that "the advertiser has the remedy in his own hands and can protect himself by requiring, either through audit associations or on his own account, exact data from publishers."[46]

Disillusioned with the government's efforts to enforce the circulation regulation, publishers and advertisers followed *Printers' Ink*'s advice and in 1914 organized their own independent auditing service—the Audit Bureau of Circulations.[47] The new auditing organization "shows that the postal law has failed," the *Duluth* (Minn.) *Herald* editorialized, "for if it had succeeded there would be no call for a private agency to furnish the protection which this bureau does so admirably."[48] As ABC worked to establish a foothold in the industry, it was frequently compared to the post office's circulation regulation. The bureau's supporters argued that the law should be repealed since it was an unnecessary, inefficient, weak duplication of ABC's work. The *New York Tribune*, for example, advertised in trade journals that the law was worthless; advertisers should instead rely on the Audit Bureau of Circulations. The regulation's proponents, on the other hand, thought the industries' efforts would be better expended on trying to strengthen and expand the law rather than on funding another auditing organization.

Stanley Clague, ABC's managing director, led the attack on the regulation. "[T]he advertiser who relies upon the safeguards provided by the postoffice [*sic*] department is gambling with every dollar he spends," Clague wrote. Relying on the government statements "would make the entire business of publishing and advertising a lottery, pure and simple."[49] Although denying that ABC was actively working for the regulation's repeal, Clague spoke before various press associations throughout the country asking members to support such a campaign. When he appeared at the Southern Newspaper Publishers Association convention, Clague met opposition. Major E. B. Stahlman, publisher of the *Nashville* (Tenn.) *Banner*, defended the law, stating that its primary purpose was public information, not enforcement. Many dailies did not belong to ABC, Stahlman reminded Clague. The regulation at least provided some means to monitor their circulations. After discussion, the organization opposed Clague's recommendation and instead resolved that Congress should strengthen the circulation regulation.[50]

Other groups came out against repeal too. "It must be conceded that the law is ambiguous and capable of valuable improvement, but we can see no reason why it should be repealed," the *Mail Order Journal* editorialized. "Just as half a loaf of bread is better than none, so is a little light on ownership and management and circulation better than none." A better solution would be strengthening the law to include all publications and to require the statements to be printed on the first page of all issues "and not hidden away in some dark corner, where readers and advertisers are apt to overlook them."[51]

As debates over the law's future proceeded, the federal government prosecuted a weekly North Carolina publisher suspected of inflating his circulation figures. A jury found A. Roscower, publisher of the *Goldsboro Headlight*, guilty of using the mails with intent to defraud after the local postmaster testified that he had counted the mailings of two issues of the paper, and each time they were under 1,000 copies. Roscower claimed he had a net paid circulation of 6,850. At the end of the trial, the district attorney told the judge that the government had no desire to punish the publisher but brought the case to demonstrate that federal law was sufficient to prosecute fraudulent circulation claims—even involving publications not covered by the Newspaper Publicity Act. The judge fined the publisher $200 and required him to publish accurate circulation data in every issue of his paper for one year.[52]

While ABC members were lobbying against the regulation,

other publishers thought that a separate auditing organization was a waste of money, particularly for dailies since they were required to publicize their circulations anyway. "Why then should a publisher allow himself to be assessed the cost of auditing his own circulation books," the *Fourth Estate* asked, "by any such an agency as the Audit Bureau of Circulations, which has no power to properly punish dishonest publishers?"[53] John Barry, ABC's eastern representative, responded: "Mr. Editor, if you go into a grocery store to buy a pound of sugar, who supplies the scales? The seller or the buyer? The A.B.C. report is the advertising scales which tells whether the man who pays gets what he pays for." The government statements, on the other hand, were generally considered "unreliable and an anachronism."[54] The *Fourth Estate* editor replied: "The reputable grocery man knows the accuracy of his scales and keeps his scales in order. He also knows that they are subject to Government inspection. The daily newspaper publisher keeps his circulation reports in order, because he knows they are subject to Government inspection." Several government investigations had occurred, the editor noted, but in every case the circulation figures were found accurate.[55] Continuing the attack, a few months later he wrote, "[I]t is ridiculous, as well as an insult to a publisher, for the A.B.C. to send a crew of men to go over his affairs and then expect him to pay the A.B.C. $500 for stating that he has not descended to lying. The whole idea of A.B.C. supervision is repugnant to the self-respect of publishers and the bureau should be abolished."[56] The bureau was not abolished, however, and neither was the regulation repealed.

The Press Gets Congress to Extend Regulation

By the early 1940s, weekly publishers—many of whom did not belong to ABC—*wanted* the government to regulate circulation disclosure.[57] The National Editorial Association, a trade organization for weekly publishers, approached lawmakers in 1946 about amending the Newspaper Publicity Act to add weeklies to the circulation requirement. Publishers hoped this action would attract national advertisers who had previously avoided many weeklies because of doubts about their circulation figures. An official of the American Association of Advertising Agencies testified before Congress that "it would be a constructive step and would be a contributing factor in helping the country press to get more advertising if annual sworn circulation statements were required by law."[58] The Senate report recommending the bill's passage actually stated that the decline of the weekly press could be partly blamed on "inadequate proof of circulation statements."[59] The bill became law on July 2, 1946, bringing with it "a large measure of control and confidence where there had been chaos and confusion," according to a newspaper management text.[60]

In 1960, Congress elected to place magazines under the circulation requirement too, seemingly with their approval.[61] The post office thought the legislation would be helpful because of many magazines' "tendency toward abuses in the practice of free circulation." The Magazine Publishers Association did not oppose the action and later supported the law.[62]

Two years later, Congress took another look at the circulation provision of the Newspaper Publicity Act at the post office's request. Postal officials wanted to make the regulation more comprehensive and precise by broadening the definition of circulation to include *all* circulation, not just paid as the 1912 law specified. They also wanted publishers to submit information on the means of distribution. Representatives of the department told a House committee that these changes would be helpful in identifying tie-in sales, illegitimate gift subscriptions, and similar abuses. Leaders of several press associations attended the hearings and asked questions, but none opposed the amendments.[63]

Lawmakers approved the law but added one curious amendment: an exemption for trade publications serving the performing arts. While these publications would still have to file statements with the post office, they would not have to publish those statements in their publications.[64] Why? The media speculated that the exemption primarily affected two publications: *Variety* and *Billboard*. But why should they be exempted?[65] *Billboard*'s president William Littleford immediately announced that the publication would not accept the "disgraceful loophole." *Variety*'s president Syd Silverman, on the other hand, said he planned to use the exemption, predicting that many other performing arts publications would also decide not to publish their circulation data.[66] Several indignant members on the House Committee on the Post Office and Civil Service told the press that they were angry with the Senate's action but did not want to jeopardize the good portions of the bill by challenging the Senate amendment. They promised, however, to try to repeal the exemption during the next session.[67]

True to their word, those lawmakers introduced legislation to repeal the law in 1964 and held hearings to find out why the Senate decided to exempt performing arts publications in the first place.[68] Although no one at the hearings was able to explain precisely why the Senate added the exemption, the general consensus was that *Variety*—the only publication using the exemption—had approached several senators with the idea. Representatives from the publication, while invited, did not attend the hearings. *Billboard*'s president, on the other hand, testified in a letter that "[n]ot having sought the legislation, unwilling to take advantage of it, seeing no reason for it, and committed to the principle of full disclosure of circulation information by all publications desiring to mail at the second-class rates, *Billboard* urges passage of [the legislation] so that the exemption for trade publications serving the performing arts will be eliminated."[69] The hearings also gave representatives from various press associations the opportunity to tell lawmakers how much they supported the Newspaper Publicity Act. Theodore Serrill, vice-president of the National Editorial Association (now the National Newspaper Association), for example, said, "[W]e feel in the half century this legislation has been on the books—having been amended during that time—it has been very helpful in making a better newspaper printing and publishing industry."[70] After the hearing, the House of Representatives voted to repeal the performing arts exemption, but the bill was not reported out of the Senate post office committee that year.[71] Lawmakers were successful in repealing the exemption in 1967.[72] Meanwhile, *Advertising Age* had regularly published *Variety*'s circulation figures.

The Audit Bureau of Circulations and similar organizations are now the first line of defense against circulation liars, although the federal government still sporadically plays a backup role. Postal officials, for example, recently investigated Paul Hensley, publisher of the weekly *Hazard Times* in London, Kentucky, after the Kentucky Press Association told them that several members had complained that Hensley inflated his circulation figures in order to win government contracts for legal advertising.[73] State law requires the contracts to go to the area's newspaper with the largest paid circulation. Hensley was convicted in 1990 for filing a false circulation statement with the U.S. Postal Service and received a suspended three-year sentence.[74] Such prosecution, while extremely rare, indicates that the Newspaper Publicity Act may still be used to protect publishers and advertisers from each other.

CHAPTER NINE

Publicity as an Antidote for Press Abuses

Despite its obscure origins, the Newspaper Publicity Act established the first important federal controls aimed directly at the press and made possible because of the postal subsidy enjoyed by most publications. The law required newspapers and magazines using the highly subsidized mail privilege to identify their owners and stockholders and to label advertisements that resembled news stories and editorials. Dailies were also forced to publish accurate circulation figures along with their ownership statements. The Supreme Court unanimously affirmed congressional authority to enact such legislation in a 1913 court case, instigated by the American Newspaper Publishers Association. Soon afterward, the press urged strict enforcement of the law, recognizing the intrinsic business advantages of supporting the press regulations. In later years, weekly and magazine publishers even asked Congress to extend the circulation requirement to them.

The Newspaper Publicity Act was fitting legislation for the Progressive years, an era known for its emphasis on government as a regulator and for publicity as a disinfectant for industrial and social ills. Proponents expected much from the law. Reformers believed the press regulations would open up the sometimes tainted news and editorial processes to readers, helping them become informed consumers of the press. Publishers and advertisers who supported the law, on the other hand, saw the regulations as a way to legitimatize their fledgling industries by exposing the "illegitimates" to public ridicule while publicizing the "legitimates" as "government-certified" publications.

141

Like many Progressive reforms, though, the Newspaper Publicity Act fell far short of expectations—a victim, in part, of reformers' naive faith in the power of publicity, industry's success in using the regulatory process, and the government bureaucracy's reluctance to assume new responsibilities.

Reformers who believed that "publicity is a great purifier" idealistically expected the law to empower readers with information—information that would give them the insight and understanding necessary to critically evaluate a publication's contents and sources, and then to act on that knowledge. As Representative Henry Barnhart, sponsor of the act's ownership and advertising provisions, told his House colleagues, "I would have the reading public know who it is and what it is that fills editorial columns, and when this is known the reliability of the editorial opinion disseminated may be easily and safely measured."[1] The Newspaper Publicity Act, then, went hand-in-hand with the democratic philosophy exemplified by such Progressive reforms as the direct election of senators, the initiative and referendum, and the public-disclosure statements of political candidates—all citizen-empowering actions.

Reformers also considered the Newspaper Publicity Act as consumer-protection legislation, even though it involved the regulation of information and ideas rather than products and services. To many reformers, including Senator Jonathan Bourne who shepherded the press regulations through the Senate, tainted news posed more of a danger to society than contaminated meat or impure food. "[A]dulterated news is more harmful to the public than adulterated milk," Bourne wrote a publisher who opposed the law. "I deem it just as important for the public to be protected from false news, as for it to be protected from impure foods, and there is just as much justification for requiring a paper to carry the names of its owners, as for requiring that a can of fruit shall bear the name of the concern that packed it."[2]

For perhaps the first time, then, the press was considered a business, subject to public scrutiny and, to a lesser extent, to government regulation similar to other businesses, the First

Amendment notwithstanding. In 1913, the Supreme Court validated this assumption, affirming the government's right to place restrictions on the press's business operations as long as the press accepted special privileges from the government— privileges like the highly subsidized second-class mail rate. Although the Newspaper Publicity Act was deemed constitutional, reformers soon discovered that mandating publicity did not automatically purify the press's business practices. Unscrupulous publishers became more devious: they hid their corporate ties behind faceless names listed on ownership statements and ran "unpaid" advertisements disguised as news stories. Furthermore, most readers did not care—or were not informed—enough to use the law as it was intended, leaving reformers disillusioned and the press basically unchanged.

Industry, on the other hand, was more successful in using the Newspaper Publicity Act than reformers were in achieving their goals. After an initial backlash, key elements of the press came to recognize the value of the act—and how it suited their interests. As Representative Barnhart, a newspaper publisher himself, candidly told his House colleagues: "[The law] will shield the great army of honest publicists from unjust suspicion which occasional impostors in the editorial profession induce; it will protect the reading public from deception by covert agencies of evil; and it will put journalism on the high plane of reliability and respectability which it ought to occupy as the greatest educational benefactor in the world."[3] Viewing the regulations from this perspective, no wonder Barnhart predicted that "every honest editor and every deserving periodical reader in our country will approve this method of compelling all editors and publishers to stand out in the broad sunlight of day."

In keeping with Barnhart's prediction, many enterprising publishers and advertisers used the law to re-enforce their legitimacy in the marketplace, but not necessarily to reform the industry as a whole. Publishers of daily newspapers, for example, advertised their "government-certified" circulation figures in trade journals without informing readers that the government had not verified the data. Advertisers and publishers also pressed the Post

Office Department to vigorously enforce the law and, when the department did not initiate investigations, they squealed on their competitors for alleged violations.

Ironically, industry also became disillusioned with the law's ineffectiveness in weeding out the "illegitimates." Many publishers and advertisers, in fact, wanted the Post Office Department to go much further in enforcing the law. They asked the government to audit the dailies' sworn circulation statements; when postal officials refused, they formed the Audit Bureau of Circulations. Industry also wanted the post office to zealously enforce the advertising provision of the law, providing publishers with an excuse for not giving businesses and organizations free publicity space. When the department did not have the resources or enthusiasm to closely monitor the nation's news and editorial columns, the industry complained and started bringing alleged violations to the administrators' attention. Even then officials vacillated, handicapped by the law's imprecision in defining what constituted an advertisement and a news story. Often they left it to the accused publisher to determine a suspected story's newsworthiness, and, consequently, the ultimate irony—his or her innocence or guilt.

The Post Office Department's lack of enthusiasm for this law was not surprising. Congress, to a certain extent, imposed the Newspaper Publicity Act on the department, correctly seeing the second-class mail privilege as the only constitutional route lawmakers could take to regulate the press. Postal officials, however, had already adopted administrative remedies to curb the pervasive second-class mail abuses that had plagued the department for years. Bureaucrats did not need—or want—the inevitable problems that would surely result from aggressively administering and enforcing the ambiguous press regulations.

In evaluating the long-term effectiveness of the law, it is easy to conclude that the press regulations proved ineffectual. Granted, more corporations own newspapers and magazines than ever before unbeknown to many readers; the distinction between advertisements and news is even more difficult to discern as the press relies increasingly on advertorials or infomercials from undisclosed special interests; and exaggerated circulation figures still anger advertisers and competitors, and occasionally spark lawsuits.

One should not, however, judge the law too harshly. While most Americans and even some members of the press may not be aware of the press regulations—and might not appreciate them if they were—that does not mean the law is worthless. Many people, for instance, will never use the freedom-of-information or open-meetings acts lawmakers have enacted to shed light on government, but they are important public policies just the same. Likewise, the Newspaper Publicity Act sets a valuable precedent that the press too must be open to public scrutiny. Representative Morris Udall (D-Utah) talked affectionately in 1962 about "the time-honored practice of requiring publications, at least once a year, in the smallest possible type, to tell the public who it is that owns and operates [them]." People who want "to strain [their] eyes on the small print" should be afforded that opportunity, Udall said.[4]

The significance of the Newspaper Publicity Act, however, lies beyond a pragmatic assessment of whether it has cleaned up the press. More important, perhaps, is appreciating how the act and the circumstances surrounding its passage enhance our understanding of the press as a business institution and of the intricacies of press-government relations during the Progressive years in American history.

This case study integrates many of the thematic threads common in studies of the Progressive era. First, it illustrates the reform hypothesis of such historians as Richard Hofstadter and George Mowry. Proponents of the regulations were unquestionably interested in curbing long-existing abuses in the press. While perhaps naive, these reformers believed that government-mandated publicity was the best way to handle business abuses, whether in the press or in banks or railroads. In hindsight, one may wonder about their political sophistication, but their motives must remain unchallenged.

Second, this research also supports aspects of the revisionist school, led by Gabriel Kolko and James Weinstein, that sees the Progressive years as more of an entrenchment of capitalistic business values than an era of reform. Clearly, segments of the press wanted government to help protect their business interests; "legitimate" publishers liked the idea of being "certified by the government," and advertisers sought legislative help in their battle to obtain accurate circulation figures. Furthermore, most members of the press actively discouraged talk of fundamentally changing the economic structure of the American press. Publishers ridiculed, for instance, reform journalist Hamilton Holt's idea of an endowed press—one free of advertisements.

Third, the study reinforces points raised by such scholars as Richard McCormick, Robert Wiebe, and Stephen Skowronek in their more structural interpretations of the Progressive years. The process by which the Newspaper Publicity Act became law, for example, bore many of the characteristics that these historians have found in their studies. First, reformers looked for models of state regulations that could be adapted for use by the federal government. Second, lawmakers looked to the "experts," in this case postal bureaucrats who had spent years finetuning administrative rules governing the second-class mail subsidy, for guidance as they crafted legislation; however, the post office hierarchy, mainly political appointees, opposed the regulations. Third, Democrats and insurgent Republicans generally aligned in support of the press regulations with Taft Republicans opposed. Fourth, people who championed the law did so for a spectrum of reasons; some simply wanted to punish hated publications, while others acted on their beliefs about the importance of untainted communication in the democratic process. And last, the object of the reforms—the press—did not uniformly oppose the law; some publishers and advertisers supported one or another of its provisions, reflecting intra-industry competition.

Most journalism histories portray the early-twentieth century American press as a crusader, working closely with reformers to weed out abuses in society. This study examines the flip side of that textbook image—the press as a business susceptible to corporate abuses as any other business at the time. From this perspective, the press is seen as a social and economic institution, reflecting the values of society as well as manifesting its broader problems. This portrayal provides balance to the press-as-a-watchdog metaphor. It also shows how some elements of the press actually invited government intervention into its business affairs in order to fight off competitors and to legitimize the industry.

Legal scholars have long been interested in constitutional limits to press freedom under the First Amendment. This study explores how the existence of a federal subsidy—the second-class mail privilege—opened the door to federal regulation of the press. Scholars such as Zechariah Chafee, Jr., Lucy Maynard Salmon, and J. Edward Gerald have addressed this issue in terms of the post office's censorial powers over obscene materials, but little attention has been given to the sweeping regulations embedded in the Newspaper Publicity Act. By accepting the privilege, for example, the press must identify its owners and stockholders, giving up its right to anonymous speech— a right that the Supreme Court upheld in the 1960 *Talley v. California* decision. The privilege also requires the press to accept content regulation over disguised advertisements (they must be marked). Surprisingly, *Lewis Publishing v. Morgan*, the 1913 case in which the High Court ruled that Congress could set these conditions on publications using the second-class privilege, has long been forgotten, lost in the 1930s and 1940s legal debate over whether the press, as a business, had to follow labor and antitrust laws, like any other business. Nevertheless, the Newspaper Publicity Act seems to be a logical place to begin the inquiry into the press as a business institution.

Finally, this study adds to the scholarship on business ethics in the media. The law was a legislative response to many of the ethical problems that publishers, editors, and advertisers discussed annually at their trade associations' conventions in the late 1800s and early 1900s. As these associations were passing their first codes of conduct and journalism programs were being started at universities, policymakers from outside the industry acted to impose their own ethical standards on the press. This outside scrutiny, on reflection, surely signified the beginning of the public debate on press responsibility that culminated in the Hutchins' Commission on Freedom of the Press in the late 1940s.

NOTES
SELECTED BIBLIOGRAPHY
INDEX

Notes

1. Introduction

1. Charles Evans Hughes, future chief justice of the United States, referred to publicity as "a great purifier" in a speech to manufacturers in 1906. Quoted in George Seldes, *One Thousand Americans* (New York: Boni & Gaer, Inc., 1947), 68.

2. Roosevelt made this comment to Washington, D.C., reporters, after reading the 1906 magazine series, "Treason of the Senate." Quoted in C. C. Regier, *The Era of the Muckraker* (Chapel Hill: University of North Carolina Press, 1932), 1.

3. Richard Hofstadter, *The Age of Reform* (New York: Vintage Books, 1955), 186; see also Richard B. Kielbowicz, "The Media and Reform, 1900–1917," in *The Media in America: A History*, ed. Wm. David Sloan and James G. Stovall (Worthington, Ohio: Publishing Horizons, Inc., 1989), 271, 273.

4. Oswald Garrison Villard, "Some Weaknesses of Modern Journalism," in *The Coming Newspaper*, ed. Merle Thorpe (New York: Henry Holt and Co., 1915), 57.

5. See, for example, Gabriel Kolko, *The Triumph of Conservatism: A Reinterpretation of American History, 1900–1916* (1963; reprint ed. Chicago: Quadrangle Books, Inc., 1967), 70–71, 121; Robert H. Wiebe, *Businessmen and Reform: A Study of the Progressive Movement* (Cambridge, Mass.: Harvard University Press, 1962) and *The Search for Order, 1877–1920* (New York: Hill and Wang, 1967); and James Weinstein, *The Corporate Ideal in the Liberal State, 1900–1918* (Boston: Beacon Press, 1968).

6. Eugene N. White, *The Regulation and Reform of the American Banking System, 1900–1929* (Princeton, N.J.: Princeton University Press, 1983); Gabriel Kolko, *Railroads and Regulation, 1887–1916* (Princeton, N.J.: Princeton University Press, 1965); Melvin Urofsky, *Big Steel and the Wilson Administration: A Study in Business-Government Relations* (Columbus: Ohio State University Press, 1969); and Nelson Gaskill, *The Regulation of Competition* (New York: Harper &

151

Brothers, 1936). Gaskill was a former chairman of the Federal Trade Commission.

7. Henry C. Adams, "What Is Publicity?," *North American Review*, December 1902, pp. 895–904; "Publicity for Industrial Corporations," *Independent*, June 5, 1902, p. 1388; Robert Luce, "Publicity and Trusts," *Review of Reviews*, September 1912, pp. 339–441; Eric F. Goldman, "Public Relations and the Progressive Surge: 1898–1917," *Public Relations Review* 4 (Fall 1978): 54–56; Ray Ginger, *Age of Excess: The United States from 1877 to 1914* (New York: Macmillan, 1965), 258; Alan R. Raucher, *Public Relations and Business: 1900–1929* (Baltimore: Johns Hopkins University Press, 1968), 6; Jean B. Quandt, *From the Small Town to the Great Community: The Social Thought of Progressive Intellectuals* (New Brunswick, N.J.: Rutgers University Press, 1970), 1, 26–27, 59–75. A few reformers, however, remained skeptical about the effectiveness of publicity in achieving real reforms. In theory, it sounded effective, they admitted, but corporations, in particular, had adopted a superficial interpretation of publicity, giving the public "chit chat" but nothing of substance. "Corporations and Publicity," *Nation*, July 4, 1912, pp. 5–6.

8. *Cong. Rec.*, April 27, 1912, 5465.

9. "Publicity and the Public Welfare," *Editor and Publisher*, July 6, 1912, p. 12.

10. Act of Aug. 24, 1912, 37 *U.S Statutes at Large* 539 at 553–54. Religious, fraternal, temperance, and scientific publications were specifically exempted from the law.

11. See generally Zechariah Chafee, Jr., *Government and Mass Communications: Report from the Commission on Freedom of the Press*, 2 vols. (Chicago: University of Chicago Press, 1947).

12. *Lewis Publishing Co. v. Morgan*, 229 U.S. 288 (1913); see also *Grosjean v. American Press Co.*, 297 U.S. 233 (1936); *Associated Press v. N.L.R.B.*, 301 U.S. 103 (1937); and *Associated Press et al. v. United States*, 326 U.S. 1 (1945). For a discussion about the significance of these cases, see generally J. Edward Gerald, *The Press and the Constitution: 1931–1947* (Minneapolis: University of Minnesota Press, 1948).

13. See, for example, Edwin Emery and Michael Emery, *The Press and America*, 4th ed. (Englewood Cliffs, N.J.: Prentice Hall, 1978), 259–77; and John Tebbel, *The Media in America* (New York: New American Library, 1974), 279–322.

14. Richard B. Kielbowicz, "Postal Subsidies for the Press and

the Business of Mass Culture, 1880–1920," *Business History Review* 64 (Autumn 1990): 460, 474–75.

PART 1. Business Excesses in the Press

1. Will Irwin, "The American Newspaper: Part III," *Collier's*, in *The American Newspaper*, ed. Clifford F. Weigle and David G. Clark (Ames: Iowa State University Press, 1969), 16.

2. According to the N. W. Ayer & Son advertising agency, daily newspapers grew from 1,836 to 2,435; weeklies went from 14,373 to 16,191; semi-weeklies from 209 to 594; and tri-weeklies from 40 to 61. See Alfred M. Lee, *The Daily Newspaper in America* (New York: Macmillan, 1937), 722–23. Figures varied, however. Mott reported dailies increased from 1,650 in 1892 to 2,250 in 1914; weeklies went from 11,000 to 12,500; and semi-weeklies from 200 to 600. See Frank Luther Mott, *American Journalism* (New York: Macmillan, 1947), 549. For magazine statistics, see Frank Luther Mott, *A History of American Magazines* (Cambridge, Mass.: Belknap Press of Harvard University Press, 1938), 4:11.

3. Quoted in Mott, *American Journalism*, 548; see also Edwin Emery and Michael Emery, *The Press and America*, 4th ed. (Englewood, N.J.: Prentice Hall, 1978), 231.

4. Corporate ownership grew to 83.2 percent by 1919. See Lee, *Daily Newspaper in America*, 197.

5. James E. Rogers, *The American Newspaper* (Chicago: University of Chicago Press, 1909), 92–93, 199–204; "Editorialene," *Nation*, June 12, 1902, pp. 459–60; "Newspapers as Institutions," ibid., July 15, 1915, p. 85; Hamilton Holt, *Commercialism and Journalism* (Boston: Houghton Mifflin Co., 1909), 36. Hazel Dicken-Garcia notes this trend in *Journalistic Standards in Nineteenth-Century America* (Madison: University of Wisconsin Press, 1989), 166, as does Jack R. Hart, "Horatio Alger in the Newsroom: Social Origins of American Editors," *Journalism Quarterly* 53 (Spring 1976): 20.

6. Rogers, *American Newspaper*, 91.

7. Gerald J. Baldasty and Jeffrey B. Rutenbeck, "Money, Politics and Newspapers: The Business Environment of Press Partisanship in the Late 19th Century," *Journalism History* 15 (Summer/Autumn 1988): 60–69; Gerald J. Baldasty, "The Nineteenth-Century Origins of Modern American Journalism," *Proceedings of the American Antiquarian Society* 100 (October 1990): 408–9.

8. Alfred D. Chandler, Jr., *The Visible Hand: The Managerial*

Revolution in American Business (Cambridge, Mass.: Belknap Press of Harvard University Press, 1977), 227, 290. See also generally Susan Strasser, *Satisfaction Guaranteed: The Making of the American Mass Market* (New York: Pantheon Books, 1989); and Richard S. Tedlow, *New and Improved: The Story of Mass Marketing in America* (New York: Basic Books, Inc., 1990).

9. Daniel Pope, *The Making of Modern Advertising* (New York: Basic Books, Inc., 1983), 31, 113, 148; Lee, *Daily Newspaper in America*, 748–49. Emery and Emery, *Press and America*, 233, however, estimate that by 1910 advertising brought in 64 percent of the revenues.

10. Will Irwin, "American Newspaper, Part IX," *Collier's*, May 27, 1911, p. 16. Holt, *Commercialism and Journalism*, 17, also noted that many newspapers received 90 percent of their revenues from advertisers. See also Joseph Blethen, "The Advertiser's Place in Journalism," *University of Washington Journalism Department Bulletin* 5 (1910): 4.

11. The newspaper was the *New York Recorder*. See *Journalist*, June 18, 1892, p. 5. According to an 1895 survey of ten leading dailies conducted by the N. W. Ayer & Son advertising agency, the reading matter/advertising ratio ranged from 25 percent advertising to 70 percent with an average of 40 percent. See Lee, *Daily Newspaper in America*, 324–25.

12. Holt, *Commercialism and Journalism*, 38. See also Rogers, *American Newspaper*, 64.

13. *Newspaper Maker*, Sept. 10, 1896, p. 4.

14. *Fame*, November 1897, p. 389; Pope, *Making of Modern Advertising*, 148.

15. For background on the muckrakers and their exposés, see generally Louis Filler, *Appointment at Armageddon: Muckraking and Progressivism in American Life* (Westport, Conn.: Greenwood Press, 1976), *Progressivism and Muckraking* (New York: R. R. Bowker Press, 1976), and *The Muckrakers: Crusaders for American Liberalism* (1950; reprint ed. Chicago: Henry Regnery Co., 1986); Richard B. Kielbowicz, "The Media and Reform, 1900–1917," in *The Media in America: A History*, ed. Wm. David Sloan and James G. Stovall (Worthington, Ohio: Publishing Horizons, Inc., 1989), 262–79; C. C. Regier, *The Era of the Muckrakers* (Chapel Hill: University of North Carolina Press, 1932); and Thomas C. Leonard, *The Power of the Press: The Birth of American Political Reporting* (New York: Oxford University Press, 1986), 137–221.

16. Robert D. Reynolds, Jr., "The 1906 Campaign to Sway Muckraking Periodicals," *Journalism Quarterly* 56 (Autumn 1979): 514–15. See also generally Herr G. Creel, *Tricks of the Press* and *Newspaper Frauds* (St. Louis, Mo.: National Rip-Saw Publishing Co., 1911).

17. James M. Lee, *History of American Journalism*, 2d ed. (Garden City, N.Y.: Garden City Publishing Co., Inc., 1923), 388, states the establishment of these associations and the subsequent codification of ethical standards were the most important changes occurring in the press during the late nineteenth century.

2. Hidden Ownership

1. Walter Lippmann, *Drift and Mastery: An Attempt to Diagnose the Current Unrest* (New York: Mitchell Kennerley, 1914), 3.

2. Richard Hofstadter, *The Paranoid Style in American Politics and Other Essays* (New York: Alfred A. Knopf, 1965), 193.

3. Quoted in "Fears a Purchased Press," *New York Times*, April 7, 1909, p. 6. See also John Tebbel and Sarah Miles Watts, *The Press and the Presidency* (New York: Oxford University Press, 1985), 342, who reported that President Theodore Roosevelt believed financiers secretly owned much of the New York press.

4. Quoted in "Newspaper Publishers Roasted by Lay Men," *New York Times*, Feb. 23, 1906, p. 4. Two years later, William Travers Jerome, a New York district attorney, warned the same publishers, "Our democratic institutions will not work out so long as we have government by the newspapers . . . dictated . . . in the counting rooms of R. H. Macy and Co., Siegel-Cooper and John Wanamaker." See "Jerome Lets Fly at the Newspapers," *New York Times*, April 24, 1908, p. 1.

5. Oswald Garrison Villard, "Some Weaknesses of Modern Journalism," in *The Coming Newspaper*, ed. Merle Thorpe (New York: Henry Holt and Co., 1915), 53.

6. Quoted in "Giving the Newspaper Readers What They Want," *American Printer*, June 1911, p. 448. Other politicians, including Senator Robert Owen from Oklahoma, speculated that corporate powers owned "in large degree many metropolitan papers and a number of magazines." George H. Shibley, "Progressive Leaders: United States Senator Robert L. Owen," *Twentieth Century*, May 1910, p. 129. See also "Bondage of the Press," ibid., October 1909, pp. 48–49; George French, "Masters of the Magazines," ibid., April 1912, pp. 501–8; Edward A. Ross, "The Suppression of Important

News," *Atlantic Monthly*, March 1910, pp. 303–11; Herr G. Creel, *Tricks of the Press* (St. Louis, Mo.: National Rip-Saw Publishing Co., 1911), 3; "Publications Change Ownership," *American Printer*, March 1911, p. 100; and *Parcel Post: Hearings Before the Subcommittee on Parcel Post of the Senate Committee on Post Office and Post Roads*, 62d Cong., 1st sess. (1911), 644–45.

7. Henry George, Jr., *The Menace of Privilege* (New York: Macmillan, 1906), 269; see also Hazel Dicken-Garcia, *Journalistic Standards in Nineteenth-Century America* (Madison: University of Wisconsin Press, 1989), 161–62; and Ferdinand Lundberg, *America's 60 Families* (New York: Vanguard Press, 1937), 244–47.

8. Herr G. Creel, *Newspaper Frauds* (St. Louis, Mo.: National Rip-Saw Publishing Co., 1911), 30.

9. Lundberg, *America's 60 Families*, 247. Ironically, some financiers became disappointed after gaining control of a publication. One told Will Irwin, " 'I bought the controlling interest in two different newspapers in those days. Something happened to them. They began to lose their pep and their interest. Within six months, they were no use to me whatever!' " Quoted in Will Irwin, *The Making of a Reporter* (New York: G. P. Putnam's Sons, 1942), 168.

10. Richard A. Haste, "The Evolution of the Fourth Estate," *Arena*, March 1909, p. 351. See also Richard S. Tedlow, *Keeping the Corporate Image: Public Relations and Business, 1900–1950* (Greenwich, Conn.: JAI Press, Inc., 1979), 8; George, *Menace of Privilege*, 280–83; Lundberg, *America's 60 Families*, 306; "Bondage of the Press," pp. 48–49; and Bernard A. Weisberger, *The American Newspaperman* (Chicago: University of Chicago Press, 1961), 126.

11. Will Irwin, "The American Newspaper, Part XII," *Collier's*, July 1, 1911, p. 18. George Seldes, *Witness to a Century* (New York: Ballantine Books, 1987), 21, revealed that he did not realize that financier Andrew Mellon was a major investor in the *Pittsburgh Leader* in the early 1900s.

12. Quoted in Albert L. Gale and George W. Kline, *Bryan the Man* (St. Louis, Mo.: Thompson Publishing Co., 1908), 104–5.

13. George, *Menace of Privilege*, 283. A trade journal also wrote about the "fascination that some railroad magnates and wire-pulling politicians have exhibited to own daily newspaper 'organs.' " "Utilizing the Press," *Journalist*, June 27, 1885, p. 4.

14. William Kittle, "The Interests and the Magazines," *Twentieth Century*, May 1910, p. 124; see also George, *Menace of Privilege*, 283.

15. Julius Grodinsky, *Jay Gould: His Business Career, 1867–1892*

(Philadelphia: University of Pennsylvania Press, 1957), 20, 336 n. 2. See also Maury Klein, *The Life and Legend of Jay Gould* (Baltimore: Johns Hopkins University Press, 1986), 135, 394; Bingham Duncan, *Whitelaw Reid: Journalist, Politician, Diplomat* (Athens: University of Georgia Press, 1975), 48–49; Weisberger, *American Newspaperman*, 126; and Tedlow, *Keeping the Corporate Image*, 8.

16. *Journalist*, April 5, 1884, p. 7; "The World's Owner," ibid., April 19, 1884, p. 4; Thomas C. Cochran and William Miller, *The Age of Enterprise: A Social History of Industrial America* (1942; rev. ed. New York: Harper & Row, 1961), 148.

17. Edwin Gabler, *The American Telegrapher: A Social History, 1860–1900* (New Brunswick, N.J.: Rutgers University Press, 1988), 18; Grodinsky, *Jay Gould*, 320; Klein, *Life and Legend of Jay Gould*, 135, 394. According to Klein, the *New York Times* reported rumors that Gould purchased the *Rocky Mountain News* in 1878 through W. A. H. Loveland and bought controlling stock in the *New York Evening Express* in 1881. Gould's Western Union reportedly controlled the *Springfield Republican*. See "The Postal Telegraph," *Telegrapher*, Feb. 19, 1870, p. 205.

18. Allan Nevins, *The Evening Post: A Century of Journalism* (New York: Boni & Liveright, 1922), 440; Weisberger, *American Newspaperman*, 126; Tedlow, *Keeping the Corporate Image*, 8; Klein, *Life and Legend of Jay Gould*, 395; Lundberg, *America's 60 Families*, 256. Lundberg reported that Villard purchased the *Evening Post* in 1883. See also James B. Hedges, "Promotion of Immigration to the Pacific Northwest by the Railroads," *Mississippi Valley Historical Review* 15 (September 1928): 199.

19. Joseph G. Pyle, *The Life of James J. Hill* (New York: Doubleday, Doran and Co., Inc. 1919), 2:101–2, 2:382–86. Hill and other railroad financiers also invested in the *Seattle Times* and *Post-Intelligencer*, and the *Portland Oregonian* and *Telegram*. See also Upton Sinclair, *The Brass Check: A Study of American Journalism* (Pasadena, Calif.: Author, 1920), 243–44; and Haste, "Evolution of the Fourth Estate," p. 351.

20. Fremont Older, *My Own Story* (New York: Macmillan, 1926), 17, 36, denied the widely circulated rumor that multi-millionaire James D. Phelen secretly owned the *San Francisco Bulletin* in the late 1890s when Older worked for that newspaper. See also W. A. Swanberg, *Citizen Hearst: A Biography of W. R. Hearst* (New York: Charles Scribner's Sons, 1961), 49; and Sinclair, *Brass Check*, 241.

21. William Salisbury, "American Journalism," *Arena*, December

1908, p. 567; Sinclair, *Brass Check*, 241–42; Lundberg, *America's 60 Families*, 274.

22. Lundberg, *America's 60 Families*, 247; Ralph W. Hidy and Muriel E. Hidy, *Pioneering in Big Business, 1882–1911: History of Standard Oil Company, New Jersey* (New York: Harper & Brothers, 1955), 212–13.

23. Sinclair, *Brass Check*, 242; Lundberg, *America's 60 Families*, 249–50.

24. William Kittle, "The Making of Public Opinion: News Bureaus and Newspapers Advocating Corporation Interests," *Arena*, July 1909, p. 442; "Corporation Control of the Daily, Monthly, and Religious Press," *Arena*, January 1909, p. 105.

25. Lundberg, *America's 60 Families*, 248–50; Ben H. Bagdikian, *The Media Monopoly* (Boston: Beacon Press, 1983), 217; Sinclair, *Brass Check*, 242; French, "Masters of the Magazines," p. 13. Page also denied that industrialist Andrew Carnegie secretly owned stock in the publication. Walter H. Page, "On A Tenth Birthday: Some Reminiscences and Gossip About the Magazine Itself," *World's Work*, January 1911, pp. 13906–907. See also Robert J. Rusnak, *Walter Hines Page and The World's Work, 1900–1913* (Washington, D.C.: University Press of America, Inc., 1982), 53.

26. The New York papers speculated that Stillman owned $100,000 out of a total of $150,000 worth of stock in *Outlook*. At first, the magazine refused to discuss the matter but then stated that Stillman held less than one-tenth of the company's stock. The magazine, however, refused to list the names and the exact holdings of its stockholders. See "Corporation Control of the Press," pp. 106–7; Bagdikian, *Media Monopoly*, 217–18; Lundberg, *America's 60 Families*, 249; and Kittle, "Interests and the Magazines," pp. 124–28.

27. Quoted in Kittle, "Interests and the Magazines," p. 126; Bagdikian, *Media Monopoly*, 217. Publisher George Gunton received $15,000 annually from Standard Oil until 1904 when the company stopped its unpublicized subsidy. See Hidy and Hidy, *Pioneering in Big Business*, 660.

28. George Seldes, *One Thousand Americans* (New York: Boni & Gaer, 1947), 67–90, quote at 70; Bagdikian, *Media Monopoly*, 217–18; Lundberg, *America's 60 Families*, 253–55; "Publications Change Hands," *American Printer*, March 1911, p. 100.

29. Bagdikian, *Media Monopoly*, 217–18; Seldes, *One Thousand Americans*, 67–90; "Corporation Control of the Press," p. 105.

30. "Corporation Control of the Press," p. 106. Some historians, however, take exception to the theory that "big business" effectively silenced the muckraking press by buying the publications. These researchers attribute the publications' decline to poor business and management practices—not to a coordinated business effort to silence the muckrakers. See Michael D. Marcaccio, "Did a Business Conspiracy End Muckraking? A Reexamination," *The Historian* 47 (November 1984): 58–71; Frank Luther Mott, *A History of American Magazines* (Cambridge, Mass.: Harvard University Press, 1930–1968), 4:209; and Harold S. Wilson, *McClure's Magazine and the Muckrakers* (Princeton, N.J.: Princeton University Press, 1970), 320–21.

31. Lundberg, *America's 60 Families*, 92–93, 252; Irwin, "American Newspapers," 69.

32. George Britt, *Forty Years-Forty Millions: The Career of Frank A. Munsey* (New York: Farrar & Rinehart, Inc., 1935), 94; see also Lundberg, *America's 60 Families*, 253.

33. Lundberg, *America's 60 Families*, 106–7, 253. The Emerys refer to Munsey as "a business-minded purchaser of newspapers who understood little of the journalistic traditions of the craft." Michael Emery and Edwin Emery, *The Press and America*, 6th ed. (Englewood Cliffs, N.J.: Prentice Hall, 1988), 280. See also Salisbury, "American Journalism," p. 566; and George Kibbe Turner, "Manufacturing Public Opinion," *McClure's Magazine*, July 1912, p. 323.

34. George Seldes, *Freedom of the Press* (Indianapolis: Bobbs-Merrill Co., 1935), 124–25; Sinclair, *Brass Check*, 241–42; Seldes, *One Thousand Americans*, 18–19. See also Richard T. Ruetten, "Anaconda Journalism: The End of an Era," *Journalism Quarterly* 37 (Winter 1960): 4–5. Ruetten's article refers primarily to the Anaconda-controlled Montana press after 1920.

35. Suspect acquisitions included: the Wanamaker family (department stores), *Philadelphia Record* and *North American*; Carson C. Peck (F. W. Woolworth Company), *Brooklyn Times*; United Shoe Machinery, *Boston Herald* and *Traveler*; Singer Sewing Machine Company, *Albany* (New York) *Knickerbocker Press*; John R. McLean (street railway and gas franchises), *Cincinnati Enquirer* and *Post*; John Spreckels (sugar), *San Francisco Call*; General Harrison Otis (owner of the Republican *Los Angeles Times*), *Los Angeles Democratic Herald*. See Lundberg, *America's 60 Families*, 255, 270, 272, 276, 305; Sinclair, *Brass Check*, 241–45, 253; Ferdinand Lundberg, *Imperial Hearst: A Social Biography* (New York: Equinox Cooperative Press,

1936), 37; and *Fourth Annual Proceedings of the Washington State Press, 1887–1890* (Hoquiam: Washingtonian Steam Book, News & Job Print, 1891), 91.

36. "Editor Hapgood Finds Flaws in the Dailies," *New York Times*, Feb. 11, 1906, p. 2. Belmont had earlier invested in the *New York Morning Star* and the *New York World*, which he used to help candidates in the Democratic party. See David Black, *The King of Fifth Avenue: The Fortunes of August Belmont* (New York: Dial Press, 1981), 84, 220; and Irving Katz, *August Belmont: A Political Biography* (New York: Columbia University Press, 1968), 17, 117.

37. Elmer Davis, *History of the New York Times: 1851–1921* (New York: New York Times Co., 1921), 193. In the mid-nineteenth century, the *New York Times* almost fell victim to a Tweed-Ring takeover. "Slippery Dick" Connolly tried to stop the newspaper's exposés of city government by offering to purchase the paper for five million dollars, five times its estimated worth. Publisher George Jones refused. See Hamilton Holt, *Commercialism and Journalism* (Boston: Houghton Mifflin Co., 1909), 79.

38. Peter Lyon, *Success Story: The Life and Times of S. S. McClure* (New York: Charles Scribner's Sons, 1963), 289–90; Robert D. Reynolds, Jr., "The 1906 Campaign to Sway Muckraking Periodicals," *Journalism Quarterly* 56 (Autumn 1979): 520; C. C. Regier, *The Era of the Muckrakers* (Chapel Hill: University of North Carolina Press, 1932), 178.

39. Donald A. Ritchie, " 'The Loyalty of the Senate': Washington Correspondents in the Progressive Era," *The Historian* 51 (August 1989): 578–79. See also Robert C. Byrd, *The Senate, 1789–1989: Addresses on the History of the United States Senate* (Washington, D.C.: Government Printing Office, 1988), 371, 380–81.

40. Ross, "Suppression of Important News," p. 305.

41. H.R. Rep. No. 376, 56th Cong., 1st sess. (1900), 4; H.R. Doc. 608, 59th Cong., 2d sess. (1907), x, 32.

42. Nathaniel C. Fowler, Jr., *Fowler's Publicity* (Boston: Publicity Publishing Co., 1900), 441. Fowler at 442, however, warned businesses that these publications often did not qualify for the second-class mail rate.

43. Ibid., 442.

44. Burton J. Hendricks, *The Story of Life Insurance* (New York: McClure, Phillips and Co., 1906), 229.

45. *National Advertiser*, April 1, 1892, p. 23. See Mott, *History*

of American Magazines, 4:364–68, for a description of these mail-order publications.

46. "Utilizing the Press," *Journalist*, June 27, 1885, p. 4.

47. Ibid., Jan. 10, 1891, p. 12.

48. "The Newspaper Stool Pigeon," *National Advertiser*, Feb. 15, 1892, pp. 207–8.

49. *Journalist*, March 21, 1891, p. 11.

50. Ibid.

51. Benjamin B. Herbert, *The First Decennium of the National Editorial Association of the United States* (Chicago: NEA, 1896), 453. Representative Owen Scott of Illinois introduced the legislation, H.R. 5068.

52. Ibid., 610–11.

53. Hiley H. Ward, "Ninety Years of the National Newspaper Association: The Mind and Dynamics of Grassroots Journalism in Shaping America" (Ph.D. diss., University of Minnesota, 1977), 227.

54. *Proceedings of the ANPA Tenth Annual Convention* (1896), 59–60.

55. Ibid., 62.

56. Ibid. (1897), 3, 35; see also *Illinois Newspaper Directory and History of the Illinois Press Association* (Champaign-Urbana: Illinois Press Association, 1934), 162. For a detailed account on how the press worked with the post office to exclude advertising sheets from the second-class mail privilege, see Richard B. Kielbowicz, "The Growing Interaction of the Federal Bureaucracy and the Press: The Case of a Postal Rule, 1879–1917," *American Journalism* 4 (1987): 5–18.

57. "To Publishers," *Fame*, April 1892, p. 41.

58. "The Press and the Post Office," ibid., March 1892, p. 10.

59. Ibid.; "The Abuse of Pound-Rates," ibid., May 1892, p. 73; "To Publishers," ibid., April 1892, p. 41.

3. Disguised Advertisements

1. Gloria Steinem, "Sex, Lies & Advertising," *Ms.*, July/August 1990, pp. 19, 26. Many advertising contracts, according to Steinem, contain "insertion orders" that specify placement and adjacent editorial copy.

2. Ibid., 27–28. See, for example, "Selling to Children," *Consumer Reports*, August 1990, pp. 518–21; Michael Hoyt, "When the

Walls Come Tumbling Down," *Columbia Journalism Review*, March/
April 1990, pp. 35–41; Randall Rothenberg, "Messages from Sponsors Become Harder to Detect," *New York Times*, Nov. 19, 1989, p.
5; Barry Meier, "TV Commercials That Go On and On," ibid., Jan.
27, 1990, p. 36; Eleanor Blau, "Whittle Distributes Books with Ads,"
ibid., Nov. 16, 1989, p. 22; and Mark Crispin Miller, "Hollywood,
The Ad," *Atlantic Monthly*, April 1990, pp. 41–54.

3. At that time, publishers, advertisers, and postal officials used
the term *reading notices* to denote paid advertisements written to
resemble news or editorials. Reading notices must be distinguished
from puffs—the practice of editors favorably mentioning advertisers
or prospective advertisers in their news columns without compensation. This, too, was a routine business practice during the early
years of the twentieth century and became even more common after
Congress required reading notices to be marked advertisements in
1912.

4. James M. Lee, *History of American Journalism*, 2d ed. (Garden
City, N.Y.: Garden City Publishing Co., Inc., 1923), 356. Other
authors mention the pervasive use of reading notices: Frank Luther
Mott, *A History of American Magazines* (Cambridge, Mass.: Belknap
Press of Harvard University Press, 1938), 3:11; Daniel Pope, *The
Making of Modern Advertising* (New York: Basic Books, Inc., 1983),
233; Silas Bent, *Ballyhoo: The Voice of the Press* (New York: Boni &
Liveright, 1927), 121; Printers' Ink, *Printers' Ink: 50 Years, 1888–
1938* (New York: Printers' Ink Publishing Co., 1938), 82; Allan
Nevins, *The Emergence of Modern America, 1865–1878* (New York:
Macmillan, 1927), 242; Ellis P. Oberholtzer, *A History of the United
States Since the Civil War* (New York: Macmillan, 1928), 2:541–42;
Louis M. Hacker and Benjamin B. Kendrick, *The United States Since
1865*, rev. ed. (New York: F. S. Crofts and Co., 1936), 695; and
George Everett, "The Linotype and U.S. Daily Newspaper Journal-
ism in the 1890s: Analysis of a Relationship" (Ph.D. diss., University
of Iowa, 1972), 77–80.

5. Richard S. Tedlow, *New and Improved: The Story of Mass
Marketing in America* (New York: Basic Books, Inc., 1990), 5, 7.

6. Publishers generally charged at least twice as much for reading
notices as for display advertisements. The *Houston Telegraph*, for
example, charged $8 per month for a display ad in 1871 and $16 for
a reading notice of the same size. "A Well-Arranged Price List,"
American Newspaper Reporter, March 27, 1871, p. 241; see also ibid.,
April 8, 1872, p. 386; and "General Table of Advertising Rates of

the Daily Newspapers of New York City," *Fourth Estate*, March 1, 1894, p. 12, which listed rates for the most expensive type of advertisement—reading notices.

7. Printers' Ink, *50 Years*, 82. Warner used the technique for years. The March 21, 1893, issue of the *Chicago Record*, for example, ran one of these reading notices under the headline, "A Dangerous Diet; How Meat May Cause Disease and Even Death." The fourth paragraph revealed the key to long life—Warner's Safe Cure.

8. Ibid.

9. Quoted in "Reading Matter Notices," *American Newspaper Reporter*, May 13, 1872, p. 512.

10. Earnest E. Calkins, *Business the Civilizer* (Boston: Little, Brown & Co., 1928), 195–96. Another writer asserted, "Many people suppose these to be the most valuable advertisements, when in fact they are the very poorest. The public generally understand that these paragraphs are paid for either in favors or cash, and estimate them accordingly." *American Newspaper Maker*, Oct. 11, 1875, p. 773.

11. "Gratuitous Advertising, and How It Wrongs the Printer," *Printers' Circular*, February 1871, p. 4.

12. "Reading Matter Notices," *American Newspaper Reporter*, May 13, 1872, p. 512.

13. Nathaniel C. Fowler, Jr., *Fowler's Publicity* (Boston: Publicity Publishing Co., 1900), 454–55.

14. Ibid., 458.

15. Ibid., 459–65. Another prolific advertising author, however, did not share this enthusiasm for the reading notice. Frank Farrington, *Retail Advertising for Druggists and Stationers* (New York: Baker & Taylor Co., 1901), 60–61, warned retailers that country newspapers would "want to publish your picture and tell a few things about your business and also . . . ask for fifteen dollars or fifty according to their news and your reputation." These reading notices were not worth ten cents, he added, but "some men are vain enough to pay the amount just to see themselves in print."

16. "The Composite Reading Notice," *Fame*, June 1897, p. 153.

17. *American Newspaper Reporter*, Oct. 11, 1875, p. 773.

18. *National Advertiser*, May 15, 1892, p. 84. Publishers in Washington Territory received cake and liquor for printing wedding notices. Barbara Cloud, "The Press and Profit: Newspaper Survival in Washington Territory," *Pacific Northwest Quarterly* 79 (October 1988): 150.

19. Quoted in Nelson A. Crawford, *The Ethics of Journalism* (New York: Alfred A. Knopf, 1924), 14.

20. Ralph M. Hower, *The History of an Advertising Agency: N. W. Ayer & Son at Work, 1869–1939* (Cambridge, Mass.: Harvard University Press, 1939), 444–45; George P. Rowell, *Forty Years An Advertising Agent, 1865–1905* (New York: Franklin Publishing Co., 1926), 29.

21. Quoted in Charles F. Wingate, ed., *Views and Interviews on Journalism* (1875; reprint ed. New York: Arno Press, 1970), 302–3; see also *American Newspaper Reporter*, Aug. 26, 1872, p. 823, for a Geo. P. Rowell & Co. advertisement, listing its rates for placing various types of advertisements in 1,225 weekly newspapers across the country. The most expensive rate—for reading notices—was $22.50 per agate line per week. See also "Concerning Local Notices," ibid., March 18, 1872, pp. 314–15; and "Relative Value of the Reading Notice," ibid., April 8, 1872, p. 386.

22. Sometimes, however, publishers would tire of the constant demands placed on them by this type of advertiser. A metro daily reported that it had "discontinued all write-ups and run [*sic*] only straight advertisements" after dry-goods houses constantly complained about the paper's treatment of reading notices. *National Advertiser*, June 1, 1892, p. 105.

23. Everett, "Linotype and Daily Newspaper Journalism," 77.

24. W. A. Swanberg, *Citizen Hearst: A Biography of W. R. Hearst* (New York: Charles Scribner's Sons, 1961), 274; see also Harry W. Baehr, Jr., *The New York Tribune since the Civil War* (New York: Dodd, Mead & Co., 1936), 36; Allan Nevins, *The Evening Post: A Century of Journalism* (New York: Boni & Liveright, 1922), 431; and *Journalist*, June 4, 1892, p. 4.

25. Jones, nevertheless, criticized other city newspapers for running similar Bell Telephone reading notices unmarked. "Newspaper Men Testify in the Telephone Investigation," *Electrical Review*, May 15, 1886, pp. 2–3. See also the editorial in *Electrical World*, May 8, 1886, p. 209, that criticized the *Times*, not for carrying reading notices, but for accepting $1,200 from Bell Telephone, a company that the paper "holds to be 'an insolent corporation' built on 'a fraud.' "

26. "Paid Criticism in Chicago," *Journalist*, Jan. 10, 1885, p. 6.

27. White stopped the practice in 1905. See Sally Foreman Griffith, *Home Town News: William Allen White and the Emporia Gazette* (New York: Oxford University Press, 1989), 82–85.

28. *Journalist*, May 9, 1891, p. 13. See also ibid., June 11, 1892, p. 9, where the journal noted that it was still accepting reading notices.

29. Ibid., June 13, 1891, p. 12. See also *Dry Goods Reporter*, Aug. 5, 1899, p. 29; and William H. Taft, *Missouri Newspapers* (Columbia: University of Missouri Press, 1964), 95.

30. Quoted in "No Passes, No Puffs," *Journalist*, April 16, 1887, p. 14.

31. "Local Readers As Advertisements," *Newspaperdom*, February 1894, p. 382.

32. *Printers' Ink*, May 21, 1890, p. 826.

33. These companies advertised in the trade journals. For example, the following advertisement for "The Telegraphic News Bureau" appeared in the *Journalist*, March 11, 1899, p. 194: "We are prepared to handle all kinds of advertising; to write and place special reading matter; design display advertisements, and act as newspaper and advertising councillors. References furnished. The Telegraphic News Bureau, 20 Liberty St., New York City."

34. "Bright Advertising Scheme," *Journalist*, Jan. 23, 1892, p. 8.

35. "The Confessions of a Managing Editor," *Collier's*, Oct. 28, 1911, pp. 20–21.

36. Quoted in "The Advertiser," *Newspaper Maker*, March 5, 1896, p. 3; see also Susan Strasser, *Satisfaction Guaranteed: The Making of the American Mass Market* (New York: Pantheon Books, 1989), 3.

37. Publicity bureaus existed in most large cities. For example, in Washington, D.C., the National News Service operated as a publicity bureau; in New York City, the Press Service Company; and in Boston, the Publicity Bureau. See "Menace of Irresponsible Journalism," *Arena*, August 1907, pp. 173–74. Railroad magnate Jay Gould hired reporters to write financial articles reflecting his perspective. Sometimes, he furnished the articles himself and paid reporters to have them published without revealing his connection. Maury Klein, *The Life and Legend of Jay Gould* (Baltimore: Johns Hopkins University Press, 1986), 136. Many journalists supplemented their low salaries this way with tacit approval from their editors. Ted Curtis Smythe, "The Reporter, 1880–1900," *Journalism History* 7 (Spring 1980): 6. Lincoln Steffens asserted that William Ziegler, millionaire founder of the baking-powder trust, bragged that "[h]e had 'got' not only legislatures and governors but chemical experts and newspapers to serve his dubious purpose for pay." *The Autobiography of Lincoln*

Steffens (New York: Harcourt, Brace & World, Inc., 1931), 447. See also "How the Reactionary Daily Press Poisons the Public Mind by Deliberate Misrepresentations," *Arena*, September 1907, p. 318; and "A New Enterprise," *Journalist*, March 22, 1884, p. 7, for a promotional article on a new publicity bureau.

38. William Kittle, "The Making of Public Opinion," *Arena*, July 1909, p. 440; see also "The Menace of Irresponsible Journalism," ibid., August 1907, pp. 170–80.

39. Samuel Hopkins Adams, "The Patent Medicine Conspiracy," *Collier's*, November 1905, pp. 14–16; Mark Sullivan, *The Education of an American* (New York: Doubleday, Doran & Co., Inc., 1938), 183–91.

40. Adams, "Patent Medicine Conspiracy," 14–16. See also Stewart H. Holbrook, *The Golden Age of Quackery* (New York: Macmillan, 1959), 118. A writer for *McClure's Magazine* speculated that newspapers were willing to participate in such practices "[a]s long as nobody called attention to it." As soon as *Collier's* publicized the agreement, newspapers in droves canceled or refused to renew the contracts. "Manufacturing Public Opinion," *McClure's Magazine*, February 1906, p. 452.

41. Griffith, *Home Town News*, 83–84. See also George Seldes, *Freedom of the Press* (Indianapolis: Bobbs-Merrill Co., 1935), 63.

42. Ferdinand Lundberg, *Imperial Hearst: A Social Biography* (New York: Equinox Cooperative Press, 1936), 107.

43. Will Irwin, *Propaganda and the News or What Makes You Think So?* (New York: Whittlesey House/McGraw-Hill Book Co., 1936), 105; Ben H. Bagdikian, *The Media Monopoly* (Boston: Beacon Press, 1983), 217; Hamilton Holt, *Commercialism and Journalism* (Boston: Houghton Mifflin, 1909), 52–53; Upton Sinclair, *The Brass Check: A Study of American Journalism* (Pasadena, Calif.: Author, 1920), 307–8. For more information on the Armstrong investigation, see Marquis James, *The Metropolitan Life: A Study in Business Growth* (New York: Viking Press, 1947), 139–65.

44. Quoted in "Manufacturing Public Opinion," p. 451. See also Kittle, "Making of Public Opinion," p. 441; and Sinclair, *Brass Check*, 307–8.

45. The original October 1906 issue, containing the exposé on Senator Dryden, was distributed to several sites before the issue was recalled and replaced with the revised edition. See generally David Graham Phillips, *The Treason of the Senate*, ed. George E. Mowry

and Judson A. Grenier (1906; rev. ed. Chicago: Quadrangle Books, 1964).

46. Quoted in Robert D. Reynolds, Jr., "The 1906 Campaign to Sway Muckraking Periodicals," *Journalism Quarterly* 56 (Autumn 1979): 515.

47. Ibid., 516–17.

48. Quoted in "Manufacturing Public Opinion," p. 451; see also Ralph W. Hidy and Muriel E. Hidy, *Pioneering in Big Business, 1882–1911: History of Standard Oil Company, New Jersey* (New York: Harper & Brothers, 1955), 660–61.

49. Sinclair, *Brass Check*, 308; Kittle, "Making of Public Opinion," p. 443. But some Kansas newspapers, including William Allen White's *Emporia Gazette*, refused to participate in the deceit. See "Manufacturing Public Opinion," p. 451.

50. Quoted in Hidy and Hidy, *Pioneering in Big Business*, 661, 802 fn. 60. See also Ferdinand Lundberg, *America's 60 Families* (New York: Vanguard Press, 1937), 248; Alan R. Raucher, *Public Relations and Business: 1900–1929* (Baltimore: Johns Hopkins University Press, 1968), 4; "Manufacturing Public Opinion," p. 451; and Sinclair, *Brass Check*, 308. Journalist Ida Tarbell discovered this contract when she was researching her series "The History of Standard Oil," published in *McClure's*. See Richard B. Kielbowicz, "The Media and Reform, 1900–1917," in *The Media in America: A History*, ed. Wm. David Sloan and James G. Stovell (Worthington, Ohio: Publishing Horizons, Inc., 1989), 267–68.

51. Quoted in Kittle, "Making of Public Opinion," p. 443.

52. James F. Doster, *Railroads in Alabama Politics, 1875–1914* (N.p.: University of Alabama Studies, 1957), 24–25.

53. Ibid., 136, 150, 158. Two years later Braxton B. Comer, the candidate the railroads opposed, successfully ran for governor of Alabama. Although still smarting from defeat, most railroads did not actively oppose his candidacy. The Southern Railway, however, did cancel a contract with the pro-Comer *Canebrake* (Uniontown) *Herald*, which gave the editor free passes in exchange for advertising space. Governor Comer successfully fought for legislation prohibiting this practice, much to the displeasure of the Alabama press.

54. Ray Stannard Baker, "Railroads on Trial," *McClure's Magazine*, March 1906, pp. 548–49.

55. Quoted in Kittle, "Making of Public Opinion," p. 443.

56. Sinclair, *Brass Check*, 309.

57. "Menace of Irresponsible Journalism," pp. 171–73.

58. Holt, *Commercialism and Journalism*, 25.

59. The *Springfield* (Mass.) *Republican* revealed the scheme. See "The Prostitution of the Daily Press by Public-Service Corporations," *Arena*, July 1905, p. 93; Kittle, "Making of Public Opinion," p. 441; "Menace of Irresponsible Journalism," p. 174; and Will Irwin, "The Advertising Influence, Part IX," *Collier's*, May 27, 1911, p. 25.

60. George Seldes, *One Thousand Americans* (New York: Boni & Gaer, 1947), 72.

61. Fremont Older, *My Own Story* (New York: Macmillan, 1926), 38–39.

62. Personal correspondence of E. H. Wells to E. W. Scripps (April 9, 1903). Ellen Browning Scripps Collection, Ella Strong Dennison Library, Scripps College (Claremont, California). The author thanks Myron (Mike) Jordan for this information.

63. Nevins, *Evening Post*, 430.

64. Holland wrote to Gilder: "No money can come to me through arrangements of the character you criticize that will pay me for hurting your feelings, or the lowering of the moral standard of the smallest man in my employ. I shall certainly do as you ask me to do." Quoted in Arthur John, *The Best Years of the Century* (Urbana: University of Illinois Press, 1981), 102.

65. *Proceedings of the Wisconsin Editorial Association—First, Second and Third Sessions* (Madison: Carpenter & Hyer, 1859), 141.

66. Quoted in Donald W. Curl, *Murat Halstead and the Cincinnati Commercial* (Boca Raton: University Presses of Florida, 1980), 39; see also Wingate, *Views and Interviews on Journalism*, 116.

67. *Proceedings of the 1881 Convention of the South Carolina State Press Association*, 16.

68. Hiley H. Ward, "Ninety Years of the National Newspaper Association: The Mind and Dynamics of Grassroots Journalism in Shaping America" (Ph.D. diss., University of Minnesota, 1977), 98; see also Thomas F. Barnhart, "The History of the Minnesota Editorial Association, 1867–1897" (M.A. thesis, University of Minnesota, 1937), 101–2.

69. Quoted in Leon N. Flint, *The Conscience of the Newspaper* (New York: D. Appleton & Co., 1925), 458.

70. "Among the Newspapers," *Journalist*, Oct. 22, 1892, p. 7.

71. Quoted in "A Criticism of the Counting Room," *Printers' Ink*, July 29, 1891, p. 86.

72. *Proceedings of the Fourth Annual ANPA Convention* (1890), 28.

73. Ibid., 42–43. Melville E. Stone, founder of the *Chicago Daily News*, noted that this policy "was adhered to religiously" since the paper's early days. "Unto Whomsoever Much is Given" in *The Coming Newspaper*, ed. Merle Thorpe (New York: Henry Holt and Co., 1915), 103. See also Donald J. Abramoske, "The *Chicago Daily News*: A Business History, 1875–1901" (Ph.D. diss., University of Chicago, 1963), 95–98. The publisher of the *Angola* (Ind.) *Magnet* adopted a similar editorial policy not "to mutilate his news columns" with reading notices. See "About Paid Readers," *Newspaperdom*, Nov. 10, 1898, p. 1.

74. Quoted in Charles H. Dennis, *Victor Lawson: His Times and His Work* (Chicago: University of Chicago Press, 1935), 139, 150.

75. *Proceedings of the Eighth Annual ANPA Convention* (1894), 28.

76. Quoted in Everett, "Linotype and Daily Newspaper Journalism," 78.

77. Quoted in "Advertisements as Reading Matter," *Newspaperdom*, August 1893, p. 198; see also Everett, "Linotype and Daily Newspaper Journalism," 79.

78. Ibid.

79. *Proceedings of the Eleventh Annual ANPA Convention* (1897), 18–19.

80. Quoted in Salme H. Steinberg, *Reformer in the Marketplace: Edward W. Bok and the "Ladies Home Journal"* (Baton Rouge: Louisiana State University Press, 1979), 22.

81. Quoted in Wingate, *Views and Interviews on Journalism*, 35. E. W. Scripps also thought it made good business sense to label all advertisements resembling reading matter. See Negley D. Cochran, *E. W. Scripps* (New York: Harcourt, Brace and Co., 1933), 239.

82. *New York Times*, Jan. 21, 1899, p. 6.

83. *New York Times*, Aug. 24, 1900, p. 6.

84. John Cockerill, "Some Phases of Contemporary Journalism," *Journalist*, Oct. 22, 1892, p. 12.

85. *Journalist*, Dec. 19, 1891, p. 3.

86. See, for example, Stanley Walker, *City Editor* (New York: Frederick A. Stokes Co., 1934), 151.

87. Quoted in O. F. Byxbee, *Establishing a Newspaper* (Chicago: Inland Printer Co., 1901), 95; and John L. Given, *Making a Newspaper* (New York: Henry Holt and Co., 1907), 309–10.

88. Quoted in Crawford, *Ethics of Journalism*, 202.

89. The industry's "truth-in-publishing" movement has been

extensively described elsewhere. See generally Printers' Ink, *50 Years*; Pope, *Making of Modern Advertising*; Max A. Geller, *Advertising at the Crossroads: Federal Regulation vs. Voluntary Controls* (New York: Ronald, 1952); and Edward J. Baur, "Voluntary Control in the Advertising Industry" (Ph.D. diss., University of Chicago, 1942).

90. *National Advertiser*, Feb. 15, 1892, p. 200. Congress enacted legislation prohibiting periodicals from printing lottery advertisements in 1890. 26 *U.S. Statutes at Large* 465. In *re Rapier*, 143 U.S. 110 (1892), the Supreme Court affirmed congressional authority to do so.

91. *Advertising Experience*, August 1899, p. 1.

92. See John B. Opdycke, *News, Ads, and Sales* (New York: Macmillan, 1914), 112, who praised the reading notice as "headlined and printed in the same text as the rest of the reading matter in a paper. Frequently, it opens like a news item and thus induces the reader to 'get' the advertisement." See also T. D. MacGregor, *Pushing Your Business: A Textbook of Advertising*, 4th ed. (New York: Bankers Publishing Co., 1911), 15; and *Newspaper Rate Book* (St. Louis, Mo.: Nelson Chesman & Co., 1911) that listed special rates for reading notices.

93. Quoted in "A Mystery Unraveled," *Collier's*, Sept. 7, 1912, p. 11.

4. Circulation Liars

1. *Western Plowman*, April 1885, p. 64, as quoted in James F. Evans and Rodolfo N. Salcedo, *Communications in Agriculture: The American Farm Press* (Ames: Iowa State University Press, 1974), 32–33. In another parody, Mr. Morse, an advertising agent, asked a publisher about his circulation: " 'Would you at that supreme moment [approaching death], state, as you have stated today, that the circulation was over 50,000?' The publisher of the *Blower* hit the table with his fist and replied: 'I'd be damned if I would.' And Mr. Morse said: 'I am sure you would' " ("A Question of Circulation," *Journalist*, June 14, 1890, p. 13).

2. Printers' Ink, *Printers' Ink: 50 Years, 1888–1938* (New York: Printers' Ink Publishing Co., 1938), 55.

3. Daniel Pope, *Making of Modern Advertising* (New York: Basic Books, Inc., 1983), 167; Daniel J. Boorstin, *The Americans: The Democratic Experience* (New York: Random House, 1973), 149. See also Michael Schudson, *Advertising: The Uneasy Persuasion* (New York: Basic Books, Inc., 1984), 169; and Frank Presbrey, *The History*

and Development of Advertising (Garden City, N.Y.: Doubleday, Doran & Co., Inc., 1929), 269, who estimated that newspapers in the late 1800s often claimed circulations five times or more their actual figures.

4. David C. Smith, "Wood Pulp and Newspapers, 1867–1900," *Business History Review* 38 (Autumn 1964): 330.

5. The *New York Morning Advertiser*, for example, awarded a $500 "insurance policy" to the survivors of anyone who died with a *Morning Advertiser* in her or his possession. See *Journalist*, Feb. 13, 1892, p. 5.

6. For examples of advertisements, see *National Advertiser*, Jan. 15, 1892, p. 176; *Advertising Experience*, September 1900, p. xxi; ibid., October 1900, p. xxvi; ibid., November 1900, p. xxx; ibid., December 1900, p. xxxii; ibid., January 1901, p. xxxi; and *Newspaper Maker*, Oct. 3, 1895, back cover. Not all publishers boasted, however. Melville Stone, founder of the *Chicago Daily News*, wrote that he "left the readers and the public to judge for themselves whether as a newspaper, or as an advertising medium, the *Daily News* was valuable." Stone believed that the "constant shouting in a newspaper 'See how we are growing' or 'See how our advertising increases,' is no more intelligent, nor more effective, than it would be for an individual to be forever parading on the street and in the company of his friends his own views of his own importance." Melville Stone, "Unto Whomsoever Much is Given," in *The Coming Newspaper*, ed. Merle Thorpe (New York: Henry Holt and Co., 1915), 107.

7. Elmer Davis, *History of the New York Times: 1851–1921* (New York: New York Times Co., 1921), 64. Davis said Raymond later regretted the challenge.

8. Charles O. Bennett, *Facts Without Opinion* (Chicago: Audit Bureau of Circulations, 1965), 10–11.

9. The *Kansas City Star*, for example, showed that its postage expenses in 1895 made up nearly one-half of the second-class revenues assessed by the Kansas City postmaster, even though eighty-one publications were sent through the city's post office. "Claims Proven," *Newspaper Maker*, Jan. 2, 1896, p. 9; ibid., Feb. 6, 1896, p. 4.

10. "False Circulation Claims," ibid., Oct. 17, 1895, p. 4 (emphasis in original).

11. Harold L. Ickes, *America's House of Lords: An Inquiry into the Freedom of the Press* (New York: Harcourt, Brace and Co., 1939), 60–63; Frank Luther Mott, *American Journalism* (New York: Macmillan, 1947), 597–98; Ferdinand Lundberg, *Imperial Hearst: A Social Biog-*

raphy (New York: Equinox Cooperative Press, 1936), 153–62; Lloyd Wendt, *Chicago Tribune: The Rise of a Great American Newspaper* (Chicago: Rand McNally and Co., 1979), 282, 317, 353. Other Chicago papers also questioned the *Tribune*'s circulation statements. The *Chicago Inter-Ocean* said the figures should be discounted about 85 percent, while the *Chicago Record* offered to give $10,000 to charity if the statements were indeed accurate. The *Tribune* refused the challenge. An employee explained: "Why should the *Tribune* accept it? . . . Everyone knows that no newspaper in Chicago really enters the names of its subscribers on its books." "Still Fighting," *Newspaper Maker*, Nov. 21, 1895, p. 1.

12. Will C. Conrad, Kathleen Wilson, and Dale Wilson, *The Milwaukee Journal: The First Eighty Years* (Madison: University of Wisconsin Press, 1964), 74–77. In 1895, the *Milwaukee Journal*'s business manager asserted, "[T]here is not a city in the country where foreign [national] advertisers are more badly duped through false circulation claims than in Milwaukee." The paper pledged $1,000 to charity if the *Wisconsin* would allow independent auditors to look at its circulation records. A. J. Aikens, *Wisconsin*'s publisher, refused on the grounds that looking at the paper's circulation records was the same as examining his bank account. Aikens also ran into trouble with postal officials for mailing thousands of sample copies to non-subscribers. "In Milwaukee," *Newspaper Maker*, Oct. 24, 1895, pp. 1, 8; "An Investigation," ibid., Nov. 21, 1895, p. 1; "Convicted Liars," ibid., Dec. 12, 1895, p. 1; "Padded the List," ibid., Feb. 27, 1896, pp. 1, 7.

13. *Journalist*, Feb. 13, 1892, p. 6; ibid., Oct. 29, 1892, p. 3; ibid., March 28, 1891, p. 7; *Advertising Experience*, January 1901, p. 2; *Printers' Ink*, Jan. 30, 1907, p. 1; "Bold Challenge," *Newspaper Maker*, Jan. 16, 1896, p. 1; "The Minneapolis Investigation," ibid., Jan. 23, 1896, pp. 3, 4; "Being Rushed," ibid., Feb. 6, 1896, p. 3.

14. "Cannot Agree," *Newspaper Maker*, June 6, 1895, p. 3; "In Cincinnati," ibid., Oct. 24, 1895, p. 5; "An Expert Test," ibid., Dec. 5, 1895, p. 1; ibid., Dec. 26, 1895, p. 4.

15. William J. Thorn with Mary Pat Pfeil, *Newspaper Circulation: Marketing the News* (New York: Longman, 1987), 45–49.

16. Audit Bureau of Circulations, *Scientific Space Selection* (Chicago: ABC, 1937), 51. Publishers using the London plan often did not bother to keep close track of the number of copies printed, sold, and given away, much to the chagrin of advertisers and postal officials.

17. Ibid., 52–53.

18. See "Who is a Subscriber?," *National Advertiser*, Feb. 15, 1892, pp. 208–9; "What Is Circulation?," *Editor and Publisher*, July 27, 1912, p. 12; and Donald J. Abramoske, "The *Chicago Daily News*: A Business History, 1875–1901" (Ph.D. diss., University of Chicago, 1963), 79. For a discussion on how the post office monitored the press's circulation claims before 1912, see chapter 8.

19. "There Should Be No Secrecy," *Newsmaker Maker*, Jan. 2, 1896, p. 6.

20. *National Advertiser*, Aug. 15, 1892, p. 191.

21. Quoted in Smith, "Wood Pulp and Newspapers," 330, fn. 6. The story appeared in the *Bangor* (Maine) *Industrial Journal* on Feb. 2, 1888.

22. *National Advertiser*, March 15, 1892, p. 8. Another advertising journal criticized a magazine that claimed a circulation of thirty thousand, but had only eight thousand. See *Kings' Jester*, February 1892, p. 193; "Smoking Out Hidden Circulation Figures," *Printers' Ink*, June 15, 1911, p. 13; "Advertisers' Right to Know Character of Circulation," ibid., p. 59; "Circulation Viewed from Behind the Scenes," ibid., July 6, 1911, p. 17; and "Deceptive Dealing," *National Advertiser*, Aug. 1, 1892, p. 182.

23. "Auditing Circulations," *Printers' Ink*, Feb. 20, 1913, pp. 92–93; "Annual Meeting of the A.A.A.," *Advertising & Selling*, February 1913, pp. 49–50.

24. The *Chicago Daily News*, under the leadership of Victor Lawson, published its first sworn circulation statement in October 1877; in January 1878, it became a regular weekly feature. See Bennett, *Facts Without Opinion*, 11; *Printers' Ink*, Jan. 18, 1905, p. 8; and Abramoske, "*Chicago Daily News*," 77–80. The Washington, D.C., Indianapolis, and Detroit papers began publishing detailed circulation statements in 1897. See *Fame*, August 1897, p. 242; and Printers' Ink, *50 Years*, 140. The *Ladies' Home Journal* sent advertisers sworn circulation statements and invited them to verify the data. See Salme H. Steinberg, *Reformer in the Marketplace: Edward W. Bok and the Ladies Home Journal* (Baton Rouge: Louisiana State University Press, 1979), 12–13.

25. Paul T. Cherington, *Advertising as a Business Force* (N.p.: Doubleday, Page & Co., 1913), 69–70.

26. Bennett, *Facts Without Opinion*, 13.

27. For a discussion of the first three categories, see Edward J. Baur, "Voluntary Control in the Advertising Industry" (Ph.D. diss., University of Chicago, 1942), 262–71.

28. "Circulation Figures," *Editor and Publisher*, July 27, 1912, p. 13. See also "What is Your Circulation?," *American Printer*, February 1911, p. 708, for this quote: "There was a time, not necessarily ancient, when to ask a publisher the circulation of his paper was as embarrassing as asking a woman her age."

29. Frank Farrington, *Retail Advertising—Complete* (Chicago: Byxbee Publishing Co., 1910), 24.

30. Nathaniel C. Fowler, Jr., *Fowler's Publicity* (Boston: Publicity Publishing Co., 1900), 362.

31. Ibid., 360–61; see also *National Advertiser*, Jan. 15, 1892, p. 161.

32. Bennett, *Facts Without Opinion*, 13, 24; Ted Curtis Smythe, "The Advertisers' War to Verify Newspaper Circulation, 1870–1914," *American Journalism* 3 (1986): 171; Baur, "Voluntary Control in the Advertising Industry," 269.

33. Bennett, *Facts Without Opinion*, 13.

34. Ibid., 6.

35. Pope, *Making of Modern Advertising*, 168; Bennett, *Facts Without Opinion*, 9; Kenneth H. Myers, Jr., "ABC and SRDS: The Evolution of Two Specialized Advertising Services," *Business History Review* 34 (Autumn 1960): 302–26; Smythe, "Advertisers' War to Verify Circulation," 167–69.

36. ABC, *Scientific Space Selection*, 51–52.

37. Quoted in Alfred M. Lee, *The Daily Newspaper in America* (New York: Macmillan, 1937), 341; see also George French, *20th Century Advertising* (New York: D. Van Nostrand Co., 1926), 153–58; and ABC, *Scientific Space Selection*, 52–53.

38. *Printers' Ink*, Jan. 23, 1907, p. 24; see also James P. Wood, *The Story of Advertising* (New York: Ronald Press Co., 1958), 143.

39. Lee, *Daily Newspaper in America*, 341. The publisher of the *Newspaper Maker* also offered $100 to anyone who could discredit the claimed circulations of twenty newspapers, including the *Louisville Courier-Journal* and *Times*, *Grand Rapids Press*, *Seattle P-I*, and the *Boston Herald*. See *Newspaper Maker*, Oct. 17, 1895, p. 3; ibid., Oct. 24, 1895, p. 2; ibid., Oct. 31, 1895, p. 3; and ibid., Nov. 7, 1895, p. 3.

40. "Address," *Journalist*, Aug. 1, 1891, pp. 2–3.

41. Quoted in Bennett, *Facts Without Opinion*, 17. Hoping to increase voluntary compliance, a few state press associations began urging their members to provide accurate circulation figures to newspaper directories. See *Illinois Newspaper Directory and History of the*

Illinois Press Association (Champaign-Urbana: Illinois Press Association, 1934), 168.

42. Quoted in "Who Cares?," *Journalist*, Sept. 19, 1891, p. 5; see also "Rowell's Methods," ibid., Oct. 3, 1891, p. 14.

43. Ralph E. Dyar, *News for an Empire* (Spokane, Wash.: Cowles Publishing Co., 1952), 135–36.

44. George P. Rowell, *Forty Years an Advertising Agent, 1865–1905* (New York: Franklin Publishing Co., 1926), 23, 410–11; Theodore Peterson, *Magazines in the Twentieth Century*, 2d ed. (Urbana: University of Illinois Press, 1964), 21; Bennett, *Facts Without Opinion*, 12; Gerald W. Johnson, Frank R. Kent, H. L. Mencken, and Hamilton Owens, *The Sunpapers of Baltimore* (New York: Alfred A. Knopf, 1937), 212; "Publishing Circulation," *American Newspaper Reporter*, Jan. 27, 1873, p. 62.

45. "Directory Ratings," *Journalist*, Oct. 24, 1891, pp. 8–9. For coverage of the court cases, see the following issues of the *Journalist*: Dec. 5, 1891, p. 4; Oct. 24, 1891, pp. 7–9; and June 18, 1892, p. 8; see also "Action for Alleged Misrepresentation of Circulation," *Newspaperdom*, September 1894, p. 109; and *Journalist*, July 18, 1891, p. 9.

46. Quoted in Sally Foreman Griffith, *Home Town News: William Allen White and the Emporia Gazette* (New York: Oxford University Press, 1989), 81.

47. Quoted in Bennett, *Facts Without Opinion*, 16–17; see also "Under Discussion by Advertisers," *Advertising Experience*, September 1900, p. 13. The New York advertisers originally called themselves the American Advertisers Association, but they merged with the American Society of National Advertising, a western organization, in 1900 and changed their name to the Association of American Advertisers. At the same time, a group of circulation managers formed the National Association of Managers of Newspaper Circulation to exchange ideas on how to combat circulation fraud. See Smythe, "Advertisers' War to Verify Circulation," 177; "The Convention of Circulators of Newspapers," *National Printer-Journalist*, July 1900, pp. 485–88; and Quentin J. Schultze, "Advertising, Science, and Professionalism, 1885–1917" (Ph.D. diss., University of Illinois, 1978), 49.

48. ABC, *Scientific Space Selection*, 54; Printers' Ink, *50 Years*, 262; Bennett, *Facts Without Opinion*, 19–20, 23; Smythe, "Advertisers' War to Verify Circulation," 177. Louis Guenther, the *Mail Order Journal*'s editor, volunteered to audit circulation figures; four publish-

ers accepted—the *Minneapolis Tribune*, *Kansas City Star*, *Davenport* (Iowa) *Times*, and the *Binghamton* (N.Y.) *Herald*. Guenther, however, had to withdraw his offer because the audits were taking too much time. "Circulation Auditing," *Mail Order Journal*, January 1914, p. 9.

49. Quoted in Bennett, *Facts Without Opinion*, 28; see also Printers' Ink, *50 Years*, 262.

50. Michael Emery and Edwin Emery, *The Press and America*, 6th ed. (Englewood Cliffs, N.J.: Prentice Hall, 1988), 222. See also Steinberg, *Reformer in the Marketplace*, 12–13; and Jan Cohn, *Creating America: George Horace Lorimer and the Saturday Evening Post* (Pittsburgh: University of Pittsburgh Press, 1989), 9.

51. Quoted in Negley D. Cochran, *E. W. Scripps* (New York: Harcourt, Brace and Co., 1933), 241, 253. Scripps, however, did not think it paid to challenge competitors. "[L]ying claims of rival publishers . . . are disagreeable but must be put up with. An attempt to prove these falsehoods only advertises the competition."

52. "What is Circulation?," *Editor and Publisher*, July 27, 1912, p. 12.

53. Quoted in Charles H. Dennis, *Victor Lawson: His Time and His Work* (Chicago: University of Chicago Press, 1935), 149. The *Daily News* was the only Chicago newspaper that consistently reported its exact circulation at the head of the editorial columns every day. When the *Chicago Tribune* challenged the *Daily News*' "bogus circulation," Lawson went to his attorney who forced the *Tribune* to print a retraction. Abramoske, "*Chicago Daily News*," 78–79. See also Stone, "Unto Whomsoever Much is Given," 105–7. Stone, the founder of the *Daily News*, began the policy of truthful disclosure.

54. Quoted in Walter C. Johnson and Arthur T. Robb, *The South and Its Newspapers, 1903–1953* (Chattanooga, Tenn.: Southern Newspaper Publishers Association, 1954), 35.

55. Ibid., 26.

56. *Publisher's Auxiliary*, July 1891, p. 5.

57. *Kings' Jester*, February 1892, p. 194.

58. *Newspaper Maker*, Oct. 17, 1895, p. 4.

59. "Great Papers in Small Cities," *Journalist*, May 9, 1891, p. 6.

60. Quoted in "The Press and the Advertiser," *Nation*, April 1, 1869, p. 252; see also Charles F. Wingate, ed., *Views and Interviews on Journalism* (1875; reprint ed. New York: Arno Press, 1970), 171.

61. The *American Newspaper Reporter* also supported legislation

similar to the New York proposal, after receiving numerous inquiries from people disgusted with circulation liars. See "Should Newspapers Furnish the Amount of their Circulation?," *American Newspaper Reporter*, March 31, 1873, p. 269; "Newspaper Circulation," ibid., July 31, 1871, p. 778; "Publishing Circulation," ibid., Jan. 27, 1873, p. 62; and "A Registry of Newspaper Circulation," ibid., Dec. 14, 1874, p. 816.

62. Quoted in Thomas F. Barnhart, "The History of the Minnesota Editorial Association, 1867–1897" (M.A. thesis, University of Minnesota, 1937), 102.

63. 1888 *Second Annual ANPA Proceedings* 6.

64. Quoted in 1890 *Fourth Annual ANPA Proceedings* 71.

65. *Newspaper Maker*, Jan. 2, 1896, pp. 1–2. ANPA members endorsing the plan included: Milton McRae, general manager of the Scripps-McRae League; Charles H. Grasty, president/general manager of the *Baltimore News*; and Charles H. Taylor, Jr., of the *Boston Globe*.

66. "False Circulation Statements," *Mail Order Journal*, February 1911, p. 12; *Journalist*, Dec. 24, 1892, p. 6. See also "St. Louis Circulations," *Newspaper Maker*, Oct. 10, 1895, p. 5, for details on how the *Post-Dispatch* tried to fool its new business manager into believing that the paper had more subscribers than it actually had.

67. Archer H. Shaw, *The Plain Dealer: One Hundred Years in Cleveland* (New York: Alfred A. Knopf, 1942), 274. Historian Ted Curtis Smythe suggests that the addition of business managers to newspaper staffs helped bring about support from within the industry to curb circulation abuses. See Smythe, "Advertisers' War to Verify Circulation," 173–76.

68. W. J. Richards, cofounder of the *Indianapolis News*, coined the phrase as quoted in Bennett, *Facts Without Opinion*, 11.

PART 2. Progressive-Era Regulations on the Press

1. Post Office Act of Feb. 20, 1792, 1 *U.S. Statutes at Large* (hereafter *Stat.*) 232. For a thorough discussion of the press/post office relationship during the early years of the Republic, see Richard B. Kielbowicz, *News in the Mail: The Press, Post Office, and Public Information, 1700s–1860s* (Westport, Conn: Greenwood Press, 1989), 13–56.

2. Quoted in Jane Kennedy, "Development of Postal Rates: 1845–1955," *Land Economics* 33 (May 1957): 98; see also Act of July 12, 1876, 19 *Stat.* 82, and Act of March 3, 1879, 20 *Stat.* 358.

For a complete discussion of the policy making behind the 1879 law, see Richard B. Kielbowicz, "Origins of the Second-Class Mail Category and the Business of Policymaking, 1863–1879," *Journalism Monographs* 96 (April 1986): 5–6. The four classes are: first, written matter (letters); second, periodical publications (newspapers and magazines); third, miscellaneous printed matter (advertising sheets, catalogs); and fourth, merchandise (products). To qualify for the second-class subsidy, a publication must be formed of printed sheets without substantial binding, regularly appear at least four times a year from a known office of publication, and disseminate "information of a public character, or . . . devoted to literature, the sciences, arts, or some special industry, and have a legitimate list of subscribers."

3. Quoted in Marshall Cushing, *The Story of Our Post Office* (Boston: A. M. Thayer & Co., 1893), 410–16; see also *Cong. Rec.*, Jan. 5, 1897, 470.

4. Leonard D. White, *The Republican Era, 1869–1901: A Study in Administrative History* (New York: Macmillan, 1958), 257–77; Lloyd M. Short, *The Development of National Administrative Organization in the United States* (Urbana, Ill.: Institute of Government Research, 1923), 344–57; Stephen Skowronek, *Building a New American State: The Expansion of National Administrative Capacities, 1877–1920* (Cambridge: Cambridge University Press, 1982), 72–78.

5. *Houghton v. Payne*, 194 U.S. 88; see also John E. Semonche, *Charting the Future: The Supreme Court Responds to a Changing Society, 1890–1920* (Westport, Conn.: Greenwood Press, 1978), 174; and Richard B. Kielbowicz, "The Growing Interaction of the Federal Bureaucracy and the Press: The Case of a Postal Rule, 1879–1917," *American Journalism* 4 (1987): 5–18.

6. For background on the Alien and Sedition Acts of 1798, see James M. Smith, *Freedom's Fetters: The Alien and Sedition Laws and American Civil Liberties* (Ithaca, N.Y.: Cornell University Press, 1956); and John C. Miller, *Crisis in Freedom: The Alien and Sedition Acts* (Boston: Little, Brown, 1951). For information on the Comstock and lottery laws, see Dorothy Fowler, *Unmailable: Congress and the Post Office* (Athens: University of Georgia Press, 1977).

7. Act of Sept. 19, 1890, 26 *Stat.* 465; re *Rapier*, 143 U.S. 110 (1892); see also Fowler, *Unmailable*, 82–87.

8. Paul L. Murphy, ed., *Political Parties in American History: 1890–Present* (New York: G. P. Putnam's Sons, 1974), 3:1001–6;

Francis L. Broderick, *Progressivism at Risk: Electing a President in 1912* (Westport, Conn.: Greenwood Press, 1989).

9. H.R. Rep. No. 627, 63d Cong., 2d sess. (1912), as cited in David Bunting, "Corporate Interlocking, Part I, the Money Trust," *Directors & Boards* 1 (Spring 1976), 7; see also Murphy, *Political Parties in American History*, 3:1001–6.

10. James Holt, *Congressional Insurgents and the Party System, 1909–1916* (Cambridge, Mass.: Harvard University Press, 1967), 5–13.

11. See generally Richard L. McCormick, *The Party Period and Public Policy: American Politics from the Age of Jackson to the Progressive Era* (New York: Oxford University Press, 1986).

5. The Press Examined

1. Preamble of the St. Louis Platform, February 1892, and the Omaha Platform, July 1892, as cited in John D. Hicks, *The Populist Revolt* (1931; reprint ed. Lincoln: University of Nebraska Press, 1959), 436, 439.

2. Robert M. La Follette, *Autobiography* (1913; reprint ed. Madison: University of Wisconsin Press, 1963), 257–59. La Follette's long-winded attack damaged his chances for the Republican nomination. See Fred Greenbaum, *Robert Marion La Follette* (Boston: Twayne Publishers, 1975), 109–10; David P. Thelen, *Robert M. La Follette and the Insurgent Spirit* (Boston: Little, Brown & Co., 1976), 90–93; "That Unfortunate Attack on the Newspapers," *American Printer*, March 1912, p. 85; and "Killed His Own Boom," *Editor and Publisher*, Feb. 10, 1912, pp. 1–2.

3. "Bryan Attacks Dailies," *New York Times*, Oct. 12, 1907, p. 2; "Publishing Notes," *American Printer*, April 1911, p. 228.

4. Chapt. CXIV, Sec. 1, 583, *California Statutes* (March 11, 1893), 132. Twelve years later, the legislature renumbered the statute but left the language unchanged. Chapt. CXIV, Sec. 1, 583a, ibid. (March 21, 1905), 686. See also Charles O. Bennett, *Facts Without Opinion* (Chicago: Audit Bureau of Circulations, 1965), 12.

5. Chapt. 178, *Session Laws of Colorado* (June 5, 1911), 526–27; Chapt. 124, *Laws of Kansas* (March 2, 1909), 228–29.

6. Pennsylvania Laws, *Purdon's Digest* (May 2, 1907), 5635–36; Chapt. 475, *Laws of New York* (June 11, 1907), 1027–28. Representative Joseph H. Moore of Pennsylvania informed House members that his state's law "tried to find out who the proprietors of the

newspapers were in order largely that men might bring libel suits."
Cong. Rec., 62d Cong., 2d sess. (April 30, 1912), 5619. The New
York legislature in 1911 also considered a bill to require signed
editorials, but it was not enacted. "We," *Independent*, Jan. 8, 1911,
pp. 1280–81.

7. Lucy Maynard Salmon, *The Newspaper and the Historian* (New
York: Oxford University Press, 1923), 76.

8. Chapt. CXXIV, *California Statutes* (March 20, 1899), 155–
56.

9. Quoted in "In Hoc Signo," *Fourth Estate*, May 6, 1897, p. 1.

10. H.R. 24136, *Cong. Rec.*, 60th Cong., 2d sess. (Dec. 15,
1908), 296; "President Likes Press Bill," *New York Times*, Dec. 19,
1908, p. 2.

11. Quoted in George H. Shibley, "Progressive Leaders: United
States Senator Robert L. Owen," *Twentieth Century*, May 1910, p.
129; S. 8874, *Cong. Rec.*, 61st Cong., 3d sess. (Dec. 7, 1910), 54.

12. Representative Frank Clark, a Florida Democrat, introduced
the first bill, H.R. 11829. The other bills were H.R. 15116 and H.R.
19545, *Cong. Rec.*, 60th Cong., 1st sess. (1908), 482, 1094, 3619.

13. Henry Schofield, "Freedom of the Press in the United States,"
*Papers and Proceedings for the Ninth Annual Meeting of the American
Sociological Society* (Chicago: University of Chicago Press, 1915), 116.

14. "Arraigns the Press," *Editor and Publisher*, March 30, 1912,
p. 1.

15. "Publicity and the Public Welfare," *Editor and Publisher*, July
6, 1912, p. 12.

16. H.R. 21279, House Rep. No. 388, 62d Cong., 2d sess.
(March 4, 1912), 2776.

17. Taft recommended a substantial postage hike for periodicals
in his first state-of-the-union message. "I very much doubt . . . the
wisdom of a policy that constitutes so large a subsidy and requires
additional taxation to meet it," he explained. *The State of the Union
Messages of the Presidents, 1790–1966* (New York: Chelsea House,
1966), 3:2362–63. For details about the president's fight to raise
second-class rates, see Henry F. Pringle, *The Life and Times of William
Howard Taft* (New York: Farrar & Rinehart, Inc., 1939), 2:566–
69, 624–25; and George Juergens, *News from the White House: The
Presidential–Press Relationship in the Progressive Era* (Chicago: University of Chicago Press, 1981), 117–21.

18. Quoted in John Tebbel and Sarah Miles Watts, *The Press and
the Presidency* (New York: Oxford University Press, 1985), 359. Taft

wrote a similar letter to Senator Frank Flint (D-Fla.). See Donald F. Anderson, *William Howard Taft: A Conservative's Conception of the Presidency* (Ithaca, N.Y.: Cornell University Press, 1968), 204–11, 221–23.

19. *Cong. Rec.*, 62d Cong., 2d sess. (April 12, 1912), 4675. The representative was Halvor Steenerson.

20. Paolo E. Coletta, *The Presidency of William Howard Taft* (Lawrence: University Press of Kansas, 1973), 140. The Taft administration was known for its emphasis on efficiency, economy, and scientific management. See Anderson, *William Howard Taft*, 86–90; Peri E. Arnold, *Making the Managerial Presidency* (Princeton, N.J.: Princeton University Press, 1986), 29–51.

21. *Cong. Rec.*, 62d Cong., 2d sess. (April 13, 1912), 4754. The representative was John L. Burnett.

22. "Democratic Diners Feel Bryan's Spell," *New York Times*, April 14, 1912, p. 1.

23. Approval of House Res. 444 allowed House members to add twelve riders to the appropriations bill, including "what are commonly known as the Goeke parcels-express bill, the Shackleford Good Roads bill, and the Barnhart newspaper amendment." See "Minutes," House Committee on Rules (April 16, 1912), 35, and "Docket on Rules," ibid. (March 8, 1912), 59. National Archives, House 62A-F34.2. Normally, a House caucus rule forbade such action. See Chang-Wei Chiu, *The Speaker of the House of Representatives Since 1896* (New York: Columbia University Press, 1928), 127–31, 155–63; Randall B. Ripley, *Party Leaders in the House of Representatives* (Washington, D.C.: Brookings Institution, 1967), 72–77, 95–96; George R. Brown, *The Leadership of Congress* (Indianapolis: Bobbs-Merrill Co., 1922), 179–81; and George B. Galloway, *History of the United States House of Representatives* (Washington, D.C.: Government Printing Office, 1965), 103, 124–26.

24. Quoted in *Cong. Rec.*, 62d Cong., 2d sess. (April 18, 1912), 5000; see also House Rep. No. 570, *Cong. Rec.*, 62d Cong., 2d sess. (April 18, 1912), 4988–90; and "Would Know Paper Owners," *New York Times*, April 16, 1912, p. 12. For information about Congressman Barnhart, see Henry A. Barnhart Papers, 1880–1940. Indiana State Library, Indianapolis, Ind.

25. *Cong. Rec.*, ibid., 4989–5009.

26. Ibid., 4994.

27. Ibid. The representative was Samuel W. Smith.

28. Ibid.

29. Quoted in ibid., 5000; see also ibid., 5008. The vote was 230 yeas, 34 nays, 5 presents, and 122 not voting.

30. Quoted in ibid. (April 27, 1912), 5465; see also ibid. (April 22, 1912), 5122, for the language of the amendments.

31. Ibid. (April 23, 1912), 5209. The congressman was Thomas F. Konop.

32. Ibid. (April 30, 1912), 5621, 5624. Thayer, however, did not offer such an amendment.

33. Ibid., 5625, 5618, 5620. The Kentucky congressman was Swagar Sherley; the South Dakota Republican, Eben W. Martin; and the Georgia Democrat, Seaborn A. Roddenbery.

34. Ibid., 5624–25.

35. Ibid., 5625.

36. Ibid., 5619.

37. Ibid. (April 27, 1912), 5465.

38. Ibid. Cox was the publisher of two Ohio papers: the *Dayton Daily News* and the *Springfield Daily News*.

39. Ibid. (May 2, 1912), 5752–53, 5755. Barnhart's proposals were amended to apply specifically to publications using the second-class mail privilege, and to require publications to identify investors with more than $550 stock, rather than $500, and to publish an ownership statement weekly rather than daily. Publications of trade unions and fraternal or benevolent societies were exempted from the requirements. For press coverage, see "Other Post Office Amendments," *Publishers' Weekly*, May 4, 1912, p. 1447; and "To Print Editors' Names," *New York Times*, May 1, 1912, p. 9.

40. Quoted in "Stop Thief! Why Should the Dishonest Publisher Be Shielded?," *Automobile Trade Journal*, May 1912; see also "How Not to Pay for What You Don't Get," ibid., July 1912; "More Reasons for Honest Circulation Statements," ibid., August 1912; and "How the Government Can Put a Stop to Fraudulent Use of the Mails by Dishonest Publishers," ibid., September 1912. National Archives, Sen. 62A-F20, Tray 108, Chilton Co. file.

41. James Holt, *Congressional Insurgents and the Party System, 1909–1916* (Cambridge, Mass.: Harvard University Press, 1967), 3–11, 36–40; see also generally Albert H. Pike, "Jonathan Bourne, Jr., Progressive" (Ph.D. diss., University of Oregon, 1957); and Arthur W. Dunn, *From Harrison to Harding: 1888–1921* (New York: G. P. Putnam's Sons, 1922), 138.

42. Bourne to supporters (April 25–26, 1912). University of

Oregon, Bourne Collection, Box 17, Outgoing Correspondence File; see also Pike, "Jonathan Bourne" 167, 171–88, 222–26.

43. Committee Print on H.R. 21279 (May 3, 1912); Hitchcock to Bourne (May 13, 1912). National Archives, Sen. 62A-F20, Trays 110 and 111, Third Assistant Postmaster General File.

44. Memorandum from [?] Turner to Bourne (June 26, 1912). Ibid., Tray 110.

45. M. Wes Tubbs to Bourne (May 17, 1912); Herbert Myrick to Bourne (May 14, 1912). Ibid., Tray 108. Myrick's letter was reproduced as a circular and sent to interested persons to encourage them to tell their senators to vote against the bill.

46. Noble to Bourne (May 20, 1912); W. C. Allen to Bourne (May 21, 1912); Doubleday to Bourne (May 24, 1912); Tessaro to Bourne (May 25, 1912, and June 3, 1912); Bourne to Tessaro (June 14, 1912). Ibid.

47. "Beware This Amendment," *Editor and Publisher*, June 22, 1912, p. 2; "Barnhart Amendment: Stricken From the Postal Bill and One Less Objectionable Substituted," ibid., July 20, 1912, p. 1; "Publishers Protest," *Publisher's Auxiliary*, July 13, 1912, p. 4; "Printing Names of Newspaper Owners," ibid., July 20, 1912, p. 139; "Senate Post Office Appropriation Bill Reported," *Publishers' Weekly*, July 27, 1912, p. 182; "Barnhart Bill Modified," *Fourth Estate*, July 27, 1912, p. 2.

48. Bill Drafts. University of Oregon, Bourne Collection, Box 29, U.S. Post Office Appropriations Bill file; "Clerk's Copy," Calendar No. 837, H.R. 21279, Senate Rep. No. 955 (July 23, 1912). National Archives, Sen. 62A-F20, Tray 111, 44–46.

49. *Cong. Rec.*, 62d Cong., 2d sess. (Aug. 10, 1912), 10667; Senate Rep. No. 955, 62d Cong., 2d sess. (July 23, 1912), 24.

50. Quoted in letters from Bourne to publishers and congressional members (July and August 1912). University of Oregon, Bourne Collection, Box 29, U.S. Post Office Appropriations file.

51. *Cong. Rec.*, Aug. 10, 1912, 10667–70; Aug. 12, 1912, 10724.

52. Ibid., 10724–26.

53. Ibid., 10725–27.

54. *Proceedings of the First National Newspaper Conference* (Madison: University of Wisconsin, 1912); see also "Conference Topics," *Editor and Publisher*, Aug. 3, 1912, pp. 1, 16–17; "Newspapers Will Be Licensed," ibid., p. 8; "Sheldon Attacks the Newspapers," ibid.,

Aug. 10, 1912, p. 6; and "Criticise Daily Papers," *New York Times*, July 31, 1912, p. 3.

55. The phrase "other consideration" in the advertising requirement was changed to "other valuable consideration," and the term *known* was inserted before "bond and stockholders" to resolve the problem of publications not knowing all of their investors' names. The Senate also approved amendments requiring the Post Office Department to furnish forms to the publications and to notify delinquent publishers by registered mail that they had ten days to file an ownership statement or lose their postal subsidies. *Cong. Rec.*, Aug. 10, 1912, 10667–70; Aug. 12, 1912, 10727.

56. The Senate conferees were Jonathan Bourne, Jr., Boies Penrose, and J. H. Bankhead; the House members were John A. Moon, chair of the House Post Office and Post Roads Committee, D. E. Finley, and John W. Weeks. *Cong. Rec.*, Aug. 16, 1912, 11046.

57. Senate Doc. No. 940, *Cong. Rec.*, Aug. 22, 1912, 11554; House Rep. No. 1242, ibid., Aug. 23, 1912, 11750; "Post Office Bill," *Editor and Publisher*, Aug. 24, 1912, p. 1.

58. *Cong. Rec.*, Aug. 23, 1912, 11760; Aug. 24, 1912, 11819.

59. Public Act 336 of 1912, 37 *U.S. Statutes at Large* 539 at 553–54. The regulations applied to publications using the second-class mail privilege, except for religious, fraternal, temperance, and scientific ones. The penalty for violating the advertising regulation was a fine of $50 to $500 for each offense. Exclusion from the second-class subsidy was the penalty for refusal to comply with the disclosure requirements.

60. See, for example, "New Publicity Law is to be Contested," *New York Times*, Sept. 13, 1912, p. 5; "How the Law Was Passed," ibid., Sept. 20, 1912, p. 6; "The Newspaper Publicity Law," ibid., Sept. 21, 1912, p. 5; "Newspaper Men Worry About the New Post Office Law," *American Printer*, October 1912, p. 246; "Efforts to Repeal Newspaper Publicity Law," *Printers' Ink*, Dec. 12, 1912, pp. 76–81; and "Publicity for Organs of Publicity," *Chautauquan*, January 1913, pp. 129–31. See also James H. Shideler, "Second Class Matter: The American Press and the Subsidy, 1879–1933" (M.A. thesis, University of California, 1938), 57–66.

61. F. H. Given to Bourne, Bourne to Given (Sept. 4, 1912). University of Oregon, Bourne Collection, Box 29.

62. See, for example, "Would Know Paper Owners," *New York Times*, April 16, 1912, p. 12; "To Print Editors' Names," ibid., May

1, 1912, p. 9; "Other Post Office Amendments," *Publishers' Weekly*, May 4, 1912, p. 1447; "Senate Post Office Appropriations Bill Reported," ibid., July 27, 1912, p. 182; ibid., Aug. 17, 1912, p. 462; "Publishers Protest," *Publisher's Auxiliary*, July 13, 1912, p. 4; "Printing Names of Newspaper Owners," ibid., Aug. 3, 1912, p. 6; "Barnhart Bill Modified," *Fourth Estate*, July 27, 1912, p. 2; "Barnhart Amendment," *Editor and Publisher*, July 20, 1912, p. 1; and "Block Postal Bill," ibid., Aug. 17, 1912, p. 1. The *New York Times*, in fact, acknowledged that it had not recognized the regulations' dire significance until after they became law. "New Publicity Law is to be Contested," *New York Times*, Sept. 13, 1912, p. 5.

63. Quoted in "Press Regulation by Congress," *New York Times*, Sept. 22, 1912, p. 16; see also "Sound Discretion," ibid., Sept. 29, 1912, p. 14; "Press Fears for Liberty," ibid., Sept. 20, 1912, p. 6; "Power Overstretched," ibid., Sept. 5, 1912, p. 8; "An Objectionable Law," *Editor and Publisher*, Sept. 28, 1912, p. 10; and "Publicity Law in Effect," *Fourth Estate*, Oct. 5, 1912, pp. 2, 14–15.

64. "Defends His Part in Newspaper Law," *New York Times*, Sept. 22, 1912, sec. III, p. 4.

65. Quoted in "Efforts to Repeal Newspaper Publicity Law," *Printers' Ink*, Dec. 12, 1912, p. 79.

66. Jonathan Bourne, Jr., "The Newspaper Publicity Act," *Review of Reviews*, February 1913, in University of Oregon, Bourne Collection, Vol. 13, National Press Clippings.

67. Bourne to Given (Sept. 5, 1912). University of Oregon, Bourne Collection, Box 29, U.S. Post Office Appropriations Bill file.

68. Bourne, "Newspaper Publicity Act," *Review of Reviews*, February 1913.

69. Nelson to Bourne (Dec. 21, 1912); Bourne to Nelson (Dec. 23, 1912). University of Oregon, Bourne Collection, Box 29, U.S. Appropriations Bill file.

70. Louis Wiley, "The Modern Newspaper," *Advertising & Selling*, January 1913, p. 36.

71. Quoted in "M'Cumber Attacks Press Publicity Law," *New York Times*, Dec. 4, 1912, p. 12; see also "Efforts to Repeal Newspaper Publicity Law," *Printers' Ink*, Dec. 12, 1912, pp. 76–81; "To Amend Newspaper Law," *New York Times*, Dec. 15, 1912, p. 2; "To Repeal Postal Law," *Editor and Publisher*, Dec. 7, 1912, p. 1; "To Amend Postal Law," ibid., Dec. 21, 1912, p. 1; "Publicity Rider in P. O. Bill," *Fourth Estate*, Dec. 14, 1912, p. 4; "Amendment to Postal

Law," ibid., Dec. 21, 1912, p. 2; "To Amend Newspaper Law," *Publisher's Auxiliary*, Dec. 21, 1912, p. 1; and "Bill to Amend 'Publicity Rider,'" *Publishers' Weekly*, Dec. 21, 1912, p. 2193.

72. Quoted in "A Question to be Decided," *New York Times*, Dec. 6, 1912, p. 14; see also "Publicity Rider in P. O. Bill," *Fourth Estate*, Dec. 14, 1912, p. 4; and "May Repeal Press Law," *Editor and Publisher*, Feb. 8, 1913, p. 1.

73. Quoted in "To Pass on Newspaper Law," *New York Times*, Sept. 24, 1912, p. 10.

74. Quoted in "Newspapers Must Give Owners' Name," *Publisher's Auxiliary*, Sept. 21, 1912, p. 1; see also "Newspaper Law to be Enforced," *New York Times*, Sept. 9, 1912, p. 7; "The Newspaper Publicity Law," *Fourth Estate*, Sept. 14, 1912, p. 2; "Ridiculous Effects of New Post Office Law," ibid., Sept. 21, 1912, p. 8; and "Publishers Object," *Editor and Publisher*, Sept. 14, 1912, p. 1.

75. "Amendments to the Postal Laws and Regulations (Sept. 13, 1912)," *United States Official Postal Guide*, October 1912, pp. 1, 6; "Order of the Postmaster General," *Daily Bulletin of Orders Affecting the Postal Service*, Sept. 14, 1912, p. 9926. An administrator of the U.S. Postal Service in 1987 confirmed that the department, in part, opposed the law because it imposed additional burdens on a small, overworked staff. Letter from Bob Boobing to author (April 6, 1987).

76. Post Office Department, Press Release No. 3 (Sept. 16, 1912). U.S. Postal Service Library, Washington, D.C.

77. "Would Have Press Label News 'Adv.'," *New York Times*, Sept. 19, 1912, p. 6; "Press Fears for Liberty," ibid., Sept. 20, 1912, p. 6; "Must Name All Owners," ibid., Oct. 5, 1912, p. 24; "Suit Started to Test Postal Law," *Printers' Ink*, Oct. 17, 1912, pp. 50–52; "Official Interpretation of Postal Law," ibid., Oct. 31, 1912, pp. 64–65.

78. Daily Newspapers—Filing Statement of Paid Circulation, 29 *Opinions of the Attorney General* 526 (Sept. 25, 1912); see also "Wickersham's View of Newspaper Law," *New York Times*, Sept. 27, 1912, p. 5.

79. Post Office Department, Press Release No. 5 (Oct. 11, 1912). U.S. Postal Service Library, Washington, D.C. See also "Publishers Obeying Law," *New York Times*, Oct. 6, 1912, sec. III, p. 13; "Access to Newspaper Data," ibid., Oct. 4, 1912, p. 13; "Washington Topics," *Editor and Publisher*, Oct. 19, 1912, p. 2; "Open Attack on Newspaper Law," *Publisher's Auxiliary*, Nov. 23, 1912, p. 1; and

" 'Publicity Law' Generally Obeyed," *Publishers' Weekly*, Nov. 30, 1912, p. 1946.

80. Quoted in "Publicity Law Up Again," *Fourth Estate*, March 15, 1913, p. 2; see also "Newspaper Law's Status," *New York Times*, March 12, 1913, p. 2; "Last Call to Newspapers," ibid., March 13, 1913, p. 1; and "To Enforce the Law," *Editor and Publisher*, March 15, 1913, p. 1.

81. Argument for Petitioners, *Journal of Commerce v. Burleson*, U.S. Supreme Court Case No. 818, 600–601; see also "Newspaper Law's Status," *New York Times*, March 12, 1913, p. 2; "Burleson is Enjoined," ibid., March 18, 1913, p. 1; "An Injunction Prevents Enforcement of the Newspaper Publicity Law," *Editor and Publisher*, March 22, 1913, p. 1; and "Supreme Court Calls a Halt," *Fourth Estate*, March 22, 1913, p. 2.

82. Alexander M. Bickel and Benno C. Schmidt, Jr., *History of the Supreme Court of the United States: The Judiciary and Responsible Government, 1910–1921* (New York: Macmillan, 1984), 3:650; John E. Semonche, *Charting the Future: The Supreme Court Responds to a Changing Society, 1890–1920* (Westport, Conn.: Greenwood Press, 1978), 278; Henry J. Abraham, *Justices and Presidents: A Political History of Appointments to the Supreme Court* (New York: Penguin Books, Inc., 1974), 145–63; Sister Marie Carolyn Klinkhamer, *Edward Douglas White, Chief Justice of the United States* (Washington, D.C.: Catholic University of America Press, 1943), 212–18; John G. Palfrey, "The Constitution and the Courts," *Harvard Law Review* 26 (1913): 0507–30; Thomas R. Powell, "Separation of Powers: Administrative Exercise of Legislative and Judicial Power," *Political Science Quarterly* 28 (1913): 47; Nathan Isaacs, "Judicial Review of Administrative Findings," *Yale Law Journal* 30 (June 1921): 795.

83. "Will Test New Law," *Editor and Publisher*, Sept. 28, 1912, p. 1; "Publicity Law Is To Be Tested," *Fourth Estate*, Sept. 28, 1912, p. 2; Edwin Emery, *History of the American Newspaper Publishers Association* (Minneapolis: University of Minnesota Press, 1950), 114–17.

84. Bill of Complaint, *The Journal of Commerce & Commercial Bulletin v. Frank H. Hitchcock, etc., et al.*, U.S. Supreme Court Case No. 818, 6–10; demurrer, 13–14; decree, 14–15; Petition of Appeal, 15; Order Allowing Appeal, 16; and Motion to Advance Appeal, 1, quote at 4. See also "Newspapers Test New Publicity Law," *New York Times*, Oct. 10, 1912, p. 24; "Newspaper Suit Goes Up," ibid., Oct. 16, 1912, p. 12; "Test of Publicity Law Begun," *Fourth Estate*,

Oct. 12, 1912, pp. 2, 14–15; "Publicity Test to High Court," ibid., Oct. 19, 1912, p. 2; "Test of 'Publicity Rider' to be Made," *Publishers' Weekly*, Oct. 12, 1912, p. 1253; and "Suit Started to Test Postal Law," *Printers' Ink*, Oct. 17, 1912, pp. 50–52.

85. Motion to Advance, *Lewis Publishing Company v. Edward M. Morgan*, U.S. Supreme Court Case No. 819, 3.

86. See, for example, "Supreme Court Gets Newspaper Briefs," *New York Times*, Oct. 20, 1912, p. 16; "Newspaper Law Hearing," ibid., Oct. 29, 1912, p. 4; "Case to Test Postal Law Goes to Supreme Court," *Printers' Ink*, Oct. 24, 1912, p. 13; "Pushing Forward Postal Case," *Fourth Estate*, Oct. 26, 1912, p. 2; and " 'Publicity Rider' Up to Supreme Court," *Publishers' Weekly*, Oct. 26, 1912, pp. 1411–12.

87. Brief for Appellant, *Journal of Commerce v. Hitchcock*, U.S. Supreme Court Case No. 818, 38–40; see also "Open Attack on Newspaper Law," *Publisher's Auxiliary*, Nov. 23, 1912, p. 1; and "Attack Postal Act," *New York Times*, Nov. 19, 1912, p. 5.

88. Brief for Appellant, *Lewis Publishing v. Morgan*, U.S. Supreme Court Case No. 819, 1–5.

89. Ibid., 21, 33.

90. Brief for the United States, *Journal of Commerce v. Hitchcock* and *Lewis Publishing v. Morgan*, U.S. Supreme Court Case Nos. 818–819, 24. See *Houghton v. Payne*, 194 U.S. 88 (1904), where the Supreme Court determined that publishers had no right to any particular classification. For a detailed discussion on how Bullitt concluded that the statute applied only to publications using the subsidy, see 3–21.

91. Ibid., 23, 26, 45, 49.

92. Supplemental Brief of Counsel, U.S. Supreme Court Case No. 818, 1–2.

93. Ibid., 11, 7.

94. Appellant's Reply Brief, *Lewis Publishing v. Morgan*, U.S. Supreme Court Case No. 819, 1–2, 7.

95. See, for example, "Says Publicity Law Leaves Press Free," *New York Times*, Nov. 29, 1912, p. 6; "Wickersham Cited Against Press Law," ibid., Dec. 1, 1912, p. 3; "A Question to be Decided," ibid., Dec. 6, 1912, p. 14; "Government Answer," *Editor and Publisher*, Nov. 30, 1912, pp. 1–2; "Brief Filed in Postal Case," *Fourth Estate*, Nov. 30, 1912, p. 2; "Constitutionality of 'Publicity Rider' Attacked," *Publishers' Weekly*, Nov. 30, 1912, p. 1947; and "The Freedom of the Press," *Outlook*, Dec. 21, 1912, p. 831.

96. "Calls Publicity Law Unfair to Dailies," *New York Times*,

Dec. 3, 1912, p. 4; see also "To Repeal Postal Law," *Editor and Publisher*, Dec. 7, 1912, p. 1; "Publicity Case in Supreme Court," *Fourth Estate*, Dec. 7, 1912, p. 2; "Periodical 'Publicity Rider' Case before Supreme Court," *Publishers' Weekly*, Dec. 7, 1912, pp. 2006–7; and Semonche, *Charting the Future*, 281–82, reports that the Chief Justice "painstakingly" considered arguments.

97. *Lewis Publishing Co. v. Morgan*, 229 U.S. 288, 33 S.Ct. 867, 57 L.Ed. 1190 (1913). Quoted in the *Annual Report of the Attorney General* (1913), 65; see also "The Newspaper Publicity Law," *New York Times*, June 11, 1913, p. 8; "Uphold Newspaper Publicity Statute," ibid., p. 3; "Publicity Law is Held Valid," *Fourth Estate*, June 14, 1913, p. 2; "Periodical Publicity Law Upheld," *Publishers' Weekly*, June 14, 1913, pp. 2117–21; "Supreme Court Decision on Newspaper Publicity Law," *Printers' Ink*, June 19, 1913, pp. 44–46; and " 'Publicity' for Publishers," *Literary Digest*, June 21, 1913, p. 1364.

98. 57 L.Ed. 1200. See also Abraham, *Justices and Presidents*, 160.

99. Ibid.

100. Ibid., 1202; see also Klinkhamer, *White*, 221.

101. Ibid., 1203.

6. Ownership Disclosed

1. Quoted in George Seldes, *One Thousand Americans* (New York: Boni & Gaer, Inc., 1947), 5.

2. Originally, publishers had to file an ownership statement with the post office twice a year, but Congress amended the law in 1933 to require annual statements in October. The Post Office Department did not object to the change, and Congress approved the amendment with little debate. See *Cong. Rec.*, 72d Cong., 2d sess. (Dec. 19, 1932), 699–700; ibid. (Feb. 25, 1933), 4983–84; House Rep. No. 1646, 72d Cong., 1st sess. (June 16, 1932), 1–2; Senate Rep. No. 1243, 72d Cong., 2d sess., 1–3; Act of March 3, 1933, 47 *Statutes at Large* (hereafter *Stat.* 1486). Congress considered the ownership provision again in the 1960s at the post office's request but left it basically unchanged. Act of June 11, 1960, 74 *U.S. Stat.* 208; Act of Oct. 23, 1962, 76 *Stat.* 1144.

3. Marshall H. Cushing, *The Story of Our Post Office* (Boston: A. M. Thayer & Co., 1893), 411–15, quote at 411.

4. 1 *Opinions of the Assistant Attorney General for the Post Office Department* (Aug. 20, 1883), 859–60.

5. Ibid. (April 16, 1884), 908–9; ibid. (June 20, 1884), 911–13; 2 ibid. (Sept. 16, 1885), 72–74.

6. 1887 *Postal Laws and Regulations* 141, sec. 333; for a copy of the application, see 2 *Opinions of the Assistant Attorney General for the Post Office Department* (Oct. 4, 1887), 479–81.

7. Cushing, *Our Post Office*, 111, 372–73, 411–15; Lloyd M. Short, *The Development of National Administrative Organization in the United States* (Urbana, Ill.: Institute of Government Research, 1923), 344–57.

8. *Cong. Rec.*, Jan. 5, 1897, 470; House Doc. No. 608, 59th Cong., 2d sess. (1907), x, 32.

9. Order No. 907, Miscellaneous Orders of the Postmaster General (Dec. 4, 1907), 12:311–26. U.S. Postal Service Library, Washington, D.C. See also Richard B. Kielbowicz, "The Growing Interaction of the Federal Bureaucracy and the Press: The Case of a Postal Rule, 1879–1917," *American Journalism* 4 (1987): 5–18.

10. Senate Doc. No. 204, 60th Cong., 1st sess. (1908), 5; see Senate Doc. No. 270, ibid. (1908), 21–43, for reprints of letters, resolutions, and published comments supporting the Post Office Department's actions. See also Frank Luther Mott, *A History of American Magazines* (Cambridge, Mass.: Belknap Press of Harvard University Press, 1957), 4:368.

11. Quoted in "Bars 'Fly By Night' Papers," *New York Times*, July 9, 1910, p. 5; see also 1909 *Annual Report of the Post Office Department*, 313–15; "A Curse of Special Privilege," *Fame*, January 1910, pp. 278–79; and "Of Counsel for the Defense," ibid., March 1910, p. 66.

12. "Book Shortage Laid to Periodicals," *Publishers' Weekly*, June 17, 1911, p. 2355. " 'No Honest Publisher Has Anything to Fear,' " *American Printer*, July 1911, p. 574, disagreed with Britt's statement.

13. Quoted in "A Marvel of Legislation," *New York Times*, Sept. 20, 1912, p. 10; "Regulation by Congress," *Syracuse Post-Standard* as cited in ibid., Sept. 22, 1912, sec. 3, p. 16; "Power Overstretched," ibid., Sept. 5, 1912, p. 8; and "Publicity Law in Effect," ibid., Oct. 5, 1912, pp. 2, 14–15.

14. Quoted in "Opinions of the New P. O. Law," *Fourth Estate*, Sept. 28, 1912, p. 13.

15. "Power Overstretched," *New York Times*, Sept. 5, 1912, p. 8.

16. Quoted in "New Law a Step Backwards," *Publisher's Auxiliary*, Nov. 9, 1912, p. 1.

17. "Believe Postal Law Should Be Repealed," *Printers' Ink*, Nov. 21, 1912, pp. 72–74.

18. "The Newspaper, the Advertiser and the Public," *Printers' Ink*, Nov. 14, 1912, pp. 33–34; "The Newspaper and the Public," *Advertising & Selling*, November 1912, pp. 16–22.

19. Quoted in "Denounces Newspaper Law," *New York Times*, Nov. 21, 1912, p. 1; and "Report of Illinois Daily Newspaper Association," *National Printer-Journalist*, Dec. 12, 1912, p. 860; see also "Iowa Editors Want New Law Repealed," *Publisher's Auxiliary*, Oct. 5, 1912, p. 1; "Declare Law is Harmful," ibid., 4; and "Opening Attack on Postal Law," *Fourth Estate*, Nov. 23, 1912, p. 23.

20. "The Freedom of the Press" Resolution (Dec. 6, 1912). University of Oregon, Bourne Collection, Box 29, Publicity Act file.

21. "Editor Would Ridicule Unjust Newspaper Law," *Publisher's Auxiliary*, Oct. 19, 1912, p. 5.

22. Quoted in "Ridicules New Postal Law," *Editor and Publisher*, Oct. 19, 1912, p. 3; James M. Lee, *History of American Journalism* 2d ed. (Garden City, N.Y.: Garden City Publishing Co., Inc., 1923), 397.

23. "*Printers' Ink* Takes Own Medicine," *Printers' Ink*, Oct. 3, 1912, pp. 82–83; "Compulsory Circulation Statements Under New Postal Law," ibid., Oct. 10, 1912, pp. 40–44.

24. Quoted in "Booth Approves of Law," *Editor and Publisher*, Sept. 28, 1912, p. 15; and "Opinions of the New P. O. Law," *Fourth Estate*, Sept. 28, 1912, pp. 13, 16.

25. Ibid.

26. Quoted in "In Favor of New Law," *Editor and Publisher*, Oct. 5, 1912, p. 2.

27. Quoted in "Newspapers Opposing Publicity," *Literary Digest*, Oct. 12, 1912, pp. 607–8.

28. Quoted in "The Newspaper Law," *Editor and Publisher*, Sept. 28, 1912, p. 10.

29. Quoted in "Publicity Law in Effect," *Fourth Estate*, Oct. 5, 1912, p. 2.

30. Ibid., p. 14.

31. "Freedom of Thought," *Red Wing* (Minn.) *Daily Republican* (Oct. 12, 1912). University of Oregon, Bourne Collection, Box 29, Publicity Act file.

32. "Press Freedom is Impossible," *Editor and Publisher*, Sept. 7, 1912, p. 21.

33. "Publicity Law in Effect," *Fourth Estate*, Oct. 5, 1912, p. 2.

34. "The Newpaper Publicity Law," *New York Times*, June 11, 1913, p. 8.

35. Edwin Emery, *History of the American Newspaper Publishers Association* (Minneapolis: University of Minnesota Press, 1950), 117–18; Alfred M. Lee, *The Daily Newspaper in America* (New York: Macmillan, 1937), 239.

36. See, for example, "Newspaper Publishers' Statements," *Editor and Publisher*, Oct. 10, 1914, p. 326; "Building for the Future," ibid., July 4, 1914, p. 40; and "Official Figures," ibid., April 3, 1915, p. 880.

37. 1919 *Annual Report of the Post Office Department* 22.

38. "Bill to Repeal Press Law," *New York Times*, Jan. 31, 1914, p. 6; "Fights Newspaper Law," ibid., March 12, 1916, p. 16.

39. Post Office Department Press Release #5 (Oct. 11, 1912). U.S. Postal Service Library, Washington, D.C.

40. "Must Name All Owners," *New York Times*, Oct. 5, 1912, p. 24.

41. 5 *Opinions of the Solicitor General for the Post Office Department* (Jan. 10, 1914), 707–715.

42. Lamar to George A. Hill, U.S. Naval Observatory (April 28, 1916). National Archives, RG 28, Entry 40, Box 12, File 43430.

43. "Newspaper Publishers' Statement," *Editor and Publisher*, Oct. 10, 1914, p. 326.

44. See, for example, anonymous, Kansas City, to Burleson (Nov. 13, 1917). National Archives, Record Group 28, Entry 40, Box 29, File 47458; J. E. Stuart, agent, to postal inspector in charge, Chicago (Oct. 17, 1917). Ibid., Box 38, File 47497; and chief inspector, Peoria, to C. F. Clyne, U.S. attorney (Sept. 6, 1917). Ibid., Box 52, File 47587.

45. *U.S. v. Smith*, 269 F. 191 (1920).

46. 7 *Opinions of the Solicitor for the Post Office Department* (March 3, 1924), 456–57.

47. "W. D. Foulke Is Troubled," *New York Times*, Feb. 18, 1914, p. 2.

48. Seldes, *One Thousand Americans*, 18.

49. Ibid., 58.

50. Ibid., 59.

51. Ibid., 59, 61.

52. Ibid., 73.

53. Quoted in Lee, *Daily Newspaper in America*, 220; see also Richard T. Ruetten, "Anaconda Journalism: The End of an Era,"

Journalism Quarterly 37 (Winter 1960): 5; and William Weinfeld, "The Growth of Daily Newspaper Chains in the United States: 1923, 1926–1935," ibid. 13 (December 1936): 358–59.

54. Michael Schudson, *Discovering the News: A Social History of American Newspapers* (New York: Basic Books, Inc., 1978), 68; "Bryan's New Attack Assails the Editor," *New York Times*, July 7, 1915, p. 22; "Not Quite Up to Date," ibid., July 12, 1915, p. 6; Walter Lippmann, *Liberty and the News* (New York: Harcourt, Brace and Howe, 1920), p. 72.

55. Robert Schmuhl, "Eliminating Anonymity in Editorials Can Make Them Sharper," *Presstime*, July 1987, p. 54.

56. *Talley v. California*, 362 U.S. 60 (1960).

57. "Filing of Information by Publications Having Second-Class Mail Privileges," *Hearings Before the House Committee on the Post Office and Civil Service*, 87th Cong., 2d sess. (Sept. 11, 1962), 4–5.

58. A few state legislatures, in fact, have enacted laws to require their state's press to disclose additional business information. New York publications, for example, must print the full names and addresses of all owners and corporate officers in every issue. New York Consol. Laws 1930, c. 21, sec. 330 as cited in William G. Hale and Ivan Benson, *The Law of the Press: Text, Statutes and Cases* (St. Paul, Minn.: West Publishing Co., 1933), 460–61. Papers in Pennsylvania, on the other hand, must identify their editors on every editorial page and must publicize the names of new owners whenever a change occurs. 54 *Pennsylvania Statutes* sec. 61, sec. 62 as cited in ibid., 461. This statute was affirmed in *Commonwealth v. Short* (38 Pa. Sup. Ct. 562, 566).

59. Peter Dreier and Steve Weinberg, "The Ties that Blind—Interlocking Directories," *Columbia Journalism Review*, November/December 1979, p. 65.

7. Advertisements Identified

1. *Bloomington* (Ind.) *Herald-Telephone*, Feb. 23, 1988, p. B5.

2. In 1985 proceedings before the Postal Rate Commission, Gary A. Triche, owner of the *Tri-Parish Journal* in Louisiana, admitted that he did not know that disguising advertisements as news stories in his publication violated federal law. U.S. Postal Rate Commission, *Transcript of Proceedings: Complaint of Tri-Parish Journal, Inc.*, C85-2 (Washington, D.C.: Aug. 26, 1985), 115.

3. Edwin Emery, *History of the American Newspaper Publishers Association* (Minneapolis: University of Minnesota Press, 1950), 115.

4. 20 *U.S. Statutes at Large* 359; see also Richard B. Kielbowicz, "Origins of the Second-Class Mail Category and the Business of Policymaking, 1863–1879," *Journalism Monographs* No. 96 (April 1986), for a detailed account of the 1879 law.

5. Wayne E. Fuller, *The American Mail: Enlarger of the Common Life* (Chicago: University of Chicago Press, 1972), 134–35.

6. 1 *Opinions of the Assistant Attorney General for the Post Office Department* (March 7, 1879), 400–407, quotes at 405, 401.

7. 1887 *Postal Laws and Regulations* 140–42, sec. 333.

8. Ibid., 139–40. Section 331 elaborated on the definition of advertising sheets:

1. Those owned and controlled by one or several individuals or business concerns, and conducted as an auxiliary and essentially for the advancement of the main business or calling of those who own or control them.

2. Those which, having no genuine or paid-up subscriptions, insert advertisements free, on the condition that the advertiser will pay for any number of papers which are sent to persons whose names are given to the publisher.

3. Those which do advertising only, and whose columns are filled with editorial puffs of firms or individuals who buy a certain number of copies for distribution.

4. Pamphlets containing market quotations, and the business cards of various business houses opposite the pages that contained such quotations.

9. Penrose-Overstreet Commission Report, House R. Doc. No. 608, 59th Cong., 2d sess. (1907), x, 32.

10. Ibid., 98.

11. Ibid., xxvii.

12. Ibid., xliii.

13. Ibid., 129, 500.

14. Ibid., 523.

15. 4 *Opinions of the Assistant Attorney General for the Post Office Department* (Aug. 21, 1907), 578–83, quote at 582.

16. John T. Schlebecker and Andrew W. Hopkins, *A History of Dairy Journalism in the United States, 1810–1950* (Madison: University of Wisconsin Press, 1957), 277.

17. "The New Newspaper Laws and the Advertiser's Interest in Them," *Mail Order Journal*, October 1912, pp. 26–27.

18. "An Objectionable Law," *Editor and Publisher*, Sept. 28, 1912, p. 10; "Opinions of the New P. O. Law," *Fourth Estate*, Sept. 28, 1912, pp. 5, 13.

19. "Newspapers Opposing Publicity," *Literary Digest*, Oct. 12, 1912, p. 608.

20. Louise Huston, "Adv.," *American Printer*, January 1913, pp. 612–13.

21. The Post Office Department noted the absurdity in a press release dated Oct. 25, 1912, edited Oct. 29, 1912. U.S. Postal Service Library, Washington, D.C. For press coverage of the case, see "May Lose Postal Rights," *Publisher's Auxiliary*, Nov. 9, 1912, p. 1; "Unexpected Result of 'Publicity Rider,' " *Publishers' Weekly*, Nov. 2, 1912, p. 1478; and "The Postal Law Case Advanced," *Fourth Estate*, Nov. 2, 1912, p. 2.

22. Quoted in "Newspapers Opposing Publicity," *Literary Digest*, Oct. 12, 1912, p. 608.

23. Ibid.

24. Quoted in "Booth Approves of Law," *Editor and Publisher*, Sept. 28, 1912, p. 15.

25. *Newspaperdom*, Sept. 26, 1912, p. 16.

26. "Congressional Regulation of Paid-For News Items a Good Move," *Automobile Trade Journal*, Nov. 1, 1912, p. 91. National Archives, Sen. 62A-F20, Tray 108, Chilton Co. file.

27. "The New Newspaper Laws and the Advertiser's Interest in Them," *Mail Order Journal*, October 1912, p. 27.

28. Brief of Counsel for Appellant, *Journal of Commerce v. Frank H. Hitchcock et al.*, U.S. Supreme Court Case No. 818, 4–7.

29. Brief in Behalf of the United States, *Journal of Commerce and Lewis Publishing Company v. Edward M. Morgan et al.*, U.S. Supreme Court Case Nos. 818–819, 5, 7.

30. As cited in brief for Appellant, *Journal of Commerce v. Hitchcock*, U.S. Supreme Court Case No. 818, 39.

31. 57 L.Ed. 1203.

32. Quoted in "Free Write Ups In Newspapers," *Fourth Estate*, Oct. 9, 1920, p. 28.

33. "Advertisers Don't Want Free Publicity," *Fourth Estate*, Jan. 13, 1917, p. 12.

34. Ibid.; L. B. Palmer, "The Press-agent Still Pursues His Wily

Ways," *Printers' Ink*, July 13, 1916, p. 73; "Publishers to War on the Press Agent," *New York Times*, April 29, 1916, p. 7; "Hunting Down the Press Agent," *Advertising & Selling*, April 1915, p. 15; Maurice L. Beresin, "New Statistics on Free Publicity," *National Printer Journalist*, January 1933, p. 60; ibid., February 1933, pp. 64–65; "Advertising Agents Condemn Free Publicity," *Printers' Ink*, April 15, 1920, pp. 196–228.

35. "Important to Publishers," *Newspaperdom*, April 28, 1921, p. 23.

36. "Advertising Agents Condemn Free Publicity," *Printers' Ink*, April 15, 1920, pp. 196–228.

37. Quoted in "Eliminating Free Publicity From Newspapers," *Advertising & Selling*, June 1917, p. 25; and *Newspaperdom*, June 14, 1917, p. 20; see also "Publicity Evils Up To Publishers," *Printers' Ink*, June 10, 1920, pp. 85–88.

38. "Law Says Free Publicity Must Be Labeled," *Fourth Estate*, Jan. 13, 1917, p. 22.

39. "Advertisers Don't Want Free Publicity," *Fourth Estate*, Jan. 13, 1917, p. 12.

40. "No Blanket Ruling on Marking Reading Notices 'Adv.'," *Printers' Ink*, Dec. 28, 1916, pp. 73–74, 111, 113, quote at 74; see also "Free Publicity Stirs Post Office Officials," *Fourth Estate*, Jan. 6, 1917, p. 12.

41. Quoted in "Circulation Publicity," *New York Times*, Nov. 22, 1913, p. 6; and "Publicity Law is Explained," *Fourth Estate*, Nov. 29, 1913, p. 2.

42. Quoted in "Post Office to Prosecute," *Fourth Estate*, April 11, 1914, p. 7.

43. Quoted in "Post Office and Newspapers," *Fourth Estate*, Jan. 13, 1917, p. 7.

44. "Post-Office Department to Enforce Law Regarding Reading Notices," *Printers' Ink*, Dec. 14, 1916, pp. 74, 76, 81.

45. Quoted in "Advertisers Don't Want Free Publicity," *Fourth Estate*, Jan. 13, 1917, p. 12.

46. *Newspaperdom*, Dec. 28, 1916, p. 15.

47. "Post Office and Newspapers," *Fourth Estate*, Jan. 13, 1917, p. 7.

48. "No Blanket Rulings on Marking Reading Notices 'Adv.'," *Printers' Ink*, Dec. 28, 1916, p. 73; "Free Publicity Stirs Post Office Officials," *Fourth Estate*, Jan. 6, 1917, p. 12; *Newspaperdom*, June 14, 1917, p. 20.

49. Quoted in "Post Office Department to Enforce Law Regarding Reading Notices," *Printers' Ink*, Dec. 14, 1916, p. 81; see also "Free Publicity Stirs Post Office Officials," *Fourth Estate*, Jan. 6, 1917, p. 12.

50. Ibid.

51. Edgar Foster, Banner Publishing Co., to postmaster E. S. Shannon, Nashville, Tenn., May 23, 1918; Shannon to Lamar, May 24, 1918; Lamar to Shannon, May 28, 1918. See also Lamar to Jacksonville, Fla., postmaster, March 14, 1916, regarding the *Florida Metropolis*, and Lamar to Dr. W. S. Hubbard, Detroit, Mich., Sept. 11, 1917, regarding a *Detroit Free Press* story about a Dr. Lewis Baker which was not labeled an advertisement. National Archives, RG 28, Entry 40, Box 12, File 43430.

52. Quoted in Foster to Shannon, May 23, 1918. Ibid.

53. "Post-Office Department to Enforce Law Regarding Reading Notices," *Printers' Ink*, Dec. 14, 1916, p. 76.

54. War Revenue Act of 1917, 40 *Stat* 300, 327–28, sec. 1101. The law established eight geographic zones. For a thoughtful discussion of the law's postal provisions, see Richard B. Kielbowicz, "Postal Subsidies for the Press and the Business of Mass Culture, 1880–1920," *Business History Review* 64 (Autumn 1990): 451–88.

55. " 'Wrinkles' in Postal Rate Law Smoothed Out by Expert of Department," *Editor and Publisher*, June 22, 1918, p. 9.

56. Ibid., 10.

57. Ibid.

58. Ibid.

59. Ibid., 11.

60. Mencken to Lamar, solicitor, July 25, 1918. National Archives, Record Group 28, Entry 40, Box 25, File 47445.

61. "Reading Matter Advertising," *Fourth Estate*, Oct. 30, 1920, p. 14; see also "U.S. Broadens Its Idea of an Ad," ibid., Sept. 18, 1920, p. 13.

62. Ibid.

63. The Illinois Press Association, for example, debated free publicity at its 1925 annual convention. See *Illinois Newspaper Directory and History of the Illinois Press Association* (Champaign-Urbana: Illinois Press Association, 1934), 229. For a discussion of the problem without reference to the law, see "Advertising in the Guise of News," *Fourth Estate*, Jan. 21, 1922, p. 8; and "Free Reading Notices," ibid., Feb. 4, 1922, p. 18.

64. Martin M. Olasky, "The Development of Corporate Public

Relations, 1850–1930," *Journalism Monographs* No. 102 (April 1987), 19, 23.

65. See H. Eugene Goodwin, *Groping for Ethics in Journalism* (Ames: Iowa State University Press, 1983), 46–49; John L. Hulteng, *The Messenger's Motives: Ethical Problems of the News Media* (Englewood Cliffs, N.J.: Prentice-Hall, Inc., 1976), 145–46, 156–57; Curtis D. MacDougall, *The Press and Its Problems* (Dubeque, Iowa: Wm. C. Brown Co., 1964), 244–47; and Ben H. Bagdikian, "Behold the Grass-roots Press, Alas!," *Harper's Magazine*, December 1964, pp. 102–10.

66. Quoted in Bagdikian, "Behold the Grass-roots Press," 102.

67. Ibid., 104.

68. Ibid., 110.

69. John Cameron Sim, *The Grass Roots Press: America's Community Newspapers* (Ames: Iowa State University Press, 1969), 93. As early as 1934, Stanley Walker, city editor of the *New York Herald Tribune*, suggested that publications should identify *all* material supplied by special interests.

70. "Shop Talk at Thirty," *Editor and Publisher*, April 23, 1966, as quoted in Sim, 94.

71. *Columbia Journalism Review*, July/August 1988, p. 18.

72. Ibid., September/October 1985, p. 22.

73. "Advertorials: Editors Discuss How to Make Them Work," *Editor and Publisher*, Nov. 17, 1990, p. 22; see also "Welcome to a New Era," ibid., p. 4.

74. M. L. Stein, "Press Releases as Paid Ads," *Editor and Publisher*, April 9, 1988, pp. 22, 52. The trade journal praised the concept of printing news releases "as is" and "as written" for a fee. "Editorial: Press Releases as Paid Ads," ibid., 8.

8. Circulation Revealed

1. Alfred M. Lee, *The Daily Newspaper in America* (New York: Macmillan, 1937), 342.

2. James E. Pollard, *Principles of Newspaper Management* (New York: McGraw-Hill Book Co., 1937), 359–61; see also Frank Thayer, *Newspaper Management*, rev. ed. (New York: D. Appleton-Century Co., 1938), 152.

3. 1879 *Postal Laws and Regulations* 74, sec. 193; see also Richard B. Kielbowicz, "Development of the Paid Subscriber Rule in Second-Class Mail" (Prepared for the U.S. Postal Rate Commission in the Tri-Parish Journal Case, Aug. 16, 1985), 19.

4. 1 *Opinions of the Assistant Attorney General for the Post Office Department* 564 (Feb. 10, 1881).

5. Ibid. 859 (Aug. 20, 1883); see also 2 ibid. 28 (June 17, 1885).

6. 1887 *Postal Laws and Regulations* 141, sec. 333; see also 2 *Opinions of the Assistant Attorney General for the Post Office Department* 479–81 (Oct. 4, 1887).

7. 2 *Opinions of the Assistant Attorney General for the Post Office Department* 443 (April 25, 1887).

8. For more information on the ensuing debates, see Kielbowicz, "Paid Subscriber Rule," 28–41.

9. 4 *Opinions of the Assistant Attorney General for the Post Office Department* 445–48 (May 9, 1907).

10. Senate Doc. 270, 60th Cong., 1st sess., 9–10 (1908).

11. "To Test Legality of Censorship Law," *New York Times*, Sept. 21, 1912, p. 5; see also "To Pass on Newspaper Law," ibid., Sept. 24, 1912, p. 10; "Calls Newspaper Law a Pretense," ibid., Sept. 25, 1912, p. 8; and "Plan to Test Newspaper Law," *Publisher's Auxiliary*, Sept. 28, 1912, p. 1.

12. For a sampling of stories, see "Post Office Bill Affects Papers," *Publisher's Auxiliary*, Sept. 7, 1912, p. 1; "Newspaper Law to be Enforced," *New York Times*, Sept. 9, 1912, p. 7; "New Publicity Law Is to be Contested," ibid., Sept. 13, 1912, p. 5; "Publishers Object," *Editor and Publisher*, Sept. 14, 1912, p. 1; "The Newspaper Publicity Law," *Fourth Estate*, Sept. 14, 1912, p. 2; and "Account for All Papers Sold," ibid., Sept. 21, 1912, p. 4.

13. "Newspapers Opposing Publicity," *Literary Digest*, Oct. 12, 1912, p. 608.

14. "Protection for Advertisers," *Editor and Publisher*, Sept. 21, 1912, p. 10; and "Editorial Comment," ibid. See also "Does Not Affect Reputable Papers," *Publisher's Auxiliary*, Nov. 16, 1912, p. 1, where J. L. Startevant, editor of the *Wassau* (Wisc.) *Daily Record-Herald*, expressed similar sentiments.

15. James Keeley, "How to Drive the Liar Out of the Newspaper Business," *Printers' Ink*, June 12, 1913, p. 7; see also "The New Newspaper Law," *Mail Order Journal*, November 1912, p. 9; *Printers' Ink*, Oct. 17, 1912, p. 35; ibid., Oct. 24, 1912, p. 65; and "Why Are They Afraid?," *Automobile Trade Journal*, November 1912, p. 95, in National Archives, Sen. 62A-F20, Tray 108, Chilton Co. file.

16. Resolution (Sept. 4, 1912). National Archives, Sen. 62A-F20, Tray 108, Chilton Co. file.

17. The organization's president was E. R. Shaw, publisher

of the Chicago-based *Practical Engineer*. "The Seventh Trade Press Convention," *Advertising & Selling*, October 1912, pp. 64–66; "The New Postal Requirement," *American Printer*, November 1912, pp. 344–45; "Meeting of the Federated Trade Press," ibid., pp. 379–81; "Asking Trade Papers to Guarantee Circulations," *Printers' Ink*, Feb. 27, 1913, p. 56. The National Trade Press Association was also known as the Federation of Trade Press Associations.

18. "To Exclude the Circulation Liar," *Printers' Ink*, March 5, 1914, p. 74; "N. Y. Trade Press Bars Dishonest Publisher," ibid., March 26, 1914, p. 32; "Trade Papers Favor Sworn Circulation Statements," *Printers' Ink*, Feb. 6, 1913, p. 90.

19. Glavis to members of the Federation of Trade Press Association (Sept. 26, 1912); "Nearing A Circulation Show Down," *Automobile Trade Journal*, October 1912, p. 89; "One Thousand Dollars for Facts," *Commercial Car Journal*, Jan. 15, 1913, p. 11; Bourne to Glavis, Jan. 8, 1913 telegram; Glavis to Bourne, Jan. 23, 1913; Britt to Glavis, Jan. 25, 1913. National Archives, Sen. 62A-F20, Tray 108, Chilton Co. file. See also George O. Glavis, "Determining Real Facts About Circulation," *Printers' Ink*, July 31, 1913, pp. 3–13; and "To Penalize the Circulation Liar," ibid., Oct. 3, 1912, pp. 49–54.

20. Quoted in "Advertising Agents for Bourne Law," *Editor and Publisher*, July 4, 1914, p. 36. The *Mail Order Journal* called the law "of greatest importance for advertisers." See "Circulation Statements," *Mail Order Journal*, November 1914, p. 3, 25+.

21. "Indorses Postal Law," *Editor and Publisher*, Dec. 14, 1912, p. 8; "Advertising Agents for Bourne Law," ibid., July 4, 1914, p. 36.

22. "The New Postal Requirements," *American Printer*, November 1912, pp. 344–45; "Meeting of the Federated Trade Press," ibid., pp. 379–81; "What Shall the Appropriation Be?," *Printers' Ink*, Nov. 21, 1912, p. 87; "Official Interpretation of Postal Law," ibid., Oct. 31, 1912, pp. 64–65, quote at 65.

23. "*Printers' Ink* Takes Own Medicine," *Printers' Ink*, Oct. 3, 1912, pp. 82–83.

24. *Newspaperdom*, April 22, 1920, p. 25. For a sampling of advertisements, see *Printers' Ink*, Aug. 21, 1913, pp. 66–67 (*Des Moines Capital*), and April 22, 1915, p. 56 (*Kansas City Star*); *Fourth Estate*, April 10, 1920, p. 7 (*New York Herald* and the *Sun*); *Newspaperdom*, Oct. 11, 1917, p. 11, and Oct. 24, 1918, p. 7 (*New York Times*), Jan. 24, 1918, p. 4 (*Cleveland News*), April 24, 1919, p. 5 (*Fort Worth Star-Telegram*), Nov. 14, 1918, p. 18 (*Fort Wayne Star-*

Telegram), and Oct. 12, 1916, p. 4 (*Philadelphia Evening Bulletin*); and *Mail Order Journal*, April 1916, p. 15 (*Detroit Sunday News Tribune*), and May 1915, p. 31 (*Georgian-American* in Atlanta).

25. "Newspaper Circulations," *New York Times*, Oct. 15, 1916, p. 10.

26. "Newspaper Publishers' Statements," *Editor and Publisher*, Oct. 10, 1914, p. 326.

27. Daily Newspapers—Filing Statement of Paid Circulation, 29 *Opinions of the Attorney General* 526 (Sept. 25, 1912); see also "To Pass on Newspaper Law," *New York Times*, Sept. 24, 1912, p. 10; "Wickersham's View of Newspaper Law," ibid., Sept. 27, 1912, p. 5; "Wickersham's Views," *Editor and Publisher*, Sept. 28, 1912, p. 14; "Wickersham Interprets New Postal Law," *Printers' Ink*, Oct. 12, 1912, p. 66; and "Wickersham Cited Against Press Law," *New York Times*, Dec. 1, 1912, p. 3. Interestingly, even though opinions of the Attorney General normally "are given weight and seldom have been overruled" in the courts, the Supreme Court determined that the law applied to second-class mail service, not all mail service, contrary to Wickersham's opinion. Homer Cummings and Carl McFarland, *Federal Justice: Chapters in the History of Justice and the Federal Executive* (New York: Macmillan, 1937), quote at 517, see also 338–39.

28. "Circulation Publicity," *New York Times*, Nov. 22, 1913, p. 6; "Publicity Law is Explained," *Fourth Estate*, Nov. 29, 1913, p. 2.

29. 30 *Opinions of the Attorney General* 244–45 (Jan. 5, 1914). See also Post Office Department News Releases, No. 21, Jan. 5, 1914, and No. 22, undated. U.S. Postal Service Library, Washington, D.C.

30. 1914 *Annual Report of the Postmaster General* 288; see also "Publicity Law Construed," *New York Times*, Jan. 11, 1914, p. 11; and "Publicity Law is Up Again," *Fourth Estate*, Jan. 17, 1914, pp. 2, 23.

31. G. H. E. Hawkins, *Newspaper Advertising* (Chicago: Advertisers Publishing Co., 1914), 56; see also "Publicity Law An Issue Again," *Fourth Estate*, Sept. 2, 1914, p. 2. For other complaints, see *Printers' Ink*, Jan. 8, 1914, p. 44; ibid., April 4, 1914, p. 52; ibid., Dec. 24, 1914, p. 52; ibid., Feb. 10, 1916, pp. 10, 12; Edward Baur, "Voluntary Control in the Advertising Industry" (Ph.D. diss., University of Chicago, 1942), 268; and Paul Terry Cherington, *The First Advertising Book* (N.p.: Doubleday, Page and Co., 1916), 395–96.

32. "Access to Newspaper Data," *New York Times*, Oct. 4, 1912, p. 13; "Government Giving Information About Circulation Figures," *Printers' Ink*, Nov. 21, 1912, p. 13.

33. Publishers were required to file two copies of their publications and completed statements with the local postmaster who forwarded one of the copies to the department's headquarters. "Publicity Law An Issue Again," *Fourth Estate*, Sept. 2, 1914, p. 2.

34. Quoted in "Post-Office Policy as to Circulation Statements," *Printers' Ink*, July 17, 1913, pp. 63–64.

35. Ibid.

36. "Agency Seeks Complete Post Office Circulation Reports In Vain," *Printers' Ink*, Feb. 10, 1916, pp. 10–12.

37. Quoted in "Uncle Sam's Bureau of Circulation," *Printers' Ink*, Dec. 24, 1914, pp. 52–55. The business manager of the Minneapolis-based *Farm, Stock & Home*, for example, wanted Congress to require the post office to open all its second-class mail records for public inspection at all times. Ibid. See also F. J. Low, "Why He Uses Trade Journals Instead of Mail Lists," ibid., Sept. 25, 1913, pp. 72–73; "Circulation from an Advertiser's Viewpoint," *Advertising & Selling*, October 1913, p. 31.

38. The "value of the list to advertisers and advertising men is inestimable," the trade journal boasted. See "A Notable Achievement," *Editor and Publisher*, April 3, 1915, p. 1; "Newspaper Publishers' Statements," *Editor and Publisher*, Oct. 10, 1914, p. 326.

39. "Circulation Statements," *Mail Order Journal*, November 1914, pp. 3, 25+; "Official Circulation Statements," ibid., May 1915, pp. 4–12; ibid., November 1915, pp. 3+; ibid., April 1916, pp. 3+; ibid., October 1916, pp. 3+. In 1917, the journal asked more than 600 papers for statements but only received 242, leading it to speculate that publishers who had not responded suffered circulation losses. "The Tenth Semi-Annual Newspaper Circulation Statements," *Mail Order Journal*, April 1917, pp. 13+. Many publications also carried reminders to meet the deadlines for filing the statements. "File Your Statement," *Fourth Estate*, Sept. 29, 1917, p. 10; "Make Post Office Reports on April 1," ibid., March 30, 1918, p. 13.

40. *Editor and Publisher*, July 4, 1914, p. 40; see also "Newspaper Publishers' Statements," ibid., Oct. 10, 1914, p. 326.

41. For example, the department received complaints from Harry R. Cook, publisher of the *Pensacola Journal* in Florida, questioning the circulation figures of rival *Pensacola News* and from E. H. Merrick concerning the *New Orleans American*'s circulation data. National Archives, RG 28, Entry 40, Box 12, File 43430. The post office again mounted a campaign to enforce the regulation in 1918. See

"Government Inspects Circulation Methods," *Editor and Publisher*, Oct. 13, 1917, p. 14.

42. Quoted in "The April 1 Official Circulation Statements," *Mail Order Journal*, April 1915, p. 3. It also indicated that the circulation reports "are authentic in such an overwhelming majority of cases that the percentage of unreliability is essentially nil." See "The Publisher's Honesty," *Newspaperdom*, Sept. 28, 1916, p. 11.

43. "Wide Range of Vital Subjects Covered by Publishers in Annual Convention," *Printers' Ink*, April 29, 1915, p. 17; see also "Publishers Oppose The Trading Stamp," *New York Times*, April 22, 1915, p. 22.

44. "Uncle Sam's Bureau of Circulation," *Printers' Ink*, Dec. 24, 1914, pp. 52–55.

45. F. J. Low, "Circulation from an Advertiser's Viewpoint," *Advertising & Selling*, October 1913, p. 31. Low was the advertising manager for the New York-based H. W. Johns-Manville Company.

46. "Compulsory Circulation Statements," *Printers' Ink*, March 19, 1914, p. 112.

47. For detailed accounts on the history of the Audit Bureau of Circulations, see generally Charles O. Bennett, *Facts Without Opinion* (Chicago: Audit Bureau of Circulations, 1965); William H. Boyenton, *Audit Bureau of Circulations* (Chicago: Audit Bureau of Circulations, 1952); and the Audit Bureau of Circulations, *Scientific Space Selection* (Chicago: Audit Bureau of Circulations, 1937). The American Newspaper Publishers Association states the Newspaper Publicity Act prompted it and other press associations to form the bureau. "With an Eye on the Past and a Look to the Future," *Presstime*, May 1987, p. 31. For a sampling of articles on what led up to the bureau, see "A.N.A.M. Chicago Meeting," *Advertising & Selling*, January 1913, pp. 62-63; "Important Step Toward Audited Circulations," ibid., April 1913, p. 41; "How the A.A.A. Conducts Its Circulation Audits," *Printers' Ink*, April 3, 1913, pp. 20–27; "Circulation Audits Considered at Conference," ibid., April 10, 1913, pp. 102–4; "A Plan to Standardize Circulation Audits," ibid., June 5, 1913, pp. 62–64; "New Audit Movement Would Include All Advertising Interests," ibid., Dec. 18, 1913, pp. 12–13, 89; "Two Audit Organizations Effect a Merger," ibid., Jan. 22, 1914, pp. 118–19; "A.N.A.M. Discusses Circulation Audits, Price-Maintenance and Objectionable Advertising," ibid., April 9, 1914, pp. 17–19; "The New Audit Association," ibid.,

April 23, 1914, pp. 108–9; and "Audit Association Formally Organized," ibid., May 28, 1914, pp. 10–12.

48. Quoted in "Circulation Law Not Enforced," *Fourth Estate*, Jan. 13, 1917, p. 19.

49. Stanley Clague, "The A.B.C. and Government Reports of Circulations," *Printers' Ink*, July 11, 1918, pp. 116–18. The former president of the Association of American Advertisers said the government statements, "even if accurate, are as worthless as a hobble skirt, and even more limited." Bert Moses, "How One Association Finds Facts about Circulation," ibid., March 5, 1914, p. 47. Ida Clarke, advertising manager of Scott's Emulsion, also campaigned against the regulation. Ida Clarke, "On the Trail of Circulation Facts," *Printers' Ink*, March 5, 1914, p. 34; see also "Annual Meeting of the A.A.A.," *Advertising & Selling*, February 1913, p. 50; and "Adventures in Search of Circulation," *Printers' Ink*, Feb. 6, 1913, p. 4.

50. At ABC's sixth convention, participants tabled a resolution "favoring the omission of circulation figures from publishers' statements to the Post Office Department." See "A.B.C. Stand for America First," *Fourth Estate*, June 28, 1919, p. 6; see also Walter C. Johnson and Arthur T. Robb, *The South and Its Newspapers, 1903–1953: The Story of the Southern Newspaper Publishers Association and Its Part in the South's Economic Rebirth* (Chattanooga, Tenn.: Southern Newspaper Publishers Association, 1954), 96.

51. "The Fight on the National Publicity Law," *Mail Order Journal*, April 1916, p. 6; see also "Newspaper Circulations," ibid., May 1915, p. 3.

52. "Mail Fraud Law Is Invoked," *Fourth Estate*, April 21, 1917, p. 8; "Uncle Sam Convicts Publisher of Circulation Fraud," *Printers' Ink*, April 19, 1917, pp. 74–76; "Circulation Figures Led Him Into Trouble," *Editor and Publisher*, April 21, 1917, p. 14.

53. "Publishers and the A.B.C.," *Fourth Estate*, Jan. 12, 1918, p. 22.

54. "In Defence of the A.B.C.," ibid., Jan. 19, 1918, p. 21.

55. "Answering Mr. Barry of the A.B.C.," ibid., Jan. 19, 1918, p. 18.

56. "The Sooner the A.B.C. Is Abolished, the Better," ibid., June 15, 1918, p. 18.

57. About one dozen weeklies belonged to the bureau in 1938. This number grew to 747 in early 1952. Thomas F. Barnhart, *Weekly Newspaper Management* 2d ed. (New York: Appleton-Century Crofts, Inc., 1952), 339.

58. Quoted in ibid., 365.

59. Senate Rep. 724, 79th Cong., 1st sess., 2 (1945); see also 1947 *Annual Report of the Post Office Department* 32.

60. Act of July 2, 1946, 60 *Stat.* 416; Barnhart, *Weekly Newspaper Management*, 365.

61. Act of June 11, 1960; 74 *Stat.* 208.

62. Quoted in House Rep. 573, 86th Cong., 1st sess., 3 (1959); see also Senate Rep. 1488, 86th Cong., 2d sess. (1960).

63. *Filing of Information by Publications Having Second-Class Mail Privileges*, Hearings Before the House Committee on Post Office and Civil Service, 87th Cong., 2d sess., 7 (1962).

64. Act of Oct. 23, 1962, 76 *Stat.* 1144, sec. 2.

65. "Circulation Disclosure Bill Passed; Who Exempted 'Performing Arts' Publications?" *Advertising Age*, Oct. 15, 1962, p. 135.

66. Quoted in "Variety; Billboard Give Opposing Views," *Advertising Age*, Oct. 15, 1962, p. 135.

67. "Circulation Disclosure Bill Passed; Who Exempted 'Performing Arts' Publications?" *Advertising Age*, Oct. 15, 1962, p. 135.

68. *Filing of Information Relating to Second-Class Mail*, Hearings Before the House Committee on Post Office and Civil Service, 88th Cong., 2d sess. (1964).

69. Ibid., 15; see also "House Unit Scrutinizes Exemption of 'Variety' in Second Class Mail Law," *Advertising Age*, March 2, 1964, pp. 1, 93.

70. Ibid., 13.

71. "House Okays Bill to Proscribe Circulation Disclosure Exemption," *Advertising Age*, June 1, 1964, p. 26.

72. "House Unit Okays Repeal of Postal Disclosure Exemption," *Advertising Age*, March 22, 1965, p. 3; Pub. L. 90-206, Title I, sec. 104 (d), Dec. 16, 1967, 81 *Stat.* 618.

73. "Weekly Publisher Indicted," *Editor and Publisher*, May 21, 1988, p. 20.

74. Hensley claimed a circulation of 9,000, 6,500 above the actual figure. "The Month That Was," *NEWSINC.*, March 1990, p. 7.

9. Publicity as an Antidote for Press Abuses

1. *Cong. Rec.*, 62d Cong., 2d sess. (April 27, 1912), 5465.

2. Bourne to Givens (Sept. 5, 1912). University of Oregon, Bourne Collection, Box 29, U.S. Appropriations Bill file.

3. *Cong. Rec.*, 62d Cong., 2d sess. (April 27, 1912), 5465.

4. "Filing of Information by Publications Having Second-Class Mail Privileges," *Hearings Before the House Committee on the Post Office and Civil Service*, 87th Cong., 2d sess. (Sept. 11, 1962), 4–5.

Selected Bibliography

Books

Abraham, Henry J. *Justices and Presidents: A Political History of Appointments to the Supreme Court*. New York: Penguin Books, Inc., 1974.

Allen, Charles L. *Country Journalism*. New York: Thomas Nelson and Sons, 1928.

Anderson, Donald F. *William Howard Taft: A Conservative's Conception of the Presidency*. Ithaca, N.Y.: Cornell University Press, 1968.

Appel, Joseph H. *Growing Up with Advertising*. New York: Business Bourse, 1940.

Associated Advertising Clubs of America. *Seventh Annual Convention Held in Boston, 1911*. Boston: Pilgrim Publicity Association, 1912.

————. *Eighth Annual Convention Held in Dallas, 1912*. N.p.: Associated Advertising Clubs, 1912.

Audit Bureau of Circulations. *Scientific Space Selection*. Chicago: Audit Bureau of Circulations, 1937.

Baehr, Harry W., Jr. *The New York Tribune since the Civil War*. New York: Dodd, Mead & Co., 1936.

Bagdikian, Ben H. *The Media Monopoly*. Boston: Beacon Press, 1983.

Barnhart, Thomas F. *Weekly Newspaper Management*. 2d ed. New York: D. Appleton-Century Co., 1936.

Bates, Ernest S. *The Story of Congress: 1789–1935*. New York: Harper & Brothers, 1936.

Bennett, Charles O. *Facts Without Opinion*. Chicago: Audit Bureau of Circulations, 1965.

Bent, Silas. *Ballyhoo: The Voice of the Press*. New York: Boni & Liveright, 1927.

Bickel, Alexander M., and Benno C. Schmidt, Jr. *History of the Supreme Court of the United States: The Judiciary and Responsible Government, 1910–1921*. 3 vols. New York: Macmillan, 1984.

207

Bing, Phil C. *The Country Weekly*. New York: D. Appleton and Co., 1917.

Boorstin, Daniel J. *The Americans: The Democratic Experience*. New York: Random House, 1973.

Boyenton, William H. *Audit Bureau of Circulations*. Chicago: Audit Bureau of Circulations, 1952.

Britt, James. *Second-Class Mail Matter: Its Uses and Abuses*. Washington, D.C.: Government Printing Office, 1911.

Broderick, Francis L. *Progressivism at Risk: Electing a President in 1912*. Westport, Conn.: Greenwood Press, 1989.

Brown, George R. *The Leadership of Congress*. Indianapolis: Bobbs-Merrill Co., 1922.

Byxbee, O. F. *Establishing a Newspaper*. Chicago: Inland Printer Co., 1901.

Calkins, Earnest E. *Business the Civilizer*. Boston: Little, Brown & Co., 1928.

Chafee, Zechariah, Jr. *Government and Mass Communications: Report from the Commission on Freedom of the Press*. 2 vols. Chicago: University of Chicago Press, 1947.

Chandler, Alfred D., Jr. *The Visible Hand: The Managerial Revolution in American Business*. Cambridge, Mass.: Belknap Press of the Harvard University Press, 1977.

Chapman, Clowry. *The Law of Advertising*. New York: Harper & Brothers, 1929.

Cherington, Paul T. *Advertising as a Business Force*. N.p.: Doubleday, Page & Co., 1913.

———. *The First Advertising Book*. N.p.: Doubleday, Page & Co., 1916.

Cochran, Negley D. *E. W. Scripps*. New York: Harcourt, Brace and Co., 1933.

Cochran, Thomas C., and William Miller. *The Age of Enterprise: A Social History of Industrial America*. 1942; rev. ed. New York: Harper & Row, 1961.

Cohn, Jan. *Creating America: George Horace Lorimer and the Saturday Evening Post*. Pittsburgh: University of Pittsburgh Press, 1989.

Coletta, Paolo E. *The Presidency of William Howard Taft*. Lawrence: University Press of Kansas, 1973.

Comer, John P. *Legislative Functions of National Administrative Authorities*. New York: Columbia University Press, 1927.

Conrad, Will C., Kathleen Wilson, and Dale Wilson. *The Milwaukee*

Journal: The First Eighty Years. Madison: University of Wisconsin Press, 1964.

Cooper, John M., Jr. *Pivotal Decades, The United States 1900–1920.* New York: W. W. Norton & Co., 1990.

Crawford, Nelson A. *The Ethics of Journalism.* New York: Alfred A. Knopf, 1924.

Creel, Herr G. *Newspaper Frauds.* St. Louis, Mo.: National Rip-Saw Publishing Co., 1911.

————. *Tricks of the Press.* St. Louis, Mo.: National Rip-Saw Publishing Co., 1911.

Curl, Donald W. *Murat Halstead and the Cincinnati Commercial.* Boca Raton: University Presses of Florida, 1980.

Cushing, Marshall H. *The Story of Our Post Office.* Boston: A. M. Thayer & Co., 1893.

Davis, Elmer. *History of the New York Times: 1851–1921.* New York: New York Times Co., 1921.

Dennis, Charles H. *Victor Lawson: His Times and His Work.* Chicago: University of Chicago Press, 1935.

Dicken-Garcia, Hazel. *Journalistic Standards in Nineteenth–Century America.* Madison: University of Wisconsin Press, 1989.

Eads, George W. *Problems of Advertising.* Journalism Series No. 17. Columbia: University of Missouri, 1918.

Emery, Edwin. *History of the American Newspaper Publishers Association.* Minneapolis: University of Minnesota Press, 1950.

————, and Michael Emery. *The Press and America.* 4th ed. Englewood, N.J.: Prentice Hall, 1978.

Emery, Michael, and Edwin Emery. *The Press and America.* 6th ed. Englewood, N.J.: Prentice Hall, 1988.

Evans, James F., and Rodolfo N. Salcedo. *Communications in Agriculture: The American Farm Press.* Ames: Iowa State University Press, 1974.

Farrington, Frank. *Retail Advertising—Complete.* Chicago: Byxbee Publishing Co., 1910.

————. *Retail Advertising for Druggists and Stationers.* New York: Baker & Taylor Co., 1901.

Faulkner, Harold U. *The Quest for Social Justice, 1898–1914.* New York: Macmillan, 1931.

Filler, Louis. *Appointment at Armageddon: Muckraking and Progressivism in American Life.* Westport, Conn.: Greenwood Press, 1976.

————. *The Muckrakers: Crusaders for American Liberalism.* 1950; reprint ed. Chicago: Henry Regnery Co., 1986.

Flint, Leon N. *The Conscience of the Newspaper*. New York: D. Appleton & Co., 1925.

Fourth Annual Proceedings of the Washington State Press, 1887–1890. Hoquiam: Washingtonian Steam Book, News and Job Print, 1891.

Fowler, Dorothy. *Unmailable: Congress and the Post Office*. Athens: University of Georgia Press, 1977.

Fowler, Nathaniel C., Jr. *Fowler's Publicity*. Boston: Publicity Publishing Co., 1900.

Fox, Stephen. *The Mirror Makers: A History of American Advertising and Its Creators*. New York: Vintage Books, 1984.

Freeman, William C. *One Hundred Advertising Talks*. New York: Winthrop Press, 1912.

Galambos, Louis, and Joseph Pratt. *The Rise of the Corporate Commonwealth: U.S. Business and Public Policy in the Twentieth Century*. New York: Basic Books, Inc., 1988.

Gale, Albert L., and George W. Kline. *Bryan the Man*. St. Louis, Mo.: Thompson Publishing Co., 1908.

Galloway, George B. *History of the United States House of Representatives*. Washington, D.C.: Government Printing Office, 1965.

Geller, Max A. *Advertising at the Crossroads: Federal Regulation vs. Voluntary Controls*. New York: Ronald Press, 1952.

George, Henry, Jr. *The Menace of Privilege*. New York: Macmillan, 1906.

Ginger, Ray. *Age of Excess: The United States from 1877 to 1914*. New York: Macmillan, 1965.

Given, John L. *Making a Newspaper*. New York: Henry Holt and Co., 1907.

Griffith, Sally Foreman. *Home Town News: William Allen White and the Emporia Gazette*. New York: Oxford University Press, 1989.

Grodinsky, Julius. *Jay Gould: His Business Career, 1867–1892*. Philadelphia: University of Pennsylvania Press, 1957.

Haber, Samuel. *Efficiency and Uplift: Scientific Management in the Progressive Era, 1890–1920*. Chicago: University of Chicago Press, 1964.

Hacker, Louis M., and Benjamin B. Kendrick. *The United States since 1865*. Rev. ed. New York: F. S. Crofts and Co., 1936.

Hawkins, G. H. E. *Newspaper Advertising*. Chicago: Advertisers Publishing Co., 1914.

Hays, Samuel P. *Response to Industrialism, 1885–1914*. Chicago: University of Chicago Press, 1957.

Herbert, Benjamin B. *The First Decennium of the National Editorial Association of the United States.* Chicago: National Editorial Association, 1896.

Hicks, John D. *The Populist Revolt.* 1931; reprint ed. Lincoln: University of Nebraska Press, 1959.

Hofstadter, Richard. *The Age of Reform.* New York: Vintage Books, 1955.

————. *The Paranoid Style in American Politics and Other Essays.* New York: Alfred A. Knopf, 1965.

Holt, Hamilton. *Commercialism and Journalism.* Boston: Houghton Mifflin Co., 1909.

Holt, James. *Congressional Insurgents and the Party System: 1909–1916.* Cambridge, Mass.: Harvard University Press, 1967.

Hower, Ralph M. *History of an Advertising Agency: N. W. Ayer & Son at Work, 1869–1939.* Cambridge, Mass.: Harvard University Press, 1939.

Ickes, Harold L. *America's House of Lords: An Inquiry into the Freedom of the Press.* New York: Harcourt, Brace and Co., 1939.

Illinois Newspaper Directory and History of the Illinois Press Association. Champaign-Urbana: Illinois Press Association, 1934.

Irwin, Will. *The Making of a Reporter.* New York: G. P. Putnam's Sons, 1942.

————. *Propaganda and the News or What Makes You Think So?* New York: Whittlesey House/McGraw-Hill Book Co., 1936.

John, Arthur. *The Best Years of the Century.* Urbana: University of Illinois Press, 1981.

Johnson, Walter C., and Arthur T. Robb. *The South and Its Newspapers, 1903–1953.* Chattanooga, Tenn.: Southern Newspaper Publishers Association, 1954.

Juergens, George. *News from the White House: The Presidential–Press Relationship in the Progressive Era.* Chicago: University of Chicago Press, 1981.

Keller, Morton. *Affairs of State: Public Life in Late Nineteenth Century America.* Cambridge, Mass.: Belknap Press of Harvard University Press, 1977.

Kielbowicz, Richard B. *News in the Mail: The Press, Post Office, and Public Information, 1700–1860s.* Westport, Conn.: Greenwood Press, 1989.

Klein, Maury. *The Life and Legend of Jay Gould.* Baltimore: Johns Hopkins University Press, 1986.

Klinkhamer, Marie Carolyn (Sister). *Edward Douglas White, Chief*

Justice of the United States. Washington, D.C.: Catholic University Press, 1943.

Kolko, Gabriel. *Main Currents in Modern American History.* New York: Harper & Row, 1976.

————. *The Triumph of Conservatism: A Reinterpretation of American History, 1900–1916.* 1963; reprint ed. Chicago: Quadrangle Books, Inc., 1967.

Krislow, Samuel, and Lloyd D. Musolf. *The Politics of Regulation.* Boston: Houghton Mifflin Co., 1964.

La Follette, Robert M. *Autobiography.* 1913; reprint ed. Madison: University of Wisconsin Press, 1963.

Lee, Alfred M. *The Daily Newspaper in America.* New York: Macmillan, 1937.

Lee, James M. *History of American Journalism.* 2d ed. Garden City, N.Y.: Garden City Publishing Co., Inc., 1923.

Leonard, Thomas C. *The Power of the Press: The Birth of American Political Reporting.* New York: Oxford University Press, 1986.

Lippmann, Walter. *Drift and Mastery: An Attempt to Diagnose the Current Unrest.* New York: Mitchell Kennerley, 1914.

————. *Liberty and the News.* New York: Harcourt, Brace and Howe, 1920.

Littlefield, Roy Everett III. *William Randolph Hearst: His Role in American Progressivism.* Lanham, Md.: University Press of America, Inc., 1980.

Lundberg, Ferdinand. *America's 60 Families.* New York: Vanguard Press, 1937.

————. *Imperial Hearst: A Social Biography.* New York: Equinox Cooperative Press, 1936.

McCormick, Richard L. *The Party Period and Public Policy: American Politics from the Age of Jackson to the Progressive Era.* New York: Oxford University Press, 1986.

MacDougall, Curtis D. *The Press and Its Problems.* Dubuque, Iowa: Wm. C. Brown Co., 1964.

MacGregor, T. D. *Pushing Your Business: A Textbook of Advertising.* 4th ed. New York: Bankers Publishing Co., 1911.

Marzolf, Marion Tuttle. *Civilizing Voices: American Press Criticism, 1880–1950.* New York: Longman, 1991.

Meier, Kenneth J. *Regulation: Politics, Bureaucracy, and Economics.* New York: St. Martin's Press, 1985.

Mott, Frank Luther. *American Journalism.* New York: Macmillan, 1947.

————. *A History of American Magazines*. 5 vols. Cambridge, Mass.: Belknap Press of Harvard University Press, 1930–68.

Mowry, George E. *The Era of Theodore Roosevelt and the Birth of Modern America, 1900–1912*. New York: Harper Torchbooks, 1958.

Murphy, Paul L., ed. *Political Parties in American History: 1890–Present*. 3 vols. New York: G. P. Putnam's Sons, 1974.

Nevins, Allan. *The Emergence of Modern America, 1865–1878*. New York: Macmillan, 1927.

————. *The Evening Post: A Century of Journalism*. New York: Boni & Liveright, 1922.

Oberholtzer, Ellis P. *A History of the United States Since the Civil War*. New York: Macmillan, 1928.

Olasky, Marvin N. *Corporate Public Relations: A New Historical Perspective*. Hillsdale, N.J.: Lawrence Erlbaum Assoc., 1987.

Older, Fremont. *My Own Story*. New York: Macmillan, 1926.

Opdycke, John B. *News, Ads, and Sales*. New York: Macmillan, 1914.

Peterson, Theodore. *Magazines in the Twentieth Century*. 2d ed. Urbana: University of Illinois Press, 1964.

Phillips, David Graham. *The Treason of the Senate*, ed. George E. Mowry and Judson A. Grenier. 1906; rev. ed. Chicago: Quadrangle Books, 1964.

Pollard, James E. *The Presidents and the Press*. 2d ed. New York: Octagon Books, 1973.

————. *Principles of Newspaper Management*. New York: McGraw-Hill Book Co., 1937.

Pollay, Richard W., ed. *Information Sources in Advertising History*. Westport, Conn.: Greenwood Press, 1979.

Pope, Daniel. *The Making of Modern Advertising*. New York: Basic Books, Inc., 1983.

Presbrey, Frank. *History and Development of Advertising*. Garden City, N.Y.: Doubleday, Doran & Co., Inc., 1929.

Pringle, Henry F. *The Life and Times of William Howard Taft*. New York: Farrar & Rinehart, Inc., 1939.

Printers' Ink. *Printers' Ink: 50 Years, 1888–1938*. New York: Printers' Ink Publishing Co., 1938.

Proceedings of the First National Newspaper Conference. Madison: University of Wisconsin, 1912.

Quandt, Jean B. *From the Small Town to the Great Community: The Social Thought of Progressive Intellectuals*. New Brunswick, N.J.: Rutgers University Press, 1970.

Raucher, Alan R. *Public Relations and Business: 1900–1929*. Baltimore: Johns Hopkins University Press, 1968.

Regier, C. C. *The Era of the Muckrakers*. Chapel Hill: University of North Carolina Press, 1932.

Richardson, A. O. *The Power of Advertising*. New York: Lambert Publishing Co., 1913.

Ripley, Randall B. *Party Leaders in the House of Representatives*. Washington, D.C.: Brookings Institution, 1967.

Rogers, James E. *The American Newspaper*. Chicago: University of Chicago Press, 1909.

Rogers, Jason. *Newspaper Building*. New York: Harper & Brothers, 1918.

Rogers, Lindsay. *The Postal Power of Congress: A Study in Constitutional Expansion*. Baltimore: Johns Hopkins University Press, 1916.

Rowell, George P. *Forty Years an Advertising Agent, 1865–1905*. New York: Franklin Publishing Co., 1926.

Rusnak, Robert J. *Walter Hines Page and The World's Work, 1900–1913*. Washington, D.C.: University Press of America, Inc., 1982.

Salmon, Lucy Maynard. *The Newspaper and Authority*. New York: Oxford University Press, 1923.

———. *The Newspaper and the Historian*. New York: Oxford University Press, 1923.

Schlebecker, John T., and Andrew W. Hopkins. *A History of Dairy Journalism in the United States, 1810–1950*. Madison: University of Wisconsin Press, 1957.

Schlesinger, Arthur M., Jr., ed. *History of U.S. Political Parties*. 3 vols. New York: Chelsea House, 1973.

Schudson, Michael. *Advertising: The Uneasy Persuasion*. New York: Basic Books, Inc., 1984.

———. *Discovering the News: A Social History of American Newspapers*. New York: Basic Books, Inc., 1978.

Seldes, George. *Freedom of the Press*. Indianapolis: Bobbs-Merrill Co., 1935.

———. *Lords of the Press*. New York: Julian Messner, Inc., 1938.

———. *One Thousand Americans*. New York: Boni & Gaer, 1947.

———. *Witness to a Century*. New York: Ballantine Books, 1987.

Semonche, John E. *Charting the Future: The Supreme Court Responds to a Changing Society, 1890–1920*. Westport, Conn.: Greenwood Press, 1978.

Short, Lloyd M. *The Development of National Administrative Organization in the United States.* Urbana, Ill.: Institute of Government Research, 1923.

Sim, John Cameron. *The Grass Roots Press: America's Community Newspapers.* Ames: Iowa State University Press, 1969.

Sinclair, Upton. *The Brass Check: A Study of American Journalism.* Pasadena, Calif.: Author, 1920.

Skowronek, Stephen. *Building a New American State: The Expansion of National Administrative Capacities, 1877–1920.* Cambridge: Cambridge University Press, 1982.

Sloan, William David, and James G. Stovall, eds. *The Media in America: A History.* Worthington, Ohio: Publishing Horizons, Inc., 1989.

The State of the Union Messages of the Presidents, 1790–1966. New York: Chelsea House, 1966.

Steffens, Lincoln. *The Autobiography of Lincoln Steffens.* New York: Harcourt, Brace & World, Inc., 1931.

Steinberg, Salme H. *Reformer in the Marketplace: Edward W. Bok and the Ladies' Home Journal.* Baton Rouge: Louisiana State University Press, 1979.

Strasser, Susan. *Satisfaction Guaranteed: The Making of the American Mass Market.* New York: Pantheon Books, 1989.

Sullivan, Mark. *The Education of an American.* New York: Doubleday, Doran & Co., 1938.

Swados, Harvey, ed. *Years of Conscience: The Muckrakers.* New York: World Publishing Co., 1962.

Swanberg, W. A. *Citizen Hearst: A Biography of W. R. Hearst.* New York: Charles Scribner's Sons, 1961.

Tebbel, John. *The Media in America.* New York: New American Library, Inc., 1974.

———, and Sarah Miles Watts. *The Press and the Presidency.* New York: Oxford University Press, 1985.

Tedlow, Richard S. *Keeping the Corporate Image: Public Relations and Business, 1900–1950.* Greenwich, Conn.: JAI Press, Inc., 1979.

———. *New and Improved: The Story of Mass Marketing in America.* New York: Basic Books, Inc., 1990.

Thayer, Frank. *Newspaper Management.* New York: D. Appleton-Century Co., 1938.

Thelen, David P. *Robert M. La Follette and the Insurgent Spirit.* Boston: Little, Brown & Co., 1976.

Thompson, John A. *Reformers and War: American Progressive Publi-*

cists and the First World War. Cambridge: Cambridge University Press, 1987.

Thorn, William J., with Mary Pat Pfeil. *Newspaper Circulation: Marketing the News*. New York: Longman, 1987.

Thorpe, Merle, ed. *The Coming Newspaper*. New York: Henry Holt and Co., 1915.

Villard, Oswald Garrison. *Some Newspapers and Newspapermen*. New York: Alfred A. Knopf, 1923.

Walsh, Richard J. *Selling Forces*. Philadelphia: Curtis Publishing Co., 1913.

Weigle, Clifford F., and David G. Clark, eds. *The American Newspaper* by Will Irwin. Ames: Iowa State University Press, 1969.

Weinstein, James. *The Corporate Ideal in the Liberal State, 1900–1918*. Boston: Beacon Press, 1968.

Weisberger, Bernard A. *The American Newspaperman*. Chicago: University of Chicago Press, 1961.

White, Leonard D. *The Republican Era, 1869–1901: A Study in Administrative History*. New York: Macmillan, 1958.

Wiebe, Robert H. *Businessmen and Reform: A Study of the Progressive Movement*. Cambridge, Mass.: Harvard University Press, 1962.

———. *The Search for Order, 1877–1920*. New York: Hill and Wang, 1967.

Wilson, Harold S. *McClure's Magazine and the Muckrakers*. Princeton, N.J.: Princeton University Press, 1970.

Wilson, James Q., ed. *The Politics of Regulation*. New York: Basic Books, Inc., 1980.

Wingate, Charles F., ed. *Views and Interviews on Journalism*. 1875; reprint ed. New York: Arno Press, 1970.

Wisconsin Press Association. *Proceedings of the Wisconsin Editorial Association—First, Second and Third Sessions*. Madison: Carpenter & Hyer, 1859.

Journals and Periodicals

Adams, Henry C. "Publicity for Industrial Corporations." *Independent*, June 5, 1902, p. 1388.

———. "What Is Publicity?" *North American Review*, December 1902, pp. 895–904.

Adams, Samuel Hopkins. "The Patent Medicine Conspiracy." *Collier's*, November 1905, pp. 14–16.

———. "Tricks of the Press." *Collier's*, Feb. 17, 1912, pp. 17–18+.

Bagdikian, Ben H. "Behold the Grass-roots Press, Alas!" *Harper's Magazine*, December 1964, pp. 102–10.

Baker, Ray Stannard. "Railroads on Trial." *McClure's Magazine*, March 1906, pp. 535–49.

Baldasty, Gerald J., "The Nineteenth-Century Origins of Modern American Journalism." *Proceedings of the American Antiquarian Society* 100 (October 1990): 407–19.

————, and Jeffrey B. Rutenbeck. "Money, Politics and Newspapers: The Business Environment of Press Partisanship in the Late 19th Century." *Journalism History* 15 (Summer/Autumn 1988): 60–69.

Blethen, Joseph. "The Advertiser's Place in Journalism." *University of Washington Journalism Department Bulletin* 5 (1910): 4–8.

"The Bondage of the Press." *Twentieth Century*, October 1909, pp. 48–52.

Bunting, David. "Corporate Interlocking, Part I, the Money Trust." *Directors & Boards* 1 (Spring 1976): 6–15.

"The Confessions of a Managing Editor." *Collier's*, Oct. 28, 1911, pp. 18–20+.

"Constitutionality of Postal Regulations as an Interference with Freedom of the Press." *Central Law Journal* 72 (Jan. 6, 1911): 27–33.

"Corporation Control of the Daily, Monthly and Religious Press." *Arena*, January 1909, pp. 105–8.

"Corporations and Publicity." *Nation*, July 4, 1912, pp. 5–6.

Deutsch, Eberhard P. "Freedom of the Press and the Mails." *Michigan Law Review* 36 (March 1938): 703–51.

DeWeese, Truman A. "From Journalism to the 'Newspaper Industry.' " *Independent*, Dec. 11, 1902, pp. 2953–56.

Dreier, Peter, and Steve Weinberg. "Interlocking Directorates." *Columbia Journalism Review*, November/December 1979, pp. 51–67.

"Editorialene." *Nation*, June 12, 1902, pp. 459–60.

Eliot, Charles W. "What Public Men Think of the Newspapers." *Collier's*, March 23, 1912, pp. 36–37.

"Fakes and the Press." *Science*, March 8, 1907, p. 391.

Filene, Peter G. "An Obituary for 'The Progressive Movement.' " *American Quarterly* 22 (Spring 1970): 20–34.

French, George. "Masters of the Magazines." *Twentieth Century*, April 1912, pp. 501–8.

Goldman, Eric F. "Public Relations and the Progressive Surge: 1898–1917." *Public Relations Review* 4 (Fall 1978): 52–62.

Hart, Jack R. "Horatio Alger in the Newsroom: Social Origins of American Editors." *Journalism Quarterly* 53 (Spring 1976): 14–20.

Haste, Richard A. "The Evolution of the Fourth Estate." *Arena*, March 1909, pp. 348–52.

Howard, C. H. "Publishers and the Postal Department." *Arena*, December 1901, pp. 570–77.

"How the Reactionary Daily Press Poisons the Public Mind by Deliberate Misrepresentations." *Arena*, September 1907, pp. 318–19.

Kennedy, Jane. "Development of Postal Rates: 1845–1955." *Land Economics* 33 (May 1957): 93–112.

Kielbowicz, Richard B. "The Growing Interaction of the Federal Bureaucracy and the Press: The Case of a Postal Rule, 1879–1917." *American Journalism* 4 (1987): 5–18.

———. "Newsgathering by Printers' Exchanges Before the Telegraph." *Journalism History* 9 (Summer 1982): 42–48.

———. "Origins of the Second-Class Mail Category and the Business of Policymaking, 1863–1879." *Journalism Monographs* No. 96 (April 1986).

———. "Postal Subsidies for the Press and the Business of Mass Culture, 1880–1920." *Business History Review* 64 (Autumn 1990): 451–88.

Kittle, William. "The 'Interests' and the Magazines." *Twentieth Century*, May 1910, pp. 124–28.

———. "The Making of Public Opinion: News Bureaus and Newspapers Advocating Corporation Interests." *Arena*, July 1909, pp. 440–45.

Luce, Robert. "Publicity and Trusts." *Review of Reviews*, September 1912, pp. 339–441.

McCormick, Richard L. "The Discovery That Business Corrupts Politics: A Reappraisal of the Origins of Progressivism." *American Historical Review* 86 (April 1981): 247–74.

Maddox, L. M., and E. J. Zanot. "The Image of the Advertising Practitioner as Presented in the News Media, 1900–1972." *American Journalism* 2 (1985): 117–29.

"Manufacturing Public Opinion." *McClure's Magazine*, February 1906, pp. 450–52.

Marcaccio, Michael D. "Did a Business Conspiracy End Muckraking? A Reexamination." *The Historian* 47 (November 1984): 58–71.

"The Menace of Irresponsible Journalism." *Arena*, August 1907, pp. 170–80.

Metcalf, James A. "Threatening the Nation's Free Press." *Publisher's Guide*, August/September 1912, pp. 35–37.

Meyer, H. H. B. "List of References on Advertising." *Special Libraries* 7 (April 1916): 61–76.

Myers, Kenneth H. "ABC and SRDS: The Evolution of Two Specialized Advertising Services." *Business History Review* 34 (Autumn 1960): 302–26.

"A Mystery Unraveled." *Collier's*, Sept. 7, 1912, pp. 10–11+.

"Newspapers as Commodities." *Nation*, May 9, 1912, pp. 455–56.

"Newspapers as Institutions." *Nation*, July 15, 1915, p. 85.

"Newspapers Opposing Publicity." *Literary Digest*, Oct. 12, 1912, pp. 607–8.

Olasky, Martin M. "The Development of Corporate Public Relations, 1850–1930." *Journalism Monographs* No. 102 (April 1987).

Palfrey, John G. "The Constitution and the Courts." *Harvard Law Review* 26 (1913): 507–30.

"The Postal Power and Its Limitations on Freedom of the Press." *Virginia Law Review* 28 (1942): 634–48.

Powell, Thomas R. "Separation of Powers: Administrative Exercise of Legislative and Judicial Power." *Political Science Quarterly* 28 (1913): 47.

"The Press and the Advertiser." *Nation*, April 1, 1869, pp. 252–53.

"The Press and the Law." *Chautauquan*, July 1903, pp. 332–34.

"The Prostitution of the Daily Press by Public-Service Corporations." *Arena*, July 1905, pp. 93–95.

"Publicity for Industrial Corporations." *Independent*, June 5, 1902, p. 1388.

"Publicity for Organs of Publicity." *Chautauquan*, January 1913, pp. 129–31.

" 'Publicity' for Publishers." *Literary Digest*, June 21, 1913, p. 1364.

"Publicity topsy-turvy." *Independent*, Aug. 17, 1905, pp. 401–2.

" 'Regulating' the Press." *Nation*, April 1, 1915, pp. 348–49.

Reynolds, Robert D., Jr. "The 1906 Campaign to Sway Muckraking Periodicals." *Journalism Quarterly* 56 (Autumn 1979): 513–20+.

Ritchie, Donald A. " 'The Loyalty of the Senate': Washington Correspondents in the Progressive Era." *The Historian* 51 (August 1989): 574–91.

Rodgers, Daniel. "In Search of Progressivism." *Reviews of American History* 56 (December 1982): 113–32.

Rogers, Lindsay. "The Extension of Federal Control through the Regulation of the Mails." *Harvard Law Review* 27 (November 1913): 27–44.

———. "Federal Interference with Freedom of the Press." *Yale Law Review* 23 (May 1914): 559–79.

Ross, Edward A. "The Suppression of Important News." *Atlantic Monthly*, March 1910, pp. 303–11.

Ruetten, Richard T. "Anaconda Journalism: The End of an Era." *Journalism Quarterly* 37 (Winter 1960): 3–12, 104.

Salisbury, William. "American Journalism." *Arena*, December 1908, pp. 564–71.

Schmuhl, Robert. "Eliminating Anonymity in Editorials Can Make Them Sharper." *Presstime*, July 1987, p. 54.

Schofield, Henry. "Freedom of the Press in the United States." *Papers and Proceedings for the Ninth Annual Meeting of the American Sociological Society*. Chicago: University of Chicago Press, 1915: 67–116.

Schultze, Quentin J. " 'An Honorable Place': The Quest for Professional Advertising Education, 1900–1917." *Business History Review* 56 (Spring 1982): 16–32.

"Second-Class Postal Rates and the First Amendment." *Rutgers Law Review* 28 (Winter 1975): 693–706.

Sheldon, Charles M. "The Modern Newspaper." *Independent*, July 25, 1912, pp. 196–201.

Shibley, George H. "Progressive Leaders: United States Senator Robert L. Owen." *Twentieth Century*, May 1910, p. 129.

Smith, David C. "Wood Pulp and Newspapers, 1867–1900." *Business History Review* 38 (Autumn 1964): 328–45.

Smythe, Ted Curtis. "The Advertisers' War to Verify Newspaper Circulation, 1870–1914." *American Journalism* 3 (1986): 167–80.

———. "The Reporter, 1880–1900: Working Conditions and Their Influence on the News." *Journalism History* 7 (Spring 1980): 1–10.

"Strangling the Magazines." *Nation*, May 2, 1912, pp. 431–32.

Turner, George Kibbe. "Manufacturing Public Opinion." *McClure's Magazine*, July 1912, pp. 316–27.

"We." *Independent*, Jan. 8, 1911, pp. 1280–81.

Unpublished Works

Abramoske, Donald J. "The *Chicago Daily News*: A Business History, 1875–1901." Ph.D. diss., University of Chicago, 1963.

American Newspaper Publishers Association. Proceedings of the Annual Conventions, 1887–1900.

Barnhart, Thomas F. "The History of the Minnesota Editorial Association, 1867–1897." M.A. thesis, University of Minnesota, 1937.

Baur, Edward J. "Voluntary Control in the Advertising Industry." Ph.D. diss., University of Chicago, 1942.

Brackeen, Louis O. "History of the Alabama Press Association." Mimeographed, prepared as a special project of the Alabama Press Association, 1951.

Everett, George. "The Linotype and U.S. Daily Newspaper Journalism in the 1890s: Analysis of a Relationship." Ph.D. diss., University of Iowa, 1972.

Kielbowicz, Richard B. "Development of the Paid Subscriber Rule in Second-Class Mail." Prepared for the U.S. Postal Rate Commission in the Tri-Parish Journal Case (Docket C85-2), Aug. 16, 1985.

Pike, Albert H. "Jonathan Bourne, Jr., Progressive." Ph.D. diss., University of Oregon, 1957.

Schultze, Quentin J. "Advertising, Science, and Professionalism, 1885–1917." Ph.D. diss., University of Illinois, 1978.

Shideler, James H. "Second-Class Matter: The American Press and the Subsidy, 1879–1933." M.A. thesis, University of California, 1938.

South Carolina State Press Association. Proceedings of the 1881 Annual Convention.

Ward, Hiley H. "Ninety Years of the National Newspaper Association: The Mind and Dynamics of Grassroots Journalism in Shaping America." Ph.D. diss., University of Minnesota, 1977.

Wisconsin Editorial Association. Proceedings of the Annual Conventions, 1869–1879.

Special Archival Collections

American Advertising Museum, Portland, Oregon

Indiana State Library, Henry A. Barnhart Papers, Indianapolis, Indiana

Library of Congress, Washington, D.C.

National Archives, Washington, D.C.
United States Postal Service Library, Washington, D.C.
University of Oregon, Jonathan Bourne, Jr., Collection, Eugene,
    Oregon

Trade Journals and Newspapers

Advertising & Selling
Advertising Experience
American Newspaper Reporter
American Printer
Chicago Dry Goods Reporter
Editor and Publisher
Fame: The Journal for Advertisers
Fourth Estate
The Journalist
Kings' Jester
La Follette's Weekly Magazine
Literary Digest
Mail Order Journal
National Advertiser
National Printer Journalist
Newspaperdom
Newspaper Maker
New York Times
Presstime
Printers' Ink
Publisher's Auxiliary
Publishers' Weekly
Telegrapher

Government Documents

Annual Reports of the Post Office Department
Congressional Record
House and Senate Documents
House and Senate Hearings
House and Senate Miscellaneous Documents
House and Senate Reports
Opinions of the Assistant Attorney General for the Post Office Department
Opinions of the U.S. Attorney General
Postal Laws and Regulations

United States Official Postal Guide
United States Postal Rate Commission, *Transcript of Proceedings: Complaint of Tri-Parish Journal, Inc., C85-2*
United States Post Office Department News Releases
United States Statutes at Large
United States Supreme Court Briefs and Pleadings

Index

tion, 124, 127–30, 132–40. See also *American Newspaper Directory*; Audit Bureau of Circulations; Newspaper Publicity Act, legislative history; United States Post Office Department, Newspaper Publicity Act, administration
Collier's, 12, 19, 44, 166n.40
Congress, 2, 3, 23–24, 30, 34, 36, 59–62, 65, 67–68, 86, 90, 91, 94, 95, 107, 110, 113, 116, 117, 118, 124, 137–40, 144, 146, 162n.3, 170n.90, 189n.2. *See also* Democrats; House of Representatives; Newspaper Publicity Act, legislative history; Republicans; Senate

Democrats, 2, 62–63, 70–74, 77, 78, 83
Disclosure, 2–4, 12, 55, 56, 66–68, 69, 76, 79, 81, 91, 94, 95, 96, 97, 98, 103–4, 107, 111, 113, 136, 139, 142, 145. *See also* Publicity
Dryden, John F., 20, 35, 166n.45. *See also* Prudential Insurance Company

Editor and Publisher, 3, 101, 121, 128, 130, 133, 134
Emporia Gazette. *See* White, William Allen

Fame, 24, 28, 94
Farmers' National Congress, 96
Federal Trade Commission, 2
Federation of Trade Press Associations, 128–30
First Amendment, 3, 4, 12–13, 59, 61, 65, 68, 86, 87, 104, 142–43, 147
Fourth Estate, 114, 115, 116, 137
Fowler's Publicity, 22, 27, 50–51
"Free publicity," 107, 111, 114–17, 121, 123

Geo. P. Rowell & Co., 29, 40–41, 52, 164n.21
George, Henry, Jr., 14, 15
Gilder, Richard W., 38, 168n.64
Gladden, Washington, 38
Gould, Jay, 12, 15–16, 168n.37

Hamilton, Holt, 10, 13, 37, 146
Hand, Learned, 86
Hearst, William Randolph, 19, 29, 47, 66
Hitchcock, Frank H., 75, 76, 83, 84, 100, 115, 131
House of Representatives, 2, 24, 62, 68–74, 139
Hutchins Commission on Freedom of the Press, 4, 147

Illinois Daily Press Association, 96
Industries: banks, 2, 15, 38, 56, 102; copper, 19; general, 15, 19, 37–38; meat-packing, 37; public utilities, 15, 37–38; steel, 2, 18, 19, 54, 102. *See also* Belmont, August; Gould, Jay; Insurance companies; Morgan, J. P.; Railroads; Rockefeller, John D.
Infomercials, 144. *See also* Reading notices
Insurance companies, 20, 22, 34–35, 38, 56, 166n.45
Interstate Commerce Commission, 36
Irwin, Will, 7, 9, 12, 14, 18, 156n.9

Journalist, 22, 30, 31, 32, 39, 42, 53, 56
Journal of Commerce, 85, 86, 113

Kansas Editorial Association, 43
Kentucky Press Association, 38–39, 140
Kings' Jester, 56

Linda Lawson is an assistant professor of journalism at Indiana University in Bloomington. Her work has appeared in the *Harvard Journal of Law and Public Policy*, *American Journalism*, *Library Quarterly*, and the *Canadian Review of American Studies*.